THE DISCOVERY OF ROMAN FORT AT CRIPPLEGATE, CITY OF LONDON

Excavations by W F Grimes 1947–68

John Shepherd

THE DISCOVERY OF THE ROMAN FORT AT CRIPPLEGATE, CITY OF LONDON

Based upon the records from excavations by W F Grimes for the Roman and Mediaeval London Excavation Council 1947–68

John Shepherd

with contributions from
Patrick Allen, Ian Betts, Joanna Bird, Trevor Brigham, Gary Brown, Stephanie Chettle, Nina Crummy, Hella Eckardt, †Jo Groves, Jenny Hall, Mark Hassall, Martin Henig, Louise Rayner, Fiona Seeley, Jane Sidell

Original artwork by †W F Grimes
with H J M Green and G Brown

artwork edited and new illustrations by †Susan Banks, Carlos Lemos and †Kikar Singh

Published by Museum of London Archaeology
Copyright © Museum of London 2012

A CIP catalogue record for this book is available from
the British Library

Production and design by Tracy Wellman
Typesetting and design by Sue Cawood
Reprographics by Andy Chopping
Copy editing by Wendy Sherlock
Series editing by Sue Hirst/Susan M Wright

Printed by the Lavenham Press

*Front cover: the excavation, in 1956, of the north tower of the fort gate (WFG5), from the north-east; Audrey Williams stands
at the back, with two of Professor Grimes's key excavators on this and other sites, Fred 'Pop' Beasley (in the hat) and Tim
Thomas, in the foreground*

*Back cover: the north tower of the fort gate in a rare colour photograph in the Grimes London Archive; graduate students from
the Institute of Archaeology, University of London, where Grimes was Director, prepare to draw the remains as part of a
fieldwork exercise*

*Frontispiece: Grimes supervising the trench in Bastion 12 (WFG1) in November 1947; the caption to this picture, published
in* The Sphere *magazine, explains that 'by patient research on these blitzed sites Mr Grimes believes it may eventually be his
privilege to rewrite much of the Roman history of London'*

Contents

Figures

Tables

Preface

This volume has been prepared in order to present the evidence for a Roman fort at Cripplegate as discovered by W F Grimes during the post-war period and is one in a series of five projects and publications prepared by the Museum of London, in conjunction with English Heritage. These volumes have been compiled from documents and finds contained in Grimes's care and in the collections of the Museum of London. From 1988, the year of Grimes's death, all of this material was generally known as the Grimes London Archive (GLA), but it is now a part of the Museum of London Archaeological Archive and Research Centre (LAARC). This extensive archive contains information, in varying quantities and quality, for each of the 63 sites evaluated and excavated by Grimes in the City of London and its immediate hinterland between 1946 and 1968, the majority of which were summarised in his interim account of his entire programme of fieldwork in *The excavation of Roman and mediaeval London* in 1968 (Grimes 1968). Two of these excavations, at Gutter Lane and Billiter Square, were carried out under the auspices of The Society of Antiquaries of London in 1945–6, but the remainder were the work of the Roman and Mediaeval (*sic*) London Excavation Council (RMLEC), with Grimes as its Honorary Director of Excavations.

The first volume in this present archiving, research and publication programme, conducted by MOLA with the full support of English Heritage, examined the clearance and subsequent excavations of the crypt at St Bride's church (Milne 1997). The second volume presented and discussed the archive for Grimes's most famous and unexpected discovery, and arguably one of the most well-known sites in the City of London, the temple of Mithras (Shepherd 1998a), while a third volume has provided a gazetteer and summary, in effect a general overview, of the entire RMLEC excavation programme and the circumstances under which the work was instigated and carried out (Shepherd 1998b). This was published alongside other gazetteers for the City (Schofield 1998) and the Greater London area (Thompson et al 1998) as part of the development programme of the Heritage Lottery Fund-financed LAARC project as a whole and has enabled, since 1998, better access to the contents of the GLA. The final two projects of the Grimes programme both examine his important work around Cripplegate in the north-west corner of the City of London. The first of these to be published examined the medieval sequence in the area (Milne 2001) while this volume, the last in the entire Grimes backlog publication programme, examines the Roman sequence in Cripplegate, with a special emphasis upon the remains of the Roman fort discovered there.

To say that this present volume has been long in the making would be an understatement. The fort was first identified over 60 years ago and this current volume was expected to be completed 20 years ago – before the end of the first millennium. My involvement with the creation of the LAARC and spin-off educational projects, related to the use of archaeological archives, in the higher education sector unfortuantely prevented this from happening. However, the Grimes London Archive has never been closed to researchers. I was always in a position, either as Curator of the GLA or Manager of the LAARC, to liaise and consult with representatives of the archaeological organisations who carried out work in the Cripplegate area during the 1990s. The work of both MOLA within the area of the fort and Pre-Construct Archaeology Ltd (PCA) outside the fort to the west was made in the light of full access to the GLA.

Now that this report on Professor Grimes's work on the Roman sequence at Cripplegate is completed, the GLA backlog publication programme is itself complete. I would like to think that Professor Grimes, for whom I worked as his research assistant in the early 1980s and from whom I received his final instructions on publication shortly before his death in 1988, would be pleased with this work. I think he would particularly like the fact that the conclusion to this volume has not been spiced up with spectacular interpretation. He was a strong advocate of the avoidance of the sensational and speculative, and believed strongly in only making public one's interpretation when one fully understood the material. Indeed, one of his maxims was 'to interpret from a position of maximum knowledge'. It is possible that Grimes was never confident that a full story of the fort could be told, because he never believed that he had enough information about it; indeed the profusion of qualifications that litter the conclusion published here emphasises one undeniable fact – although we have a lot of information for the fort, we still know very little about its status and purpose. It is interesting to observe that the more recent excavations at Cripplegate, though adding significantly to the quality of the data available for study, still tell us little more than what Grimes reported as observable fact in his 1968 volume. They might have cleared up one or two nagging suppositions about the fort – they confirmed, for example, that there was no timber predecessor to the masonry fort and that the fort was not in existence from the early to mid 3rd century AD onwards. But why exactly was a fort located here? What was its relationship with the port facilities on the Thames? Which units garrisoned it? Did the governor use it? Or what of the procurator and his staff? And, really, what did it have to do with the rest of Roman London? At times I feel that the answers to these questions are just as elusive now as they were in 1968 when Grimes first published his interim account. If only we had an inscription or two …

John Shepherd
Woodford Green, 2011

Acknowledgements

This volume has been long in the making. Professor Grimes made a start on it during the 1970s, but a lack of funding prevented him from completing it. I brought it close to completion in the late 1990s before transferring to the LAARC team in the Museum of London. Now, with the continued support of English Heritage, the account of the discovery of the fort is now completed.

Because of the time span for this project, from the late 40s when the first signs of the fort began to reveal themselves to the present, many people have been involved. To begin with, I wish to remind the reader of those who worked closely with Grimes in the field during the post-war period – especially Fred (Pop) Beasley, George Faulkner, A J Haydon, George Rybot and Audrey Williams. He and his team received considerable support from the Executive Committee of the RMLEC, in particular R Asheton MP, Sir H Bell, Sir A Bossom, D A J Buxton, N Cook, P Corder, N Davey, G C Dunning, C Harrison, Dame K Kenyon, Sir J Mann, G Nicholson MP, A H Oswald, Sir I A Richmond, R Syme and Miss M V Taylor. He received a great deal of additional support and assistance from four other members of the Executive Committee, R Smith, the Librarian and Curator of the Guildhall, F J Forty, the City Engineer whose vision and efforts during the war enabled the survival during the post-war period of reconstruction of so many parts of the city wall in the Cripplegate area, B H St John O'Neil, the Chief Inspector of Ancient Monuments and his successor, and P K Baillie Reynolds. A special debt is due to the Council's Secretary, J A Giuseppe, and Treasurer, J F Head. Their efforts enabled so much to be achieved by Grimes and his small team before the speed of redevelopment in the late 1950s and 60s overpowered them and many other archaeological teams around the country. Also on the administrative side, Grimes was very ably supported by his secretaries at the Institute of Archaeology, London, Jean McDonald and Margery Hunt.

Following the work in the field, Grimes was supported in his post-excavation work by Joanna Bird, whose samian identifications are reproduced in this volume, and Sarah Macready. I too benefitted from their efforts and much of the order of the archive that was stored over the decades at the Museum of London is due to their work.

For my part, I would particularly like to thank Roger Thomas and Barney Sloane of English Heritage, and also Gill Andrews who patiently oversaw the entire Grimes backlog programme. It should be emphasised here that, of all the organisations that supported Grimes and the RMLEC, English Heritage and its predecessor bodies (Ministry of Works (MoW), Department of Environment (DoE) and Historic Buildings and Monuments Commission (HBMC)) have always been at the fore. This has not just been in the form of money for his fieldwork and post-excavation work, but also since his death in 1988 in a generous allocation of funds to archive his field notes and finds and produce the final publications of his work. It is and always has been greatly appreciated.

I would also like to thank the former directors of the Museum of London, Max Hebditch CBE and Simon Thurley CBE for all of their help and support, especially while I was seconded on to other projects such as the creation of the LAARC. I must also thank my friend and colleague Jenny Hall for all her support and management of the Grimes projects. Nick Merriman, Kate Starling, Roy Stephenson and Hedley Swain have also given much support. Alan Thompson, Cath Maloney and Steve Tucker gave me much support in the London archive.

For this report, I would like to thank Joanna Bird, Jo Groves (sadly no longer with us), Louise Rayner, Beth Richardson and Fiona Seeley for their work on the pottery; Nina Crummy and Hella Eckardt for the small finds reports; Ian Betts for the building materials; Jane Sidell for advice on the animal bone from the sites in this volume – although the poor sampling process for this material meant that it was not useful for study. Trevor Brigham and Gary Brown gave me invaluable help in connection with their own research work on the fort, Patrick Allen for 29 Noble Street 1973, Gina Porter and Andrew Westman for their work on the west and north walls of the fort, Natalie Cohen for work on Grimes's documentary archive, and Gus Milne and Mike Webber for assistance and useful discussions while they were working, with Natalie, on the medieval levels of the Cripplegate area. An earlier draft was read by Michael Fulford and I am most grateful for the constructive comments he had to make.

The final production of this volume has benefitted from the skills and talents of many people at MOLA. David Bowsher has managed the final stages and Sue Hirst has patiently helped to bring work of the 1950s up to a modern standard. The illustrations have benefitted from the work of Hannah Faux, Carlos Lemos, Sandra Rowntree, and Andy Chopping has accomplished wonders with 50s material as well as producing new work. As always, the skills and patience of Tracy Wellman must be mentioned here. However, I am sure they would all like me to make a very special mention to our former colleagues, Susan Banks and Kikar Singh, who both passed away at too young an age. Susan did so much of the preparatory work on Grimes's drawings for this and its companion medieval volume, Kikar worked on the finds drawings for this volume. To them, and to Jo Groves, I would like to dedicate this final part of Professor Grimes's post-war work in the City of London.

Summary

The Roman and Mediaeval London Excavation Council was formed immediately before the end of the Second World War to tackle the perceived threat to countless archaeological sites in the City of London by the imminent redevelopment of properties destroyed by enemy action. Grimes was its Honorary Director and he led a campaign of work, from 1944 to 1968, which examined over 63 sites in total. Twenty-five of these were in the Cripplegate area, a region of London that had not been examined in much detail previously but which contained long stretches of the Roman and medieval city wall. Grimes believed that work here would reveal a great deal about these historic defences.

His earliest work revealed a number of discrepancies in the construction of the city defences, which became clear when the south-western corner of a Roman fort was revealed at Noble Street. Material associated with the fort construction suggested that it was built early in the 2nd century AD. It was evident that the fort pre-dated the city defences as a whole but that the north and west walls of the fort had been incorporated into them at the time of their construction, towards the end of the 2nd century AD or early in the 3rd.

His work revealed detail of the fort defences, including the western gateway and internal interval towers. Some parts of the internal buildings were excavated, but the loss of archaeology through deep basements in this area frustrated his efforts to create a detailed plan of the interior. Subsequent analysis of the finds from his sites, coupled with the results of more recent work in the vicinity, suggest that the fort went out of use early in the 3rd century AD.

Little use was made of the Cripplegate area during the 3rd and 4th centuries AD. The ditch of the fort on the south side was backfilled during the 3rd century AD; some of the internal areas were covered by a deposit of dark earth.

The post-Roman sequence is discussed in a separate volume (Milne 2001).

Résumé

Le Bureau des fouilles du Londres romain et médiéval fut formé juste avant la fin de la deuxième guerre mondiale dans le but de protéger les innombrables sites archéologiques de la ville de Londres, que l'on pensait être menacés par le réaménagement imminent des propriétés détruites par l'attaque ennemie. Grimes fut son directeur honoraire et il mena une campagne de travaux, laquelle, entre 1944 et 1968, examina plus de 63 sites en tout. Vingt-cinq de ces sites se trouvaient dans le quartier de Cripplegate, une partie de Londres qui n'avait guère été examinée dans le détail auparavant mais qui contenait de longues portions du mur romain et médiéval de la ville. Grimes estimait que de travailler là en révélerait beaucoup sur ces défenses historiques.

Ses premiers travaux révélèrent un certain nombre de divergences qui furent tirées au clair lorsque l'angle sud-ouest d'un fort romain fut révélé à Noble Street. Le matériel associé à la construction du fort suggérait qu'il avait été construit au début du IIe siècle apr. J-C. Il était évident que le fort était antérieur aux défenses de la ville dans leur ensemble mais que les murs nord et ouest du fort avaient été intégrés dans les défenses à l'époque de leur construction, vers la fin du IIe siècle apr. J-C. ou au début du IIIe siècle.

Ses travaux révélèrent des détails des défenses du fort, y compris la porte ouest et les tours d'intervalle intérieures. Certaines parties des bâtiments intérieurs furent fouillées mais la perte d'archéologie due aux sous-sols profonds dans ce quartier a fait que, malgré ses efforts, il ne réussit pas à formuler un plan détaillé de l'intérieur. Une analyse ultérieure des découvertes provenant de ces sites, ajoutée aux résultats de travaux plus récents aux alentours, suggéra que le fort cessa de fonctionner au début du IIIe siècle apr. J-C.

Le quartier de Cripplegate ne servit pas à grand chose au cours du IIIe et du IVe siècle apr. J-C. Le fossé du fort sur le côté sud fut remblayé au cours du IIIe siècle apr. J-C. ; certaines zones intérieures étaient recouvertes d'un dépôt de terre foncée.

La séquence post-romaine est traitée dans un volume séparé (Milne 2001).

Traduction: Charlette Sheil-Small

Zusammenfassung

Der Ausgrabungsrat für das römische und mittelalterliche London wurde unmittelbar vor Ende des Zweiten Weltkriegs gegründet, um der drohenden Gefährdung zahlloser archäologischer Stätten in der Londoner Innenstadt durch bevorstehende Sanierungen von Gebäuden, die durch Kriegseinwirkung zerstört worden waren, entgegenzuwirken. Grimes war der ehrenamtliche Direktor und leitete von 1944 bis 1968 eine Arbeitskampagne, die insgesamt über 63 Ausgrabungsstellen untersuchte. Fünfundzwanzig davon befanden sich in Cripplegate, einem Bezirk Londons der bisher nicht genauer untersucht worden war, der aber lange Abschnitte der römischen und mittelalterlichen Stadtmauer umfasste. Grimes glaubte, dass die Arbeit hier eine Menge über diese historischen Verteidigungsanlagen enthüllen würde.

Seine ersten Arbeiten enthüllten eine Reihe von Abweichungen im Bau der Stadtbefestigung die deutlich wurden, als in der Noble Street die südwestliche Ecke eines römischen Kastells freigelegt wurde. Fundmaterial, welches mit der Konstruktion des Kastells in Zusammenhang stand, deutete auf eine Erbauung im frühen 2.Jh. n.Chr. hin. Es war offensichtlich, dass das Kastell als Ganzes noch in die Zeit vor der Stadtbefestigung datierte, dass aber die Nord- und Westwände des Kastells zum Zeitpunkt der Erbauung der Stadtbefestigung, gegen Ende des 2.Jhs n.Chr. oder Anfang des 3.Jhs, in diese eingebunden worden waren.

Seine Arbeit enthüllte Elemente der Befestigungsanlage des Kastells, einschliesslich der westlichen Toreinfahrt und der inneren Zwischentürme. Einige Teile der Innenbebauung wurden ausgegraben, doch der Verlust an archäologischer Substanz aufgrund der tiefen Kellergeschosse die hier existierten, machte seine Bemühungen, einen Detailplan des Innenbereichs zu erstellen, zu Nichte. Die anschliessende Analyse der Ausgrabungsbefunde, zusammen mit den Ergebnissen neuerer Ausgrabungen aus der näheren Umgebung, lassen vermuten, dass das Kastell ab dem frühen 3.Jh. n.Chr. nicht mehr in Gebrauch war.

Während des 3. und 4.Jhs n.Chr. wurde der Bereich um Cripplegate nur wenig genutzt. Der Graben auf der Südseite des Kastells wurde während des 3.Jhs n.Chr. verfüllt; Teile der internen Bereiche wurden von einer Schicht Dark Earth bedeckt.

Die nachrömischen Schichtabfolgen werden in einem separaten Band (Milne 2001) behandelt.

Übersetzung: Iris Rodenbuesch

1 Professor Grimes's London Archive and Cripplegate

1.1 The Roman and Mediaeval London Excavation Council

Though I was given a CBE [for the discovery of the temple of Mithras] I do not conceal the fact that in the conditions of the time the discovery was in the nature of a fluke. ... I shall always rate the other important Roman discovery ... – the Cripplegate fort – as archaeologically the more satisfying achievement. (Grimes 1968, 237–8)

The application of carefully planned and controlled excavation [in London] has also had notable successes. The discovery and elucidation of the Cripplegate fort in 1947–65 by Grimes must always rank as one of the triumphs of archaeological method ... (Biddle and Hudson 1973, 10)

The Roman and Mediaeval London Excavation Council (RMLEC) evolved slowly over a two and a half year period. In May of 1944 Kathleen Kenyon, acting as Secretary of the Council for British Archaeology (CBA), drew attention in the London and national press to the need for controlled archaeological examinations of the many bomb-damaged sites in London prior to their anticipated imminent redevelopment. Raymond Smith, the Librarian and Curator at the Guildhall and a member of the CBA, also realised the need for such work to be carried out even though, he added, Kenyon's expectation to carry out immediately an excavation in 'the region of Ludgate Hill' (*Evening Standard* 1944) was premature. Ironically the area she suggested, part of the Fleet valley, was only to be redeveloped for the first time since the Second World War after archaeological excavations had been carried out by the Museum of London's Department of Urban Archaeology (DUA) during the late 1980s. It was probably one of the last remaining major blitzed sites to be developed.

In May 1945 James Mann, the Director of the Society of Antiquaries of London, and Ian Richmond, then the Vice-President of the society, informed the Lord Mayor that the Society of Antiquaries of London wished to form a joint committee, under the presidency of the Lord Mayor, to carry out archaeological research in the City of London. This initial overture for the formation of a committee was not met with much enthusiasm by the Corporation of London and its senior officials. In fact, they were very cold to the idea of such a venture. However, after a few months, and with some testing difficulties, the Improvements and Town Planning Committee of the Corporation of London was persuaded to allow a deputation consisting of James Mann, Ian Richmond and William

Grimes, the Assistant Archaeology Officer to the Ordnance Survey (OS), to attend a meeting on 13 July 1945. Their intention was to put forward the case for the setting up of a 'joint committee with regard to the excavation of Roman London'. The result of this meeting was that Raymond Smith, the Librarian, was permitted by the Improvements and Town Planning Committee to serve on this joint, archaeological committee. At this initial phase, it was to be called the 'Roman London Committee' (GLA, pers corr, 1945).

In the same year (1945), Grimes became the Keeper and Secretary of the London Museum. At the same time, on behalf of the Roman London Committee of the Society of Antiquaries of London, he began some small-scale trial work on the two sites in the City referred to above ('Preface') – at Gutter Lane (LAARC site code WFG25) and Billiter Square (WFG51). A new approach was made to the new Lord Mayor, The Rt Hon Sir Bracewell Smith, to act as President of the committee (since renamed the Roman London Excavation Committee (RLEC)) to enable Grimes to work in the developing City with his authority and, again with the Lord Mayor's seal of approval, as a means of attracting additional sponsorship. This second appeal was very successful and the Lord Mayor's willingness to act as President of the RLEC led to a formal inaugural meeting in the Mansion House on 26 September 1946. It should be noted that, before this meeting it was Grimes, as 'Director of Excavations', who proposed changing the title from the 'Roman London Excavation Committee' to the 'Roman and Mediaeval London Excavation Council' (RMLEC) so that:

a) with the title of 'Council' it might be seen to be a 'parent body rather than an *ad hoc* appendage to a pre-existing organisation' and
b) the inclusion of 'mediaeval' [*sic*] would 'avow clearly our concern also with the later periods' (GLA, pers corr, 18 September 1946).

This title was duly adopted with the archaic spelling of the later period in the title – not Grimes's preferred spelling, it should be noted – insisted upon by an influential member of the Council (Grimes 1968, 221). Immediately efforts were begun to raise support and funds for the examination and excavation of archaeological sites in the City of London. Then, as now, the greatest support always came from the relevant government departments concerned with heritage and ancient monuments through annual grants for excavation and post-excavation work – first from the MoW, then their successors, the Ministry of Public Buildings and Works, the DoE, the HBMC and, most recently, English Heritage. It has to be stressed and acknowledged here without qualification, that without this support from these departments, so often vilified in the context of other programmes of work elsewhere in the country, none of Grimes's work in the City, the sporadic post-excavation work conducted in the late 1960s, 1970s and early 1980s, nor the more recent post-excavation research, archiving and publication programme could have been carried out at all.

With the solid assistance of the Executive of the Council and a number of skilled and trusted employees, especially Gordon Atkinson, Fred Beasley, A J Haydon, George Rybot and Audrey Williams, Grimes examined a further 61 sites in and around the City of London under the auspices of the RMLEC. He always insisted on employing staff to work on his site, rather than accepting casual volunteers. He was mindful of the need for speed and accuracy in the often-dangerous surroundings of his excavations and felt that such places were not conducive as training excavations or the venues for volunteer programmes. Not that he was against such programmes – he oversaw the work of George Rybot, who collected a volunteer and student work force to examine sites WFG6 and WFG7 in the Noble Street length of city wall between the west gate (WFG5) and the south-west corner of the fort (WFG9). The results of that work are included in this report (Chapter 6.1).

The 61 RMLEC sites were excavated while he was still the Director of the London Museum and, subsequently from 1955, Director of the Institute of Archaeology, University of London. Not surprisingly, he put a lot of trust in individuals such as Audrey Williams, who were on site daily, and often his contribution to the individual excavations would be sporadic visits when, in between his museum and university duties, he would manage to get down to site. It is for this reason that photographs of him on RMLEC sites often show him in a suit – not his normal dark blue boiler suit which he usually wore when in the field – see for example photographs of him at Sutton Hoo (Suffolk) and, in 1944, at Gutter Lane (Fig 1). In 1962, however, the decision was made to wind up the excavation policy of the previous 15 years, although the church of St Mary the Virgin, Aldermanbury, was to be excavated by the RMLEC in 1967 (WFG22a; Chapter 9.5), and to concentrate upon the processing and publication of the large volume of data that he and his assistants had accumulated. It was always his intention to precede the full and detailed publication of the London sites with a general survey of the activities of the RMLEC, and his 1968 book was the result. In that book, he emphasises the interim nature of its contents and makes the point in a number of places that full study of the results of the excavation was still to be carried out for many of the sites he had examined. Unfortunately, Grimes himself was never able to complete his own goal of seeing all his work prepared into a final, publishable format but this was not for the want of trying or due to any neglect on his part of his

responsibilities. To suggest otherwise, as some who worked in the City during the 70s and 80s, is unnecessary, wrong and – now early in the 21st century, over 30 years in many instances since their own fieldwork, compared to just the 15 or so when Grimes's record was the subject of comment – is, perhaps, hypocritical to the extreme.

As mentioned above, the post-excavation analysis of his work was never neglected. Since the late 1960s this large quantity of data has been steadily processed and analysed by a succession of research assistants, many at the beginning of their careers, such as Joanna Bird, Sarah Macready, Percival Turnbull, Ahmed Youssef, and the present author, John Shepherd. However, throughout the 1970s and the early 1980s, as the costs of archaeological excavation and research rose alarmingly, his honest intentions so often expressed in his 1968 volume to produce a definitive account of his work became more and more idealistic. Paradoxically his ambitions were not helped by a new generation of archaeologists who, for the most part, laudably accelerated the rate of research and excavation thus putting additional pressure on the few public funds which were available for post-excavation and research. As new work was being conducted and attracted funding, Grimes's work was demoted to the status of 'backlog', for which at the time there were few

Fig 1 Grimes at Gutter Lane, 1944

incentives for funding. Priorities lay elsewhere and, unfortunately, Grimes himself was excluded from the debate as to what these priorities should be (W F Grimes, pers comm). But while he was receiving scant support from the City, archaeologists and Corporation alike, he continued to receive support from the DoE and its successors. The comment made above about the continuing support of the government departments in the 1970s and early 80s must be repeated here. The importance of his work was always acknowledged and some funds made available so that, even if the work was not completed during this period, the RMLEC archive was at least maintained and processed. As 'Anno Domini crept up on him', as he would say, the task of getting the material into a format which could be properly published became ever greater. But the RMLEC archive was never neglected.

1.2 The Museum of London and the Grimes London Archive

In January 1988, W F Grimes, Hugh Chapman (then the Deputy Director of the Museum of London) and Peter Marsden (then Section Head of Field Section I in the Museum's DUA) signed an agreement that would agree the transfer to the Museum of London the full responsibility for ensuring the maintenance and the publication of the RMLEC material. In June 1988, the present author spent three days with Grimes sorting through his papers and receiving his instructions as to how he envisaged the material to be published, including for example his personal desire that as much of his own original artwork, of which he was justifiably proud, should be included in the publications. This material was to be called the Grimes London Archive (GLA) in order to differentiate it from the other parts of his professional archive that included material from his many other excavations around the country, for example his work as archaeologist to the OS on the airfield sites during the war, and was placed in the care of the then Prehistoric and Roman Department of the Museum of London, now the Department of Early London History and Collections, with the Roman Curator Jenny Hall as Manager and the present author, the last of Grimes's full-time research assistants during the early 1980s, as Curator of the archive. As mentioned above, Grimes left a number of specific verbal instructions on what should be published and how certain elements of the archive should be presented, but he allowed the Museum of London the freedom to determine the proper publication strategy. Sadly, W F Grimes died, aged 83, on Christmas Day 1988, just six months after the transfer of his archive into the public domain (Fig 2).

In 1990 the Museum of London began working in coordination with English Heritage (especially Gill Andrews and Roger Thomas) to ensure the correct archiving and processing of the GLA. By 1992, full assessments of the records and finds from the total 63 sites conducted by Grimes in the City and as Director of Excavations of the RMLEC had been completed and proposals for publication had been submitted. This work was carried out in keeping with English Heritage's (1991) *Management of archaeological projects* (MAP2), although the application of the principles contained in MAP2 on Grimes's archive, excavated according to a non-single context system, required some pragmatism in its application, resulting in a few very successful compromises. For example, from the archiving point of view, while it was possible to subdivide the Grimes material into specific components it was evident that certain components, so important in modern archives and research projects, were missing and unlikely to ever be available. Their absence was not allowed to prevent the progress of the project to publication stage.

1.3 The London Archaeological Archive and the RMLEC

Although the Roman temple of Mithras at Walbrook, which he and Audrey Williams excavated between 1952 and 1954 (Shepherd 1998a) is undoubtedly the best known of Grimes's discoveries in the City of London and for which, much to his bemusement (quoted above, 1.1), he was awarded Commander of the Order of the British Empire (CBE), he was the first to point out that he would much rather have had an award bestowed upon him for the discovery of the Roman fort in the Cripplegate area. This is not to say that he was ashamed of his work at the Walbrook and was very proud of the honour bestowed upon him – on the contrary, the efficiency and detail with which the building was examined, along with the other areas of the Walbrook site, were an important factor that made the publication of the site possible. It was rather that, in his own words, the temple discovery was in the nature of a 'fluke' and as such was a discovery made in marked contrast to the careful planning and research which went into the discovery and the elucidation of the Cripplegate fort.

It is the intention of the following volume, therefore, to present the information that he recorded during his campaign of work in the Cripplegate area of the City. This extended over a long period of time, from 1946 to 1968, in fact, for as long as the RMLEC's fieldwork programme was in existence, and his records contain a variety of recording methods as well as the work of a large number of individuals, especially Audrey Williams. His early work reveals what has to be described as a casual, almost naive approach to the recording of some of the stratigraphy he encountered. Only select layers are described and finds survival was not regarded as a priority to record – finds were also selected. Later, from the late 1950s onwards, his recording becomes more detailed and involved and

Fig 2 Professor W F Grimes, 1905–88 (photograph by Peter Marsden)

even later in his campaign, especially on his work on the temple of Mithras in 1954, one can see the beginnings of a recording system which, had it been allowed to evolve, might well have resulted in the introduction of something similar to the single context recording system a full 15–20 years before it was introduced by Museum of London's DUA. However, such a study of his comparative recording strategies is not for the present volume. Because of the variability in his recording methods, as well as the variability in the quantity and quality of the archive components available for each of his sites examined in the Cripplegate area, the format of this volume is more in the format of the presentation of the data from each site, with a short synthesis, thus allowing subsequent researchers to understand these variables that exist in the GLA for the Cripplegate area. Such summaries are included here with references to the relevant parts of the archive itself. All of Grimes's documentation and

the associated finds from his work in the City of London is available for study in the London Archaeological Archive and Research Centre (LAARC), part of the Museum of London, together with the archives and finds from the more recent work in the area. Full use has been made here of Professor Grimes's own artwork to his instructions, but – as for the temple of Mithras report (Shepherd 1998a) – we have digitally altered some of his artwork, many of which were his working drawings and site records, in order to make them more presentable and accessible for publication. The graphical conventions used in this report are shown on Fig 3. Once again, the originals from which the annotated copies published here are available for consultation and study in the LAARC.

One very important feature of GLA is the relative completeness in terms of the sequence he attempted to record of the archive for each site. This is in keeping with his desire to change the name of the RLEC to include the archaeology of later periods – and indeed, he recorded not just medieval sequences but even sequences up to the early modern period. To a certain degree, the reason why he did this in the Cripplegate area was, as will be seen, the close proximity of the Roman archaeological levels to his contemporary working levels – such as the basements of the blitzed Victorian warehouses and buildings along Noble Street and at the back of Bastion 14 and Barber-Surgeons' Hall (Fig 5, WFG2, WFG4, WFG6–WFG9). Therefore, in his efforts to ensure that the Roman levels were not overlooked or damaged by his activities, and in order to objectively record the fine details of the Roman sequence of the Cripplegate fort once he found it, Grimes saw to it that the complete archaeological sequence for each site was recorded. This resulted in a thorough review of the post-Roman phases on the same sites discussed here, with some additional analysis of the city ditch profiles and fills excavated by Grimes at, for example, Fore Street and Cripplegate Buildings (WFG17 and WFG18); they are presented in the companion volume to this (Milne 2001).

The Roman fort at Cripplegate, located as it was to the west of the contemporary Roman town sometime during the early 2nd century AD, is a rather uncomfortable appendage to Londinium (Fig 4). In part this is due to the rare, but not unique, occurrence of such a military structure in such close proximity to a civilian centre – and, in this case, in the southern part of the province of Britannia, at some distance from the more established military centres of the province. It can be argued, however, that its presence might be an important link in the lines of communication of the army on the frontier and elsewhere in the province, connecting it with its main supply bases along the south-east coast of Britain, perhaps including Londinium itself. However, the fact that we know so little about the role of this fort might also be due to a lack of study of the area, which has only recently become the focus of renewed archaeological activity during the 1990s, as those buildings which succeeded Grimes's fieldwork, constructed in the 1950s, became redundant to a new generation of computer-assisted businesses in the City. This work has now been published (see especially Howe and Lakin 2004); and

the work by Howe and Lakin in particular, more so than Grimes's work that focused primarily on the now scheduled or inaccessible areas of the defences of the fort itself, has once again drawn attention to this enigmatic part of the City.

Whether the recent work has much to add to that conducted by Grimes, other than in detail, is open to debate, but that does not deny the fact that the work of the 1990s has been critical in our understanding of the history of the fort and, by extension, the role of the fort and the nature of its relationship with the civilian zone to the immediate east. The following volume, long overdue, is presented here as a complement to the more recent work, presenting the evidence from Grimes's work on those sites on which he first elucidated the outline of a fort. The finds data from these sites, sadly scant in its survival, is also presented to make the accumulative study complete for future researchers to reassess the evidence. What is easy to agree is that, as a result of the work of the RMLEC presented here, along with the medieval sequence presented by Milne and the work of the various archaeological units that has been published in a variety of places, the Cripplegate area will once again attract the kind of attention that led Grimes to open the first trench of his extensive research excavation campaign in that area in July 1947.

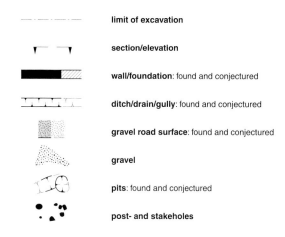

Fig 3 Graphical conventions used in this report

2 Cripplegate before Grimes

2.1 Another unexpected discovery

It is a fundamental fact of archaeological fieldwork that, until that work commences, it is often very unwise to attempt anything more than a tentative prediction about what might be found in the course of the excavation. Desktop evaluation might give one a clue, and trial excavation might be revealing, but both these methodologies are known to be flawed, at the cost to many an embarrassed archaeologist around the world, especially in urban contexts. How many have discovered that their predictions have been proved to be misleading or under-representative of the real nature of the extant archaeological evidence? How many post-excavation programmes have also suffered from pre-negotiated and capped levels of funding because of misleading, supposedly objectively quantified, predictions of the anticipated quantity of evidence to be discovered? It is also generally understood that, even as the archaeology is being recorded *in situ* during the excavation itself, the picture that is gathered is often so fragmentary that any conclusive interpretation must await the post-excavation stage of the process. And yet there are times when the story that the archaeology presents, even as an excavation is underway, contrasts so dramatically with any prediction, is so unexpected and has such an immediate impact upon previous understandings and interpretations, a paradigm of discovery no less, that all previous interpreters of the available data can be forgiven for their failures to see, what in hindsight, is so obvious the case.

This 'unexpected' phenomenon, a feature of any experimental or exploratory process, has always played a major role in British archaeology – in fact, one can perhaps say in archaeology in general – and, arguably, it is the chance of revealing the unexpected that probably attracts so many, from all walks of life and in all manner of ways, to archaeology as a discipline and hobby in itself. The excitement of the discovery and the immediate advancement of knowledge is a great catalyst for anyone's interest. There is no respite to the surprise factor that thrills and excites all of us involved in archaeology. Even in the City of London, one of the most thoroughly archaeologically explored areas of the country with a vast archive of information and data, an accumulation of over 300 years of work, ranging from casual observations to antiquarian comments and, more recently, scientifically recorded stratigraphic sequences and new discoveries continue to cast new light on the lives of those who previously inhabited the region of London. Often, this is in the form of a simple, single item, such as an item of personal adornment from a grave, perhaps, or a scrap of waste material from a craft or industry, but it can still be in the form of something large and, quite simply, staggering to our understanding of London.

A recent and well-known example of the latter was the discovery of the Roman amphitheatre in the area of the Guildhall, City of London, in 1988. The scale of this building demonstrates only too well how it is possible for archaeological features of major proportions to remain hidden for so long. In this case, we now know that a post-war observation and an earlier formal excavation by the DUA had located elements of the amphitheatre, but at the time, no one ever had been able to make the interpretive leap from those scant remains to a Roman amphitheatre. Only with hindsight, in the light of the discovery of recognisable elements of a Roman amphitheatre, is it possible to see that the combination of the large open area of Guildhall Yard itself, the eccentric orientation of the church of St Lawrence Jewry, the location of the medieval Guildhall and the medieval road system skirting around an elliptical zone demonstrate that the presence there of a substantial topographical feature was perhaps obvious. One need only to suggest a structure with a large open space on the interior at a short distance from the fort to the north-west, and then compare and contrast with another British site such as Caerleon (Monmouthshire) in south Wales, to suggest that the medieval topography perhaps sealed an amphitheatre. So much for hindsight, but many generations of antiquarians and archaeologists, even those who had their offices in or near the Guildhall itself, failed to make the connection. This is not a criticism, merely an illustration of how the obvious so often eludes the archaeologist.

The unexpected, too, played a very large part in the discovery of the temple of Mithras alongside the Walbrook in 1954 and, indeed, Grimes confessed to this (Chapter 1.1). His original intention on that site was to record an east–west profile through the valley of the Walbrook watercourse, an important topographic feature in the City of London that had previously been variously described as anything from a minor stream to a major river. The remains of the temple became apparent as soon as he lifted the basement slab in his trenches in 1952, but the apsidal building was not identified as a Mithraeum until the very last day of excavation in 1954 (Shepherd 1998a, 165–7) when the head of Mithras himself, one of Roman London's iconic images, was discovered. However, the existence of a Mithraeum in the vicinity should have been anticipated because of the presence of three sculptures in the London Museum collections, which included a Mithras Tauroctonos relief (MOL acc no. A16933) found in 1889, with a 'Walbrook' provenance. Perhaps Grimes had remarked the provenance of these sculptures before he began work, it is unlikely that he would have overlooked them, but his thoughts about what he anticipated finding are restricted to matters related to his original intention of examining the Walbrook valley. He genuinely never expected to locate the building itself – and certainly not in such a good state of preservation so high up in the archaeological sequence on the site (W F Grimes, pers comm).

However, of all the major discoveries which have been made in London since the Second World War, one of the most startling and unexpected to all involved in the study of the archaeology and history of London at the time, has to be the discovery of the Roman fort in the north-west corner of the City of London, generally known as the Cripplegate area and named after Cripplegate Ward, which itself is named after medieval Cripplegate which originally straddled Wood Street. There had been no finds previously of any sort to suspect a military encampment there – in actual fact, there had been few Roman finds in the area at all (below, 2.2). Yet, once again, as soon as the all-important piece of evidence was discovered, in this case the interval tower at the south end of Noble Street (WFG9; Fig 4) had been discovered in 1949, all of the pieces of the puzzle began to fall into place – even those pieces which had been visible for, literally, centuries but had never been regarded as being of any great significance other than anomalies in the general fabric of Roman (and, subsequently, medieval) London.

Cripplegate is located in the north-western corner of the City of London and takes its name from the gate on the northern part of the wall linking London Wall with Fore Street (Fig 4). Aldersgate and the Museum of London border the area on the west side, the church of St Giles Cripplegate, the Barbican and Fore Street are located to the north, London Wall, Moorgate, Aldermanbury and the Guildhall are to the east and Gresham Street is to the south (Fig 5; Fig 6). When Grimes examined the site in the 1940s and 50s, the main thoroughfares in the area were Wood Street, which ran south from Cripplegate to Cheapside, and Silver Street and Addle Street, which both ran approximately east–west, to converge at the junction with Wood Street in a location that approximates with the centre of the Roman fort. Aldermanbury skirted down the east side of the area and Falcon Square (no longer in existence) was located on the west side. Cripplegate Buildings was a small road on the north side of the gate at Cripplegate itself that continued the line of Wood Street and made a junction with Fore Street to the north. Fore Street itself marks the north side of the position of the city ditches in this area and London Wall, running parallel with Fore Street, was located inside the city wall and evidently grew from a road at the foot of the city wall bank. On the west side

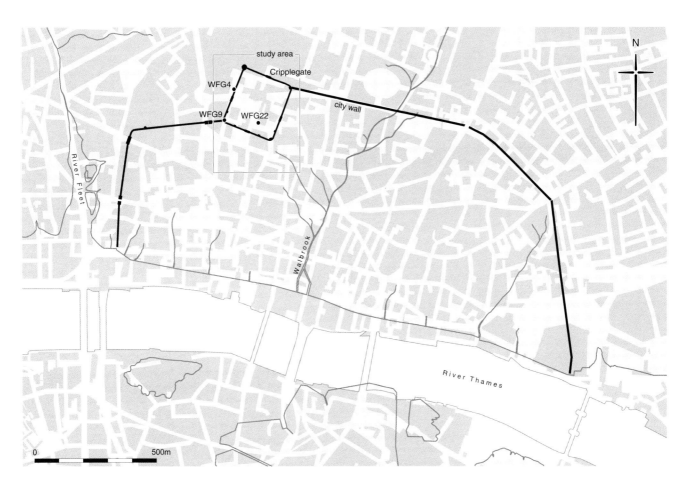

Fig 4 Plan of London showing the location of the Cripplegate study area (with location of three of Grimes's sites shown) in the north-west corner of the City; modern Thames shoreline and bridges shown in lighter tone (scale 1:15,000)

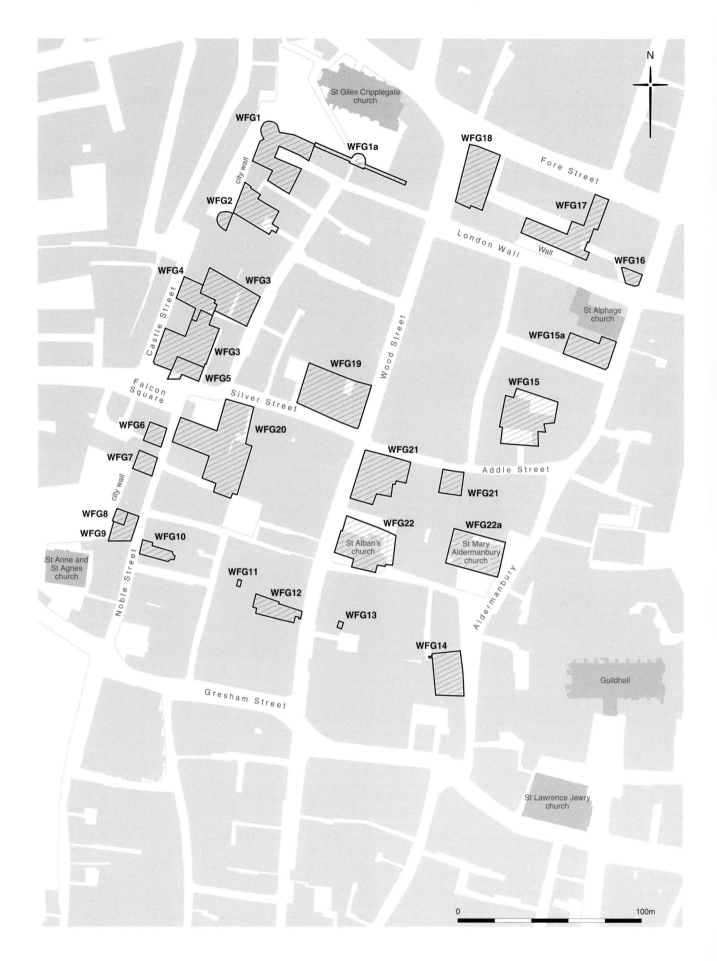

Fig 5 The locations of the RMLEC sites superimposed on the contemporary street plan (see Table 1 for site details) (scale 1:2000)

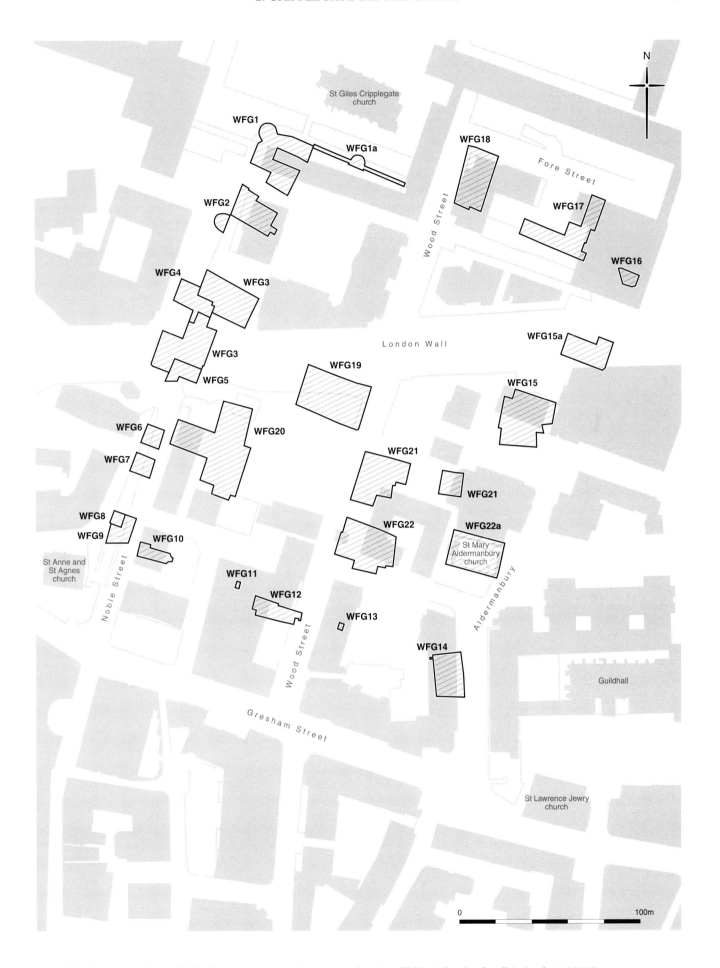

Fig 6 The locations of the RMLEC sites on a modern street plan (see Table 1 for site details) (scale 1:2000)

of the study area, Noble Street also appears to have evolved from an intramural road. Numerous small alleys and lanes of medieval foundation intersected the entire area, like much of the rest of the City of London. Many of these still survive in the modern cityscape despite the intensive rebuilding (Fig 6; see Milne 2001 for the medieval sequence at Cripplegate).

2.2 Archaeology in Cripplegate before the Blitz

In his 1968 volume Grimes makes reference to the fact that his interim account had 'a limited purpose and does not attempt to take in all the evidence, whether of recent or more remote origin, on which a complete study of early London would require to be based' (Grimes 1968, 1). In truth, although this statement might be relevant to other areas that he examined, such as at Cheapside, Paternoster Square or Queen Victoria Street, all in the City of London, where there had been numerous earlier discoveries and observations, it is difficult to see exactly what earlier evidence he had in mind for Cripplegate. Very little earlier work had been conducted there and, just as his work on the interior of the fort was to demonstrate, there would appear to have been little to discover there in the first place! During the 19th century, when large and deep-cellared buildings were being constructed across the City, the distribution of discoveries of the remains of mosaic pavements or even simply walls from buildings seem to stop far short of the Cripplegate area. As Grimes was to discover when he carried out his initial assessment of the areas available for excavation, Cripplegate had also received its fair share of deep-cellared buildings, but there is not a single antiquarian discovery or record of any kind associated with the interior of the zone surrounded by the city wall. However, the same was not the case for the area outside the city wall, although these observations are few. The first part of the following section examines briefly, therefore, these few records in order to make a more complete study of this area as Grimes intended.

Briefly, however, and before presenting these antiquarian observations, reference should be made to one of the earliest attempts to create a map of Roman London – if only to point out what at first sight appears to be a remarkable, though coincidental, piece of speculation. With a degree of certainty that was in marked contrast with the evidence available at the time, Stukeley recorded on his map of 1722 the presence of a 'castrum exploratorum' in the north-west corner of the City (Fig 7). One could be forgiven for thinking that the label was describing the area of Cripplegate itself, but closer analysis shows a small flag on a mound in what is now the Barbican area. Harben (1918) explains that the first definite mention of 'Barbecanstrut' occurs in 1348 (*Cal Husting Wills* i,

525) and 'seems to have derived its name from the tower which once stood on the north side, fronting Redcross Street'. There is also a reference to the tower, by Stow, as being pulled down (by Henry III in 1267) then probably rebuilt and the site given (by Edward III) to Robert Earl of Suffolk in 1336 by the name of his manor of Base Court, commonly called Barbican (Stowe 1956). For example, 'Bas Court, Barbican', is described as 'A house with gardens called "La Bas Court" by Crypelgate' (*Cal Pat R Edw III*, 1330–4, p 106). Wherever this house and the tower were located, it is likely that Stukeley regarded it as a feature that had a Roman precedent.

Irrespective of this possible extramural feature, one important structure in this area that frequently attracted the attention of the artist and, later, the photographer was the wall and horseshoe-shaped bastion (Bastion 12) in the churchyard of St Giles Cripplegate. This churchyard was one of the largest in the area and, no doubt, was a quiet retreat from the hustle and the bustle of 18th- and 19th-century London. There are many views of the medieval defences there, some of which show in great detail the diaper brickwork of the late 15th-century rebuild of Mayor Jocelyn. As an open, consecrated area, the churchyard escaped development in the late 19th century and continued to be a site of interest, even meriting its own postcard (Fig 8). The curve of Bastion 13 can also be seen at the rear of that view; all of the buildings pictured were to be destroyed in 1940.

The construction of the warehouses and offices in the Cripplegate area in the 19th century, many with deep, even double basements as mentioned above, revealed no details of any note other than the quite spectacular unveiling of Bastion 14 (Fig 9). This, though, was soon engulfed again in the new building work only to reappear following the devastation of 1940.

Of more significance to this study, however, is the reference to a coin hoard and other Roman remains in Well Street/Jewin Street, 'close by the Old London Wall, a few yards from the outside of the circular bastion still remaining in Cripplegate Churchyard' (Anon 1847, 272–3). The north end of the Museum of London coincides with the former position of Jewin Street. The coin hoard, exhibited by a Mr Chaffers, consisted of 68 silver denarii. There was one of Galba, five of Vespasian, five of Domitian, one of Nerva, 21 of Trajan, 21 also of Hadrian, two of Sabina, eight of Antoninus Pius and, finally, four of Faustina the Elder. It was further noted that the latest issues were in almost mint condition. Therefore, a mid 2nd-century deposition date, contemporary with the life of the Cripplegate fort, can be suggested. In the same street, Mr Chaffers also discovered 'sepulchral internments from which some urns, one containing burnt bones, were exhibited' (ibid, 273). Two ceramic vessels in the Museum of London's collections, both described in the accession registers as 'cinerary urns' come from Well

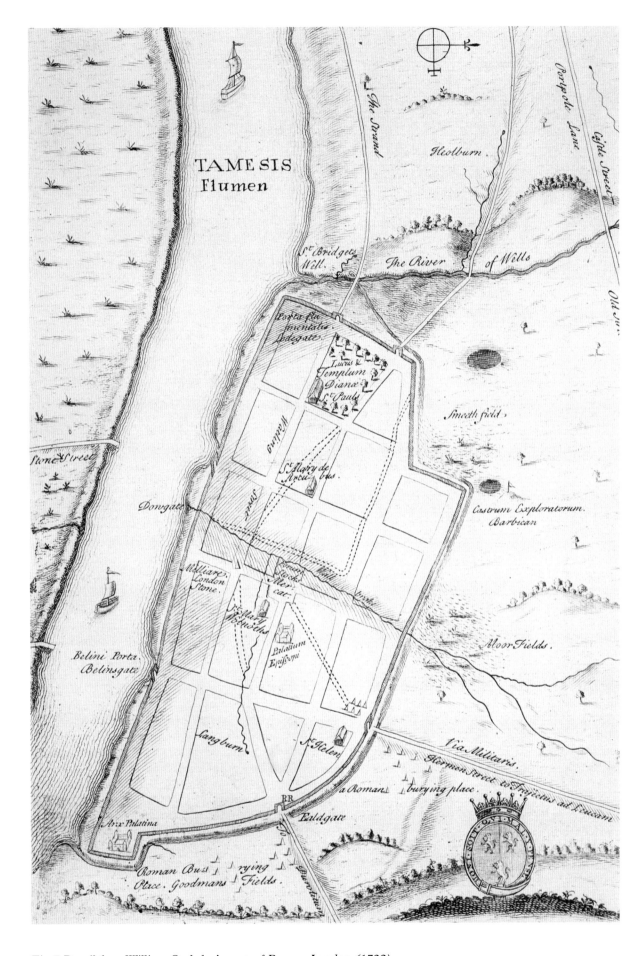

Fig 7 Detail from William Stukeley's map of Roman London (1722)

Fig 8 The Cripplegate Bastion (Bastion 12) just before the First World War, view looking south-west

Street. A grey coarse gritted domestic cooking pot, a Thameside Kent hook-rimmed jar (MOL acc no. 21993) *c* 190mm high, was found in 1846 (Fig 10). Such vessels were often used as cemetery grave goods (eg Barber and Bowsher 2000, 236, CB785), and can be broadly dated to *c* AD 180–300 (B Richardson, pers comm). The second (MOL acc no. 22006) is a coarse cup of creamy yellow ware, *c* 100mm high. Sadly, this vessel can no longer be located in the Museum of London's collections.

In the late 19th century, major rebuilding of the area stretching between Bastion 13 (WFG2) and westwards towards Aldersgate took place following a devastating fire. This too, unfortunately, failed to attract much antiquarian attention. John Terry examined the exterior of Cripplegate Bastion (Bastion 12; Terry 1906) and he also carried out a small excavation at its foot, which, from his observations, he determined to be Roman in origin. This work did not reveal a great deal because his small trench was located over the 17th-century backfilling of the city ditch. The only feature he recorded in detail was a large brick drain, which he believed was built to drain the ditch

itself. Baddeley (1921, 10) equated this with the record in the 'Remembrancia' that in 1634 the City Authorities, with the assistance of Inigo Jones, proposed that a 'vaulted sewer of four feet [1.2m] in breadth at the bottom and six feet [1.8m] at least in height should be made from Moor-ditch to the Minories and so to the Thames'. He believed that Terry's discovery evidently showed that the scheme was also carried out to the west of Moorgate.

This dearth of evidence for the Roman period in the Cripplegate area prior to Grimes's work resulted in very few references in the Royal Commission volume on Roman London (RCHM(E) 1928). Terry's erroneous dating of Bastion 13 is repeated verbatim without comment (ibid, 104) and other references relate to medieval wall fragments in the region. However, one important passage is repeated below in full.

One further point may be noticed here. The curious planning of the landward wall on the N.W. side, with its deep re-entrant angle between Cripplegate and Newgate, has never been

*Fig 9 Bastion 14 revealed in 1865 (*Illustrated London News *1865)*

satisfactorily explained and no definite explanation will be here attempted. It may, however, be noted that the two walls of the right-angled salient, W. of Cripplegate, are parallel or at right angles to the fairly well authenticated road between Newgate and the Walbrook-crossing at Bucklersbury. It is possible, therefore, that this salient represents a skirting, by the wall, of a quarter already definitely laid out before the wall was built. (RCHM(E) 1928, 79)

The last sentence of this paragraph, written by none other than Mortimer Wheeler, proved to have a semblance of truth about it. As will be seen, although the wall did not skirt around a previously laid out area, its course was certainly designed to include a pre-existing zone of use.

When Grimes and his team first approached this

Fig 10 Thameside Kent hook-rimmed jar (MOL acc no. 21993) discovered by Mr Chaffers in 1846 at Well Street (scale c *1:2)*

area, therefore, there was very little evidence for the Roman period available for it. Indeed, other than the expectation to confirm that the foundation of the wall was indeed Roman in date, there were no preconceptions whatsoever of the real nature or extent of the Roman remains there. Grimes was in the fortunate position of knowing that, whatever they did in this area, it was guaranteed to increase the sum of knowledge about Cripplegate.

2.3 War comes to the City

It is well documented that the area at Cripplegate became available for archaeological excavation as a result of the destruction caused by enemy action during the Second World War (Ministry of Information 1942; Johnson 1980; Ramsey 1988; see also Fig 11 for a schematic drawing showing the extent of the damage in the area of the City of London). This began, on a relatively small scale, on 25 August 1940, during the first half hour after midnight, when a total of 40 bombs were recorded by the Home Office Security Appreciation as falling on the Fore Street area of the City of London. Indeed a plaque on the north wall of

Roman House, at the junction of Fore Street and Cripplegate Buildings, records this as the location of the very first bomb to hit the City of London during the Second World War.

However, on Sunday 29–Monday 30 December 1940, a combination of munitions was dropped that was to have a devastating effect on Cripplegate and many other neighbouring areas. Visibility that night was moderate to poor, but it was fair over London and only became cloudy by dawn. On the Continent, visibility was poor to moderate due to a fresh, strong westerly wind with lowering cloud, which brought rain and drizzle. In these favourable conditions, between 18:17 and 21:30 hours, 136 bombers (107 of Luftflotte 3 and 29 of Luftflotte 2, consisting of Junker 88s, Heinkel 111s and Dornier 17s) attacked the City and government areas of London with 127 tonnes of high explosives. The attack was compressed to ensure that aircraft could return to base before the anticipated arrival of bad weather conditions on the Continent.

The attack was commenced by 10 Heinkel 111 aircraft and Luftflotte 3 with the dropping of an initial 10,470 incendiaries – just under half of a total of 22,068 incendiary bombs that were dropped throughout the entire raid. At one point during this

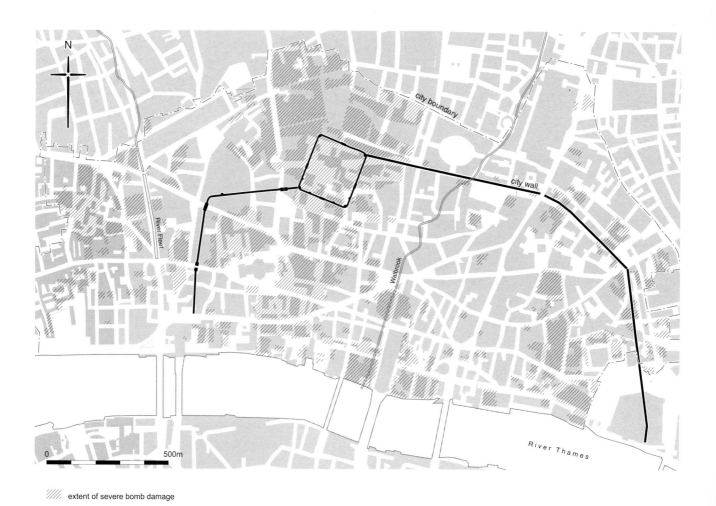

///// extent of severe bomb damage

Fig 11 Extent of Second World War severe bomb damage within the area of the City of London (scale 1:15,000)

initial assault, 300 incendiary bombs were striking the City each minute. The intention of this preliminary incendiary run was to begin fires so that following groups of aircraft, arriving in the 30 minutes up to 18:50 hours, were able to line up on their targets using the light of the fires below. It was a very successful stratagem. Pilots reported afterwards that a total of 54 large fires could easily be seen at that time, 17 of them were very large, and by the end of the attack at 21:30 hours the final crews over the area reported that the number of fires visible from above had risen to well over 100. On the ground, however, a total of 1500 individual fires were recorded throughout the evening and night. Initially breaks in the cloud made it possible for pilots to bomb visually, but later in the raid the thick black smoke emanating from the fires made it difficult to see even the explosions of the bombs that were being dropped. As on so many other nights during the Blitz of 1940–1, the anti-aircraft fire from the ground – impressive though it must have sounded to the Londoners nearby – caused very few problems to Luftflotten 2 and 3 of the Luftwaffe. A total of 4000 rounds were fired by anti-aircraft batteries throughout the evening at enemy aircraft flying from 9000ft to 25,000ft (2743m to 7620m). Batteries on the Medway, Thames, around Slough (Buckinghamshire), the Solent, Portsmouth and the Isle of Wight (all in Hampshire) were all involved but no enemy aircraft were reported as being destroyed. Only one German aircraft was lost, a Junker 88 crashed on landing at its home airfield.

In the City, thousands of offices and warehouses built of brick, mortar and timber, all at least 50 years old, contained highly combustible contents: paper, wooden furniture, panelling and stairs. Old cities burn easily, a fact known to the Luftwaffe, so their tactic was not chosen at random. The initial hail of incendiaries shattered through the roofs of these buildings, setting alight the dusty loft spaces and upper parts of the structures. Eyewitnesses reported that there were very few people about in the City, it being a Sunday evening, and even firewatchers appear to have been thin on the ground. Herbert Mason (Ramsey 1988, 359), the photographer of the iconic picture of the dome of St Paul's Cathedral wreathed by the smoke of buildings burning all around it (Fig 12), noted that:

Fig 12 St Paul's Cathedral wreathed in fire and smoke, 29–30 December 1940, view looking east (photograph by Herbert Mason, by permission of Daily Mail*)*

The tragedy of this second great fire of London was the fact that there were so few firewatchers. Single-handed I could have prevented thousands of pounds' worth of damage being done, but the buildings were locked, there was nobody present to force an entry. There were so few people. It was pathetic.

The addition of high explosives to this cocktail of destruction broke open the buildings and helped to spread the fires across properties. As the fires intensified the heat from them caused neighbouring properties to combust into flames. The fire services struggled all night to get sufficient water, and water pressure, to tackle the fires. The Thames tide was at an abnormally low ebb at the start of the raid making it difficult to pump water from the river. Initially fire crews found they were able to get some water and good pressure from the mains, but as the draw on the water from numerous crews around the City became greater, the pressure subsided. The results of high explosives hitting roads also broke many mains supplies. In many cases, it was simply impossible for the fires to be tackled and properties had to be left to burn themselves

Fig 13 Detail from the London County Council bomb damage map showing the extent of damage in the Cripplegate area; the circle to the north-west of St Giles Cripplegate (top left corner of figure) indicates the point of impact of the 1944 V1 flying bomb (LMA: LCC war damage maps sheet 62)

out. As the evening wore on, and the tide rose, the work of the fire crews was made slightly easier, especially closer to the Thames, but so many fires were burning that it was anticipated that the next wave of attacks would simply add to the destruction already caused. However, the Luftwaffe did not return that night – fog on the Channel coast grounded all their aircraft.

One massive conflagration burnt over an area extending in the north from Aldersgate Street underground station (now Barbican station) across to Moorgate station down to Cheapside in the south (Fig 13). On this night alone, London lost its medieval Guildhall, a number of company halls including Barber-Surgeons' Hall, eight churches including St Alban on Wood Street, St Mary Aldermanbury in the Cripplegate area, St Bride and St Lawrence Jewry. Guy's Hospital, Southwark, had to be evacuated as were eight other hospitals. Telecommunications were severely disrupted as a result of the loss of the Central Telegraph Office, and the destruction of a modern telephone exchange in Wood Street had what was to be the worst effect on the telecommunications infrastructure throughout the entire war. St Paul's Cathedral survived, recorded at the time by Mason, even though incendiary bombs struck the dome and some, unexploded incendiaries, got stuck in the

cathedral gutters. Because the City was largely empty of people that Sunday evening, casualties there were low but 16 firemen were killed and 250 injured. However, bombing in more populated areas nearby, at Millwall, Victoria and the London Docks, resulted in 163 civilian deaths and 509 injuries.

The Cripplegate part of the City was to be struck by bombs again during the next few years but there was simply nothing much left to destroy after that night (Fig 14; Fig 15). A V1 flying bomb (doodlebug), for example, struck *c* 200m to the immediate north-east of St Giles Cripplegate in 1944. By the end of the war, a vast area extending north–south from just south of Old Street, in the Jews Garden area of the Barbican, to Carter Lane near St Paul's Cathedral and east–west from Cheapside and Old Change to the temple had been destroyed. Rather than describe what was destroyed in the Cripplegate area, it is far easier to simply list the buildings that survived: they were 12, 16 and 17 Noble Street; 37, 63, 64 and 85–89 Wood Street; 2–4 Little Love Lane; and 61–64 Aldermanbury.

It was in this devastated area that Grimes and the RMLEC were to focus their initial efforts of their campaign of work begun immediately after the war and in which the majority of their fieldwork was conducted over the coming 20 years.

Fig 14 (below and facing) View south towards St Paul's Cathedral of the destruction at Moorgate (left), Barbican (centre) and Cripplegate (distant) (LMA, Cross and Tibbs Collection, 1942, cat no. m0020324cl; reproduced with the permission of the Chief Commissioner of the Metropolitan Police)

*Fig 15 View west from Moorgate, looking down the line of the city wall at London Wall, towards Cripplegate (*Illustrated London News *1957)*

3 Finding the Roman fort in Cripplegate

3.1 The RMLEC's plan of attack

When the RMLEC, in its earliest manifestation as the RLEC, was formed towards the end of the war, they had numerous objectives. It was evident that the City's Roman past could be elucidated but, as described (Chapter 1.1), it was made more than apparent by Grimes himself that the study of the medieval history of the City was also a priority. Intent on recording both of these periods, therefore, the stretch of the city wall in the Fore Street, Cripplegate, London Wall, Falcon Square and Noble Street region was an obvious and tempting monument for study. Grimes was aware, however, that this exercise – examining the city wall of a town – was traditional in its approach. He wrote (Grimes 1968, 15–17) that:

> This decision (to commence with the city wall) was not of course governed entirely by the practical requirements of the immediate situation. In the nature of things, the defences of a city are not normally as productive of occupation-material as are the actual dwelling-sites and it is upon occupation-material that the dating of the different elements depends.

In 1947, therefore, Grimes was free to begin examining those basements that were clear of rubble and other clutter in the belief that a rebuilding programme on these sites was still a few years away. Having arranged permission from the Barber-Surgeons' livery company, the freeholders of the majority of properties on the western side of the area, especially the Barber-Surgeons' Hall itself (WFG2) and Windsor Court (WFG3), he was able to begin a programme of work that can be said to have initiated scientific excavation, recording and analysis of London's archaeology. As elsewhere on his sites in London, hired workmen under the supervision of a trained and trusted individual carried out this work. In the early years this was Mr A J Haydon with the role passing over to Fred (Pop) Beasley when Haydon died. In 1953, following a successful programme of work in St Albans (Hertfordshire), Grimes was joined by a truly professional archaeologist in the form of Audrey Williams.

In all, the RMLEC examined 25 sites in this study area (Fig 5; Fig 6); site addresses are shown in Table 1.

Grimes's first work was in the north-western corner of the Cripplegate area around Bastion 12 (WFG1) and the ruins of the Barber-Surgeons' Hall (WFG2) (Fig 17a and b). The nature of this work was

Table 1 The 25 sites in the study area with site addresses; for locations see Fig 5 and Fig 6

Site code	Site address
WFG1	Cripplegate Bastion (Bastion 12), 7 Wood Street Square, St Giles Cripplegate churchyard, EC2, City of London
WFG1a	Bastion 11A, 1–4 Hart Street, 4 Cripplegate Buildings, St Giles Cripplegate churchyard, EC2, City of London
WFG2	Barber-Surgeons' Hall (Bastion 13), 34–35 Monkwell Street, 12 Nicholl Square, EC2, City of London
WFG3	Windsor Court and Castle Street, 38–40 Monkwell Street, Monkwell Street chapel, 3–9 Castle Street and 1A Windsor Court, EC2, City of London
WFG4	Bastion 14, 7 Castle Street, EC2, City of London
WFG5	Falcon Square, EC2, City of London
WFG6 and WFG7	20–28 Noble Street, EC2, City of London
WFG8	Bastion 15, 31 Noble Street, EC2, City of London
WFG9	31–32 Noble Street (south-west tower), EC2, City of London
WFG10	Lillypot Lane (fort wall), EC2, City of London
WFG11	Staining Lane (fort wall), EC2, City of London
WFG12	Wood Street (fort south gate), EC2, City of London
WFG13	Wood Street (fort wall), EC2, City of London
WFG14	70a–71 Aldermanbury (fort south-east corner), EC2, City of London
WFG15	Brewers' Hall, Addle Street, EC2, City of London
WFG15a	Aldermanbury (fort wall), EC2, City of London
WFG16	Aldermanbury Postern, EC2, City of London
WFG17	St Alphage churchyard, Fore Street, EC2, City of London
WFG18	Cripplegate Buildings, Roman House, Wood Street, EC2, City of London
WFG19	Silver Street (headquarters building), EC2, City of London
WFG20	15–17 Silver Street, EC2, City of London
WFG21	Addle Street, EC2, City of London
WFG22	St Alban's church, Wood Street, EC2, City of London
WFG22a	St Mary the Virgin, Aldermanbury, EC2, City of London

straightforward – a series of trenches was located perpendicular to the line of the city wall with the intention of revealing a full section through the city defences. The results of this work are well documented in his 1968 volume but it is worth considering the hardships that his team had to contend with during this era in London's archaeological study. The resources of the RMLEC, and the simple unavailability of plant in this post-war period of strict rationing and hardship, meant that every task had to be carried out by hand – including the breaking up of the concrete slabs of the basements. George Faulkner, one of his hired hands who was to join him during 1952–3 and continue with him for almost five years, recalled that:

> I was told when I applied for the job that it wasn't only scratching the earth away, but all the concrete breaking etc had to be done by hand by the team available.
>
> I started on the Roman fort site by helping to mark out 40 feet by 5 feet [12.2 × 1.5m] along the concrete floor of the cellar, about 6inches [0.2m] thick, if I remember right, and was appalled by the tools – or lack of them – that were to do the job. I suggested a compressor, as the contractors used, but was told they cost so much.
>
> So it was down to two 14lb hammers, tongs and a couple of very blunt chisels and points, and as I saw, the tools had never been sharpened. Try knocking out 40' by 5' of 6" concrete with chisel ends the size of your thumbs! (G Faulkner, pers comm, 1994)

And it would appear that everyone pulled their weight – or at least tried to:

> … to give him full credit, Professor Grimes picked up a 14lb hammer to help do 'some bashing'. Timmy [Thomas] turned round to me and said 'Do you want to hold the tongs George?' Grimes said 'No – George is a real hammer man so we'll need him using one as well'. To cut a long story short, Grimes had a few swings – tongs and chisel-head about evens – then laughed and said he'd better pack it in when a 'wag' from the on-looking crowd called out 'You nearly got it that time Guv'nor!' But he – Grimes – at least took his coat off and tried. (G Faulkner, pers comm, 1994)

Such hardships were, and still are, common to many organisations with limited resources at their disposal and Grimes's decision to make use of, primarily, hired labourers to tackle these onerous tasks is also well recorded (Grimes 1968, 223–8). But there were disadvantages with this strategy which George Faulkner well remembered – evidently with the frustration of

someone who approached his work conscientiously and fully appreciated the purpose of what he was supposed to be doing. When the RMLEC was fully stretched during the mid 1950s, with work going on in the Cripplegate area, on the temple of Mithras site in the centre of the City and at St Bride's church on the west side of the Fleet river, not every site was properly supervised. This lack of supervision led to some severe liberty-taking by some of the workmen. Both of the following episodes, retold by George Faulkner in 1994, were also recalled by Grimes in his epilogue (1968, 224–5).

> When I first came to work there were labourers employed there and a senior man named Tom used to amaze me by going to the top (i.e. off the site) with the crowd and sell some of the 'bits and pieces' to those willing to buy. I didn't think too much of this, and thought to put him off the dealing by saying that those who were connected with the Council along with the sponsors usually came round (unannounced) to see how things were going.
>
> Unfortunately we did have two or three men who came, got paid as the rest of us, but 'hopped' off for an hour or two around Smithfield Market, and didn't like too much of the heavy work. I found out from friends in the market, that it was customary for one or two from our site to go 'barrow pushing' – a perk job when someone had a heavy load to push. When I protested to one individual I was told I wasn't in charge and he knew what he was doing – wasn't mad – had papers to prove it (he showed me a signed statement of discharge from some 'psycho hospital'). I said if Mr. Grimes asks you about your frequent disappearing acts then you'd better show him that. He must have done because Grimes came and told us how he and Audrey had a good laugh when the fellow told him that despite what letters Grimes had, he hadn't a form to say he was sane!

Grimes 'released' the fellow with the certificate after encountering him returning to work after 'an unduly prolonged and mildly alcoholic dinner-break'. Tom also departed after being confronted with his offence, 'without ill-feelings on either side', according to Grimes – and this came as no surprise because Grimes felt that, on sighting him a little while later dressed in more prosperous attire, Tom appeared to be doing quite well for himself (Grimes 1968, 225).

3.2 The start in Cripplegate

In 1947, the main objectives at Cripplegate were to date the foundation of the city wall, to record and date its many alterations, to date and determine the size and

Fig 16 RMLEC workmen breaking out a basement slab at Windsor Court (WFG3) in 1947

position of the city ditch, and to examine the nature and history of the occupation on either side of the city defences. This was a broad and all-encompassing brief. The main areas were at the Cripplegate Bastion, now called Bastion 12 (WFG1), Barber-Surgeons' Hall incorporating another bastion, Bastion 13 (WFG2) and a third bastion, Bastion 14 (WFG4) facing Castle Street (coinciding now with the eastern frontage of the Museum of London). Windsor Court (WFG3) was in the area behind WFG4 (Fig 5; Fig 16; Fig 17). These bastions are persistently called 'late Roman' in Grimes's notes and site records up until 1965, almost the end of the campaign, when Bastion 11A (WFG1a to the east of Cripplegate Bastion) was discovered. His work there showed that this particular bastion was medieval in date (Shepherd 1998b, 33–4). On the basis of plan and location, he concluded that the other bastions in the Cripplegate area were probably of the same date. Subsequent work has done nothing to alter this opinion (Milne 2001, 30–4).

An early and most unexpected discovery at WFG2 was the unusually high level of the original natural surface in the Cripplegate area relative to the modern ground surface. It was a mere 2.45–2.75m below the modern street level and over a large part of the area it had been truncated by the digging of Victorian cellars. While this reduced the amount and volume of information that could be obtained, it also made any extended excavation of the area unnecessary. The absence of deep stratigraphy had inadvertently affected the state of preservation of the wall, which in both the cellars and in many places above ground level had been completely removed and replaced by modern brick walls along the same line. In contrast to this, the ancient fabric of the three visible bastions (Bastions 12–14) had been well preserved behind 19th- and 20th-century brickwork.

Grimes discovered completely undisturbed deposits, however, on two of these initial sites, namely in the Barber-Surgeons' Hall area (WFG2) and at the southern end of the site around Windsor Court (WFG3). It was, therefore, in these two areas, with a trench across Bastion 14 (WFG4), that he concentrated the efforts of his team. Work was hampered by various modern encumbrances, such as foundation stanchions and drains, and the impossibility

a

Fig 17 The three bastions visible in 1947: a – Cripplegate Bastion – Bastion 12 (WFG1), view looking east; b – Barber-Surgeons' Hall bastion – Bastion 13 (WFG2), view looking west; c – bastion at 7 Castle Street – Bastion 14 (WFG4), view looking west

b

c

of examining the ground in detail outside the city wall in 1947 made it difficult to arrive at any conclusions about the date of the numerous alterations he recorded in the fabric of the city wall itself. It has to be admitted that, although the GLA contains a great deal of data about his excavations, there is an unfortunate dearth of detail about the standing remains themselves. It is unclear whether he never got around to recording the standing building remains or there is a serious gap in the archive itself.

As to the defences of the City themselves, it should be emphasised here that Grimes was, during his first season at Cripplegate in 1947, totally unaware that the earliest foundation of the city wall in the Barber-Surgeons' Hall (WFG2) and Bastion 14 (WFG4) area was the western wall of a Roman fort. He observed a number of different fabrics to the wall (Fig 18), one line of wall apparently butting parallel to another, and this led him to note that there may have been extensive rebuilding on a number of occasions in the history of the city wall itself. Furthermore, he recorded that the Roman wall was backed by an earthen bank (composed of material cast up from the external ditch), behind which was a layer of gravel which suggested that there had been a road at the foot of the bank, running parallel with the line of the city wall. He recorded, however, that the wall itself was set unusually high, its foundations being in the bank rather than in the natural ground beneath it. This led him to believe at this early stage in his campaign that it was a later version of a wall on a slightly different line than an earlier one and was narrower, scarcely 1.50m compared to 2.50m, than the city wall seen elsewhere in the City. It was evident that the history of the City's defences was more complex than he had realised. These initial results encouraged him to maintain a presence in this area to disentangle the complex sequence. Although there were few positive conclusions about the history of the city wall itself, the Council's first season of work had given, for the first time in the City of London, an insight into the

Fig 18 The two parallel walls as first seen in 1947 at Bastion 14 (WFG4), view looking west

history of one small area over the full course of the City's existence.

Over the following three years the work of the RMLEC was made all the more difficult by the growing speed of redevelopment – something which appeared to take Grimes and the RMLEC Executive, even with the Lord Mayor as patron, slightly by surprise. This meant that he had to tackle sites upon which building was soon to take place, in order to get as much information from them as possible in advance of their redevelopment, rather than having time to carefully examine the archaeology on these sites. It became evident that this state of affairs, the ever increasing pace of redevelopment, would continue and almost certainly accelerate over the short term. His programme of fieldwork, based largely upon evaluation trenches rather than open excavations, was to change. This acceleration in the pace of redevelopment was also to have a serious effect upon the Council's limited infrastructure, which, apart from the small nucleus of paid labourers, still at that time had no other permanent staff. An attempt was made during the late 40s, therefore, to prepare for such developments by organising a fund-raising drive from the many businesses, institutions and individuals associated with the City of London. A similar drive was initiated in 1954 following the positive publicity for the Council's work with the discovery of the temple of Mithras.

The main focus of interest at this time, during the late 1940s, for the RMLEC was still around Cripplegate,

which continued to produce valuable information to inform Grimes's understanding of the complex sequence of stratigraphy he encountered there. The differences between the city wall at Cripplegate and the remains already recorded elsewhere in the City of London (eg Tower Hill) were twofold. In the first place, as he saw in 1947, the wall itself was not constructed in the same way. Further work at Bastion 14 (WFG4) in 1948–9 had shown that the higher, eastern, of the two side-by-side walls lacked the bonding-courses of tile, which is such a distinctive feature of the city wall elsewhere. Secondly, and of even more importance, this higher wall was clearly later than the internal bank which everywhere appeared to be composed of the material from the external ditch: the base of the secondary wall foundation stopped short at least 300mm above the natural surface, with bank deposits seemingly associated with an earlier wall passing beneath it. This earlier wall, on the outside of the city wall, was even narrower than the higher wall – only *c* 1.25m. The construction trench of the higher wall, which had been dug into the bank of this earlier wall, was now clearly visible in section. This evidence, that the wall uncovered the previous year was not the first wall on the site, was strengthened by two other discoveries: firstly on the ground surface beneath the first bank a scatter of mortar showed that there had been previous building activity along the same line; and secondly a number of shallow pits for mixing mortar, all containing traces of different 'mixes', were also found.

On this evidence it could only be concluded that

there had been an extensive renewing or rebuilding of the north-western defences of the city at a date some time after the mid 2nd century AD, a date conveniently supplied by a coin of Lucius Aelius (d AD 138) embedded in the mortar of the city wall thickening. This date was to be revised later by a worn coin of Commodus, <S14> dated AD 183–4, coming from a layer immediately sealed by the city wall thickening itself (Falcon Square, WFG5; Chapter 5.6, 'Period 4'). It had, therefore, become important to explore the matter further, both to determine the extent of the rebuilding and to collect any available evidence regarding its date and character. To the north it was clear that the same features were present, though much damaged, on the Barber-Surgeons' Hall site (WFG2); and here as well as in Windsor Court (WFG3) a lower foundation contemporary with the first bank was recorded. In both places also there was evidence for the gravelled road 6–6.5m wide at the foot of the bank presumably intended to provide ready communication with different parts of the defences.

3.3 The fort reveals itself

The extent of deep basements and accessible areas suggested that in order to explore further this two-wall phenomenon the best results would be obtained on the south side of the initial study area. There, in the basements of Victorian warehouses and workshops on the west side of Noble Street, at its southernmost end (WFG8 and WFG9), several cuttings were made. The site at 31–32 Noble Street (WFG9), behind the angle of the Aldersgate re-entrant, produced the results, which at once explained everything so far uncovered. At this point both the earlier outer wall and the higher, inner Roman wall, post-dating c AD 180 were found and their longitudinal junction could be clearly seen. But their behaviour on plan was most surprising: instead of both turning westwards to follow the known line of the city wall as it crosses Aldersgate Street, both had begun to curve gently towards the south-east, in fact towards the interior of the city (Fig 19).

Here the first complete section clarified the whole

Fig 19 Aerial view of the south-west corner of the fort at 31–32 Noble Street (WFG9), showing the curving outer wall and square internal corner tower, looking west (3ft (0.91m) scales)

position, the key to which was the relationship of the two walls to the earliest Roman rampart bank. For while the inner wall, though Roman, was later than the bank, it was now possible to see that the outer wall had clearly been added to that. In other words, outer wall and early bank were contemporary; the inner wall was a later addition to them with its own bank piled up on the first. Furthermore, it looked increasingly likely that both of these walls were Roman in date, but at this stage an absolute date for the first wall, the outer wall in the sequence, was not forthcoming.

The course of these walls as they left the known line of the defences was pursued, and it was found that while the later, inner and higher wall quickly ended, the curve of the outer, earlier wall continued towards the east, evidently to complete a right angle. Though much

damaged by later activities the curve of the wall could be seen to be beautifully laid in good Roman style, the wall itself being *c* 1.25m wide; and built against it on the inside curve was a small building, rectangular against the wall in plan but which, at parapet level, would have been about 4.5m square. This arrangement was typically that of a corner of a Roman fort; the rounded angle and small square corner tower having many parallels in western and northern Britain as well as beyond. The southern fort wall, as it can now be called, was traced for a distance of over 120m from the corner at Noble Street (WFG9) to a point on the east side of Wood Street (WFG13). Its course was parallel with that of the outer city wall on the north side between the Cripplegate Bastion (WFG1) and Aldermanbury Postern (WFG16) (Fig 20).

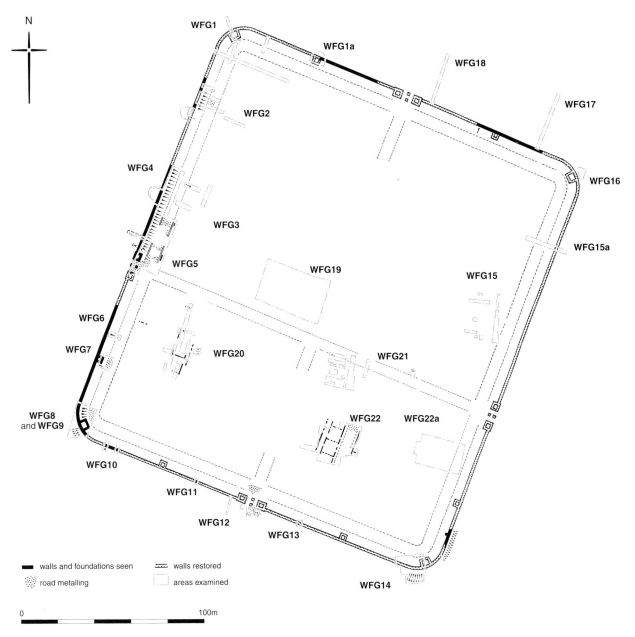

Fig 20 The plan of the fort as published by Grimes in 1968, with numbered excavation areas 1–22, now WFG1–22 (scale 1:2000)

Once the outer wall was seen to curve in the Noble Street (WFG9) trench, problems in interpretation began to dissolve and the significance of a number of long-noticed, but often ignored, features became apparent. Though the ancient structure of Cripplegate had never been seen by modern eyes, and still remains a mystery, there is reason to believe that the medieval gate of Cripplegate was built on a Roman predecessor. In a corresponding position on the south side of the circuit of the fort, a carefully located trench on the west side of Wood Street (WFG12) revealed a break in the line of the wall of the fort. This represented the position of the south gate. With this information it was then possible to suggest the course of the east wall of the fort. Taking these two gates as being on the long axis of the fort, Grimes was able to calculate that the approximate position of the east wall could be determined as probably lying along the line of, or just to the west of, Aldermanbury. Confirmation of this could be found in the fact that this point coincides with a hitherto unexplained change in direction of the city wall along London Wall, where both property and parish boundaries also changed their courses slightly (Fig 21). An examination of the likely site of the junction of the east and north walls was carried out in 1958 at Aldermanbury Postern (WFG16), but the results were disappointing. The disturbed condition of the ground just there and the depth of the cellars made excavation futile.

The overall dimensions of the fort are c 220 × 215m, a total area of about 4.5ha: these dimensions raise it out of the class of normal auxiliary forts. A date for the construction of the fort, c AD 120, was still not available until the pottery, in particular the samian sealed by the fort bank, had been examined by Joanna Bird in the

1970s (Chapter 5.3). However, even though this date was not known, the evidence Grimes had at his disposal showed that it was certainly too late to belong to the first occupation of the site of London by the Romans. Rather it belonged to a time when the main military presence in the province was much further to the west and the north. The GLA contains a succinct summary of Grimes's interpretation of the development of Roman London presented to the Council in 1950. It is reproduced here in full as it offers a rare glimpse of Grimes's interpretation of the development of Roman London as a whole.

The following sequence seems at present the most likely one to fit the facts. The first Londinium was centered around the Walbrook Stream and a comparatively limited area on the eastern hill opposite the bridgehead. It was destroyed by Boudicca [*sic*] in AD 61, but was gradually rebuilt on a grander scale, though still probably concentrated in very much the same area. At this time London was still an unwalled city; but perhaps with the memory of Boudicca before them, perhaps to provide a military depot near the port, the authorities in due course built a military station, locating it on the highest part of the area away from the growing civil settlement and at the same time within easy reach of the most important roads to the interior.

For some time, therefore, military fort and civil settlement were physically distinct. But the latter undoubtedly grew with the years and when in the second century the wall was thrown round the city the fort was incorporated in the enclosed area. The main city wall was carried to its

Fig 21 View looking eastwards showing the angle in the street-line of the former London Wall; this point represents the junction of the north wall of the fort with the city wall

northeast and southwest corners and the north and west walls of the fort then became part of the external defences. Whether or not the fort continued to enjoy a separate existence remains to be seen. At any rate its external walls were thickened and strengthened to bring them into line with the new city wall; and this is the explanation of the inner late wall, which in Noble Street ends when the fort wall ceases to face outwards, and has the effect of increasing its width to 8 feet [2.4m] more or less, which was the standard dimension of the main wall elsewhere (Fig 22). The internal bank and road were added to at the same time, the actual date (and therefore presumably the date for the city's main defence as a whole) being within a few years of AD 140.

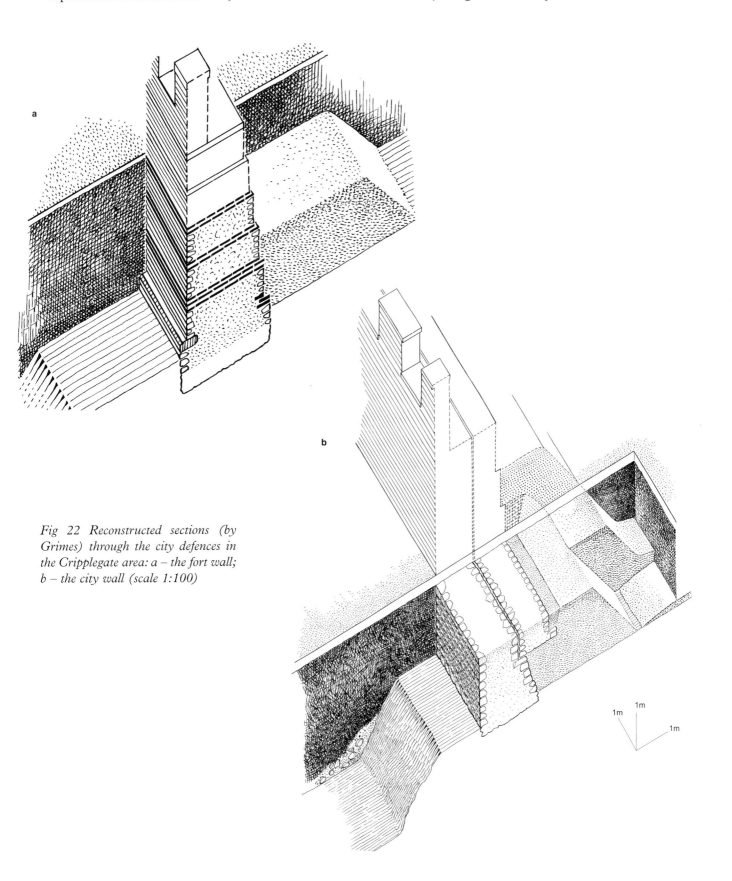

Fig 22 Reconstructed sections (by Grimes) through the city defences in the Cripplegate area: a – the fort wall; b – the city wall (scale 1:100)

Take note that Grimes revised the dating for the city wall to the late 2nd century AD following the discovery of the worn coin of Commodus dated AD 183–4 from the fort gate site (WFG5), conveniently discovered immediately below the city wall thickening (Grimes 1968, 51; Chapter 5.6).

Throughout 1952–4 the RMLEC continued its detailed examination of the sites in the Cripplegate area. It was also during this period that the Council extended its activities much further across London. Work began in the Dutch church of Austin Friars (WFG50), a large bombed area called the Bucklersbury House redevelopment site on the west side of Walbrook (WFG44 and WFG45) on which the temple of Mithras was to be found, the total excavation of the church of St Bride, Fleet Street (WFG62) (all in the City of London), and a section across the line of Stane Street near the Elephant and Castle, Southwark (WFG60). Progress in Cripplegate was often disrupted because of the demands made by these many other excavations. Notwithstanding these other pressures, however, once the fort had been identified, a finely tuned programme of research excavation was conducted to elucidate further the plan of the Cripplegate fort.

As mentioned above, at Wood Street (WFG12) further attention was given to the line of the north–south road through the fort. Only a very limited area was available for examination and the archaeological sequence had been severely disrupted by deep basements and closely set foundation stanchions. However, part of the south gate of the fort and the line of the fort ditch on the south side of its defences was located. At Aldermanbury (WFG14) it was established that the south-east corner of the fort lay under the street just to the south of the church of St Mary Aldermanbury. A length of the fort ditch was cleared and could be seen beginning to make the curve for the south-east corner of the fort as it passed under the street. Though cut by medieval rubbish pits, the ditch was very well preserved. Its Roman filling was found to be undisturbed in several places, yielding pottery which, recent analysis has shown, dates to the late 2nd century AD in its earliest fills and to the early part of the 3rd century AD in its upper fills. This now suggests that the fort ditch here was filled, or allowed to fill, over a short period of time, probably during the early 3rd century AD. The wall that accompanied the ditch at Aldermanbury was very poorly preserved as a result of robbing. This robbing phase could not and still cannot be dated.

On the north side of the Cripplegate area, in what was the eastern end of the northern side of the fort, it was possible to examine the elevation of the city wall at St Alphage churchyard (Fig 23). It was here that the RMLEC worked in close cooperation with

Fig 23 The city defences today at the site of the church of St Alphage, view looking west

representatives of the Corporation of London, in particular the City Engineer, Francis J Forty, and the Ancient Monuments Department of the MoW that undertook the repair and consolidation of this section of wall for permanent preservation. This successful working relationship was to repeat itself on a number of occasions resulting in the preservation of the city wall remains in the Noble Street and Barbican areas today. Grimes and Forty were to work closely throughout the 1950s on a great many other projects, not least the preservation of the west gate of the fort in the late 1950s.

3.4 The fort gate – a crisis avoided

After the spectacular discovery of the temple of Mithras in 1954, and the even more spectacular reaction to it (Shepherd 1998a, 19–20), concerted attention was focused once again upon the Cripplegate area. In 1956–7 work was continued in greater detail and the surviving portion of the west gate of the Roman fort was fully excavated at Falcon Square (WFG5) (Fig 24). This proved to be remarkably well preserved, even though the site suffered from a great many post-medieval intrusions. In the area examined, the north tower, built of massive blocks of purple sandstone and smaller dressed ragstone blocks, and the north roadway with

the whole of the central foundation (*spina*) had survived. A complete reconstruction of the plan of the gateway was possible, and an important new element, therefore, was added to the plan of the fort. In the course of this work, and the examination of the surrounding area, two important pieces of datable evidence emerged. A coin of Vespasian of AD 71 had been found beneath the bank of the fort (Grimes 1968, 38), thus confirming the date for its building as not before *c* AD 80 (as mentioned above, 3.3, Grimes at this time was not aware of the samian dates which would place the construction of the fort in the Hadrianic period; Chapter 5.6). Secondly, the well-worn coin of Commodus of AD 183–4 was found in the material into which the foundation of the later wall thickening had been built (Chapter 5.6). Since this thickening was equated with the building of the city wall proper, the latter find supplied a *terminus post quem* of *c* AD 185 for the date for the building of the city wall of London. In 1966, excavations by Marsden on an interval tower on the west side of the city wall, near the Old Bailey, revealed a small cache of coin moulds, which appear to have been deposited there *c* AD 220–5 (Marsden 1980, 126). These two numismatic finds, of Grimes and Marsden, provide the accepted date range for the construction of the city wall from *c* AD 185 to *c* AD 225. Take note, however, that the coin of Commodus supplying the first of these dates is very worn.

Fig 24 Grimes and Williams, with Faulkner behind, examining the fort gate in 1956, view looking north

Through the efforts of Grimes and the City Engineer, Francis Forty, this gateway is now preserved at the west end of the car park beneath the modern thoroughfare called London Wall (not on the same alignment as the pre-war road of the same name; cf Fig 5 and Fig 6). However, coming so soon after the discovery and crisis over the temple of Mithras (Shepherd 1998a, 13–26) it is not surprising to note that the gate too attracted some attention at a much higher level – though not, it seems, attracting the same sort of press and public clamour for preservation as the temple.

Throughout the early part of the campaign in Cripplegate Forty and Grimes worked closely together to ensure that as much as possible of the city wall remains were not only exposed but retained. In actual fact, Forty found in Grimes a very useful ally in trying to accomplish the aims of the Corporation's preliminary draft planning proposals prepared in 1944. The following, reproduced in full, is a statement made by Forty to the Executive Committee of the RMLEC in 1952 regarding the remains Grimes had worked on at St Alphage churchyard, London Wall and its vicinity, at Fore Street (WFG17) and Cripplegate Buildings (WFG18). It is reproduced here in full as it gives an interesting insight into the Corporation's ambitions with regards to the city wall in the north-west corner of the City.

To: The Executive Committee of the Roman and Mediaeval London Excavation Council

From: The City Engineer, City Engineer's Office.

I do not think it necessary to excuse myself for saying that when the bombing of the City of London started in 1940, one of my earliest thoughts was of the opportunity which would most likely present itself to expose, and keep visible in the future, parts of the ancient Town Wall of London which for long, indeed for centuries, had been buried or built upon, and to create where possible, public open spaces near such lengths of the Wall so that it would be visible in perpetuity for future generations of Londoners to see. I discussed the possibility of such action with Mr. O'Neil, Inspector of Ancient Monuments, on many occasions during his frequent visits to the City in those troubled times. I recommended this course to the Improvements and Town Planning Committee of the Corporation who were entirely sympathetic with the principle involved. In the meantime steps were taken to protect from weather the Wall where exposed. Later, in the Report on Reconstruction in the City of London published in 1944 [ie the Corporation preliminary draft planning proposals], there were included

paragraphs leading to this end. Many of you are familiar with the Report which you will recollect was not accepted by the Minister. Relevant passages of which I need quote only in extract, e.g. para.96 to 98, as follows:

(96) 'Of other architectural traces of the City's long past, enemy action has served to expose one monument to an extent to which it cannot have been seen for many hundreds of years, namely, the London Wall, in the north-west part of the City. There stands today, mainly above ground level a stretch of the Town Wall, including three bastions, from Falcon Square to St Giles Cripplegate churchyard and then turning eastwards as far as Aldermanbury Postern. Except for a small stretch next to the churchyard of St Giles and on the north side of the churchyard of St Alphage, the whole of this wall was incorporated in buildings on either side'

(97) 'This is an unequalled opportunity to purchase (the wall and property being, for the greater part, privately owned at present) and preserve for all time a major trace of the historic past. On drawings Nos.1, 2, 3, 3A and 3B [not reproduced here] is shown a scheme involving as little acquisition as possible but still retaining the most interesting views of the Wall between the churchyard of St Giles and Falcon Square. On Drawing No.3B a suitable position for a car-park or multi-storey garage is indicated closely associated with the ring route [Route 11, later to readopt the name of London Wall]. The alternative proposal (as in drawings Nos. 4 and 4A) [also not reproduced here] would maintain its present degree of exposure by acquiring land on either side which could be laid out as open space, with some part possibly devoted to car-parking without detracting from the general panorama envisaged.'

(98) 'We have appreciated the interest and assistance given by the Ancient Monuments Departments, Ministry of Works and Buildings in the temporary protective works which the Court have authorised to the portions of the Wall exposed as a consequence of enemy action'.

It was, of course, through the good influence of Mr. O'Neil that this helpful co-operation of the Ministry was secured.

Since those days, when although war was raging, we were full of hope as to the future rate of progress in such works as this, and indeed as to the rate of post-war reconstruction generally in the City, optimism as to the speed of such works has indeed waned.

Enthusiasm for the work has however always remained, and it was therefore with the keenest satisfaction that, following a talk with him, there came a letter from Mr. W. F. Grimes regarding his views expressed at a meeting of the Roman and Mediaeval London excavation Council as to the possibility of doing work on the Wall. I could not indeed have welcomed any suggestion more, which was so much in accord with the idea in the 1944 report, and that it should now have the active and enthusiastic support of our Honorary Director of Excavations whose work and discoveries in connection with Roman London have been of such intense and momentous interest in the past few years, was immensely helpful.

Such work as was desired would be costly and nothing whatever could be done without the active and keen support, first of the Improvements and Town Planning Committee of the Corporation and then of the Court of Common Council itself. Accordingly I first reported to the Committee upon the matter providing estimates of costs of the work, which would probably be necessary to make a start with the proposal. I further discussed the matter with Mr. Grimes and also with your Vive President [*sic*] Sir Frederick Tidbury Beer who was warmly in support. The estimate for the initial works was in the neighbourhood of £3,000 and included a considerable amount of excavation of debris lying in basements of demolished buildings abutting the north side of the Wall. In regard to this particular work there was some expectation of partial reimbursement from the War damage Commission. The Improvements and Town Planning Committee took a favourable view of the matter and presented it to the rates Finance Committee and forwarded it subsequently to the Court of Common Council, with the result that the Corporation approved an expenditure of £2,925, on works which included the removal of a large quantity of excavation debris from the basement area on the side of the Wall, the demolition of modern brickwork screening the mediaeval wall and provision for some expenditure on preservation works.

As to the actual method of operation, while all the work would be under my general direction and the general clearance work could be done by contract with the general supervision of my own department, I felt that with the skilled and specialised work upon the fabric of the Wall itself, it would be most helpful to have the practical co-operation of the Ministry of Works, Ancient Monuments Section whereby skilled

workers should be attached to my department (as had been done on earlier protective works on the Wall which I had found most helpful). Further, that we should have the advantage of the continuous advice and the supervision of personnel by Officers of the Ministry of Works, Ancient Monuments Department. We are indeed grateful to Mr O'Neil, for his cooperation in this matter. Following the initial clearance in September 1951, I have had the help of the Ministry of Works officers and am glad to be able to refer to their much-appreciated assistance in the work, which has been done. I wish also to refer to the great keenness and enthusiasm and desire to help of the foremen and skilled workmen of the Ministry. In our own house there has always been manifested the interest and support of Mr Raymond Smith, the City Librarian and Curator and a prominent member of this Council.

I am glad to say in connection with the possibility of the creation of an open space on the north side of the Wall ensuring that in perpetuity such sections of the ancient wall as could be exposed would remain visible, the principle of the creation of an open space having been fully approved by the Improvements and Town Planning Committee, I am at present time in conjunction with the City Planning Officer, preparing an appropriate layout to merge satisfactorily with the planning of the area.

I will now refer to the work carried out on the Wall:

After the initial clearance of debris and careful and thorough cleaning to basement level in August/September 1951, the protective exploratory work decided upon was commenced. The independent skin wall, part of the previously existing commercial structure, which extended from the basement to the full height of the old wall and varied in thickness from 18 inches to 22 1/2 inches [0.46–0.56m] has been demolished together with the basement division walls.

On the south side a considerable quantity of debris banked against the wall in the churchyard has been moved revealing the mediaeval wall in its full thickness (but not to the full height).

On the north face the lower section of the wall has been restored, loose stonework being taken out and rebuilt, and where it had been faced with modern brickwork the brickwork has been cut away and the wall left with the core exposed. On the upper section, which is of brick, some 30 feet [9.2m] of wall has been preserved both north and south faces being cleaned and restored and the embrasures opened up in their original form. Again any modern brickwork has been cut out and the wall left as core work.

The work has necessarily been very costly as the wall was found in many places to be unsafe but it is hoped that the Corporation will be prepared when they see what has been achieved to proceed with the whole of the preservation works to these parts of the wall, which are now exposed.

During the progress of the works I have taken many photographs, which illustrate what has been accomplished in the various stages, and these are available today for inspection by any member of the Committee interested [here, Fig 25; Fig 26].

I think at this point I should add that my remarks in this memorandum are related only to execution of work on and around the Wall. I am not touching upon the question of ownership, as there are complications here which need not concern this Council. Suffice it to say that I have approached all parties whose consent might appear to be necessary for the execution of work and that I have no doubt that ultimately the Wall and the land adjacent to it will become the unquestioned property of the Corporation of London.

Time, since receiving warning of the Committee

today, has not allowed of more than this brief statement, but I hope in due course to give the Council a fuller report embodying some of the closer details of the work which has already been done and of any subsequent operations.

This report from Forty describes, then, the original ambition to preserve and display as much of the wall as possible in the north-west area of the City, and the successful efforts to preserve the first section to be tackled in this way at St Alphage. All of this work was going on successfully and quietly behind the scenes, with very little attention being drawn to it by the public. However, the identification of the temple of Mithras in 1954 and the outcry that resulted from its threatened destruction, during September and October 1954 (Shepherd 1998a, 13–26), brought the ancient remains in the City under closer scrutiny. As early as 1955, immediately in the wake of the Mithras crisis, a question was asked in the House of Commons about what plans were in place for the preservation of other remains. For example:

> **Captain Pilkington** asked the Minister of Housing & Local Government to what extent those parts of London Wall, excavated since the war, are to be preserved in the rebuilding of the City.

The response was quite succinct and reflected the work the Corporation had already committed itself to:

> **Mr Sandys** In accordance with the London Development Plan the principal remains of the Roman Wall now exposed are to be preserved in

Fig 25 View of ruined exterior of St Alphage church, London Wall, with the city wall to the right, 1959 (LMA, Photograph Collection, cat no. m0026674d)

open settings. (*Hansard* 1955–6, vol 558, 469)

However, progress regarding the preservation exercise was very slow, if not at all, at this time. Mr E Fletcher, the MP for Islington East, the constituency just to the north of Cripplegate, took up the case. On the 17 December 1957, over two years after Pilkington's first question, Fletcher raised the issue again:

Mr. E. Fletcher asked the Minister of Works what steps he has taken in conjunction with the City Corporation to ensure the preservation and proper display of the remains of the Roman London wall and fort in Falcon Street, Cripplegate.

Mr. Molson The Corporation of the City of London is proceeding with the scheme for the preservation of the wall and gate to which I referrcd in reply to the hon. Member's Question on 12th February 1957. It will be possible for the public to inspect the remains, which will be in a chamber underneath Route 11.

Mr. Fletcher Is the right hon. Gentleman aware that, notwithstanding his answer in February, nothing has been done since then? Has he observed the very interesting suggestion put forward by Lord Mottistone for the preservation of this interesting relic of antiquity as a memorial of London of deep significance, by sinking the external level to the old level and thereby providing a very attractive piece of evidence and possibly a centre of interest to tourists from all over the world?

Mr. Molson I have not seen the suggestion made by Lord Mottistone. What it is proposed to do is in general accordance with the advice given by the Ancient Monuments Branch of my Ministry. It would be thoroughly well preserved and readily accessible to anyone interested in it. I am sorry that here has been a delay in this matter, but that has been due to the time we had to wait for Route 11 to reach that point. (*Hansard* 1957–8, vol 580, 175)

This response reflected the work that Forty and Grimes had already put in motion, although (see immediately below) Grimes was not enamoured by the Mottistone plan, which would have required the remodelling of a large volume of archaeology-bearing ground.

But progress was still slow, in Fletcher's opinion, and he did not ease up with the pressure. On 4 March 1958, he raised the issue again:

Mr. E. Fletcher asked the Minister of Works if, in conjunction with the City of Corporation, he would now arrange for the excavation and preservation, in a suitable sunken garden, of the exterior face of the Roman Wall of London between Falcon Street and Cripplegate.

Mr. Molson I understand that, since this section of the wall was revealed by bombing in 1944, it has always been the intention of the City Corporation to consolidate and preserve it, with an open space on both sides, so that the remains can be seen by the public. The City Corporation is the owner and the responsible authority,

Fig 26 View looking north-east along London Wall showing bomb damage and work in progress on the Roman and medieval wall at St Alphage church, 1942 (LMA, Cross and Tibbs Collection, cat no. m0018650d)

although the preservation work, which entails excavation, will be done with the advice of my Ancient Monuments Branch. The precise layout and timing are matters for the City Corporation, but there will be full consultation with my Department.

Mr. Fletcher I am much obliged to the Minister for that Answer. Will he bear in mind the importance of something being done reasonably soon about this matter? Will he do anything he can to assist the City Corporation before it is too late?

Mr. Molson We shall certainly do anything we can to assist. I have inquired of the City Corporation, and it says that it cannot yet give a date for starting. (*Hansard* 1957–8, vol 583, 945)

However, even before starting the preservation on the west side of the fort, some things did not go as smoothly as they should have. The rapid rate of clearance and preparatory work by contractors in the Cripplegate area during the mid 50s, virtually all of it without invigilation, resulted in the loss of some of the medieval fabric of the wall. Indeed on a number of occasions Grimes intervened to prevent medieval masonry at Windsor Court and Bastion 14 being removed during the removal of much later brickwork by poorly briefed demolition crews, but one section to the north of the west gate was lost. This incident came immediately to the attention of Fletcher. He raised this in the House of Commons on 20 May 1958 as follows:

London Wall

Mr. E. Fletcher asked the Minister of Works what steps he has taken to prevent the threatened destruction of an important section of the Roman Wall of London.

The response was:

The Minister of Works (Mr. Hugh Molson) I assume that the hon. Member is referring to a section of the London Wall between Cripplegate and Falcon Square. Three bastions consisting largely of Roman work are scheduled under Ancient Monuments Acts and notice is accordingly required of any intention to carry out works affecting them.

Adjoining the southernmost of these bastions and to the south of it a short stretch of wall was also scheduled. Although there may be Roman remains below ground, this consisted mainly of the upper parts of the mediaeval city wall; the lower parts had been cut away and modern brick substituted. This piece of wall and its junction

with bastion 14 were recently demolished inadvertently in connection with the construction of Route 11 and there was minor damage to the bastion itself. My inquiries of this incident are not yet complete.

Mr. Fletcher I appreciate that as soon as this regrettable incident came to the notice of the Minister and the City Engineer, steps were taken to prevent further damage. Will the hon. Gentleman bear in mind the constant danger of destruction? Will he also bear in mind that the real solution is to proceed immediately with the plan, already agreed in principle, for the creation of a sunken garden to bring the wall down to the level of the inner ditch?

Mr. Molson I am examining means of preventing an incident of this kind from occurring again. The City of London has been most cooperative in this matter and regrets what has happened as much as I do. I will consider further what the hon Gentleman has said. (*Hansard* 1957–8, vol 588, 1092)

Another question, not from Fletcher this time, asked again on 10 June 1958:

Mr. Parker asked the Minister of works when further action is to be taken to preserve the London Roman Wall between St Giles, Cripplegate and Falcon Square, in view of the recent damage done to it.

Mr. Molson As I said on 4th March, in reply to the hon. Member of Islington East (Mr. E. Fletcher), the timing of any scheme for preserving this stretch of the wall is a matter for the City Corporation, although my Ancient Monuments Branch will advise on the work itself. I am keeping in touch with the City Corporation.

Fletcher himself did not ease up, and just a few weeks later, 24 June 1958, he pressed the Minister again:

Mr. E. Fletcher asked the Minister of Works if he has now completed his inquiries regarding the recent destruction of a stretch of the Roman Wall of London between Cripplegate and Falcon Square; what steps he is taking to prevent further demolition; and if, in conjunction with the City Corporation, he will proceed immediately with the plan for the creation of a sunken garden to preserve and expose the external face of the wall down to the level of the ancient city ditch.

Mr. Molson Yes, Sir. I am satisfied that the

recent demolition of a fragment of London Wall near Falcon Square was inadvertent. With the object of avoiding another such incident, the City Corporation has repaired and strengthened the fencing round the remains of the wall in this vicinity and will provide any further protection which may appear necessary. It is also reaffirming its instructions that those concerned with operations near the wall should be most careful to keep clear of it. As the hon. Member knows, it is the intention of the City Corporation to preserve and display this stretch of the wall with a public open space adjoining it. I understand that the City Corporation proposes to carry out this work when it can best be fitted into the general redevelopment of this area.

Mr. Fletcher I thank the Minister for that reply, but will he suggest to the City Corporation that it would be desirable to complete this work, which it can quite conveniently do, in advance of its general scheme of development in the area?

Mr. Molson I am approaching the City Corporation with the suggestion that it might be desirable for further exploration to take place before large-scale building work begins in the neighbourhood. (*Hansard* 1957–8, vol 590, 215)

It is more than apparent by these statements from the Minister, just as Forty had presented to the RMLEC a few years previously, that there had been a plan to preserve as much as possible of the city wall in this area from Bastion 12 in the north to Bastion 14 and to create a public open space for a considerable period of time – but it was still taking a long time to implement. As Milne explains (2001), this programme of preservation was extended to the area south of the new London Wall as and when the Roman remains of the fort in Noble Street became visible.

In between these two zones, the first to the north of Falcon Square and the other in Noble Street, and directly under the proposed line of Route 11, as the new London Wall was called at the development stage, lay the site of the fort gate. Initially, there was never any intention to preserve any of the remains under the line of the road, even though it was known to cross the line of the city wall and a proposed subterranean car park would certainly require the removal of any wall or remains surviving there, in addition to those already 'inadvertently' demolished. The presence of the well-preserved gate, therefore, did cause some concern and a reasonably restrained debate about its future ensued.

Grimes initiated the discussions, reporting to the 41st meeting of the Ancient Monuments Board for England on the 5 October 1956 (TNA: PRO, WORK 14/2200 1954/1960) that:

… he had been excavating the west gate of the

Roman Fort in the City of London, and he hoped that it would be possible to arrange for its permanent preservation. The site lay in the path of Route 11, and it might possibly be preserved in a car park beneath the new road. He was about to open discussions in the City Corporation and he asked for the Board's support in his proposals.

The Board agreed and welcomed these proposals. However, on the 7 December 1956 (TNA: PRO, WORK 14/2200 1954/1960), in matters arising, he reported that:

… he had not yet been able to obtain the assent of the City Corporation to his proposal. Their reaction had not been favourable, and they had pointed out the preservation of the fort would limit the size of the proposed underground car park. He hoped to hold further discussions with the Corporation and he would report further to the Board.

As with the temple of Mithras debate some two years earlier, the impact of preservation of ancient monuments upon the necessities of modern London – office space and rents in 1954, car parking spaces in 1956 – predominated the discussions. The value of the remains as an ancient monument and any ethical considerations came second. However, the Rt Hon Fletcher MP, in his questions to the Minister had on a couple of occasions pointed out the potential tourist benefits of preserving the remains in the Cripplegate area. Almost a year after Grimes had reported to the Ancient Monuments Board that his meetings were not progressing well, Fletcher had asked his question about the Mottistone plan, quoted above.

Grimes was concerned about the Lord Mottistone plan, namely to truncate all the archaeology in the surrounding area in order to display the wall as best as possible, and the remains as they can be viewed now represent the compromise which Grimes brokered with Forty – much being preserved *in situ* beneath the open spaces. In this compromise the basement slabs were lifted and only certain areas were carefully landscaped to show off the wall to better effect. The construction of the Museum of London on the west side of these remains during the late 60s and early 70s helped to enhance this effect.

By the time Fletcher invoked the Mottistone plan, however, Grimes and Forty had already reached an agreement over how the fort gate could be preserved. Early in 1957 new plans of the west end of the underground car park were drawn up (with the loss of 12 car parking spaces and the rents they would have accrued!). This new plan allowed Molson, the Minister of Works, to report in his next exchange with Fletcher on 17 December 1957 that 'It will be possible for the public to inspect the remains which will be in a chamber underneath Route 11' (*Hansard* 1957–8, vol 580, 175).

The matter was settled and a large section of the city wall, together with the gate, was preserved. For the record, however, it is worth reporting that Fletcher continued to press the Minister over the delay in making these accessible. In July 1959, just as Grimes was excavating the south tower of the gate in advance of the construction of the new chamber for the display of the fort gate, he asked the new Minister (Rt Hon H Nicholls) a very familiar question (*Hansard* 1958–9, vol 6098, 1039):

Roman Wall, Cripplegate

4. **Mr. E. Fletcher** asked Minister of Works what arrangements he is making with the City Corporation to ensure the preservation of a length of the Roman Wall of London near Cripplegate, abutting on the proposed new Route 11.

The terse reply from the Minister suggests impatience with the Member for Islington East:

Mr. H. Nicholls I understand that the position remains as stated in my right hon. Friend's letter of 8th August 1958, to the hon. Member. The City Corporation intends to open up the wall and its bastions between Cripplegate and Falcon Square and to preserve them as part of an open space.

But this did not deter Fletcher:

Mr. Fletcher Can the hon. Gentleman now tell us when this will be done?

Mr. Nicholls It is really a matter for the City Corporation. We shall make quite certain that the archaeological part of it is taken fully into account, but the decision is for the City Corporation.

Fifty years later the fort gate, property of the Corporation of London, is still preserved and protected beneath London Wall (Route 11) and is made accessible by arrangement with staff of the Museum of London on a basis that even they regard as far from adequate (Fig 27). It is unlikely that such limited accessibility is what Fletcher envisaged in his exchanges with the Minister in the 1950s.

However, many of the sections of the fort and later city defences are easily accessible in the Cripplegate area as a result of the collaboration of Forty and Grimes; these are listed in Chapter 11.3.

Fig 27 The fort gate preserved in its chamber below London Wall, looking north-east (photograph by G Milne)

3.5   Returning to the archaeology

Back on site in Cripplegate during this period much time had been devoted to the examination of an area in the angle of Noble Street and Silver Street (WFG20; Fig 5; Fig 20; Chapter 9.2), in the hope of learning more about the periods of occupation of the fort. Here the Roman remains had been much destroyed by later activity, but parts of a stone building had been found overlying earlier occupation, which included timber structures. The amount of this later stone building available for examination was too limited to enable its character to be determined. At the time of discovery some of its features, such as copious quantities of wall plaster and hearths, suggested a domestic rather than military use, but its alignment was parallel with the west wall of the fort and dated to the 2nd century AD, thus making it contemporary with the fort defences themselves. Fragmentary remains of stone buildings were also discovered during the investigation of the gateway briefly described above. It seems likely, therefore, that there were many more buildings of stone in the fort.

Excavation was also carried out in the north-east angle of the Wood Street–Silver Street junction (WFG19; Fig 5; Fig 20; Chapter 9.1) where it was believed that the site of the headquarters building was located. Here, as elsewhere in the area, all traces of Roman structures had been swept away, apart from the lower parts of one or two gullies and some pits.

In 1957–8 the main focus of attention of the RMLEC was again in the area of the fort – but time was against the Council due to the impending development of this area with the building of the new London Wall (Route 11). All efforts were made, therefore, to concentrate on those sites in the fort area where the levels were such that there was some possibility of Roman features being preserved.

The Brewers' Hall (WFG15; Fig 5; Fig 20; Chapter 8.1) had been completely destroyed in the Blitz and a considerable part of the site appeared to be undisturbed to modern street level. However, the results of the excavation, from the point of view of the Roman sequence, were extremely disappointing. Later, medieval, occupation had severely truncated and damaged the earlier levels (see Milne 2001 for a discussion on the medieval results, including the medieval Brewer's Hall).

A similar situation occurred at Windsor Court (WFG3; Fig 5; Fig 20; Chapter 5.4). Deposits apparently intact to modern street level had in fact been disturbed to depths of 4.5m or more by medieval pits, some of which could not be pursued to their full depth (once again, see Milne 2001). Again the hope of obtaining a full datable sequence was not realised. However, traces of a Roman building were seen, which aligned with those further south near the west gateway, suggesting a long narrow building parallel with the west wall of the fort and flanking the eastern side of the perimeter road – perhaps another barrack block.

Further cuttings were also made inside the wall at Noble Street (WFG6 and WFG7; Fig 5; Fig 20; Chapter 6.1), primarily with the intention of augmenting the dating material for the defences, but also in preparation for the preservation scheme which the Corporation had adopted for this part of the city wall, following the results of the collaboration between Forty and Grimes. This work was done by volunteers under the leadership of Mr George Rybot, site survey by Michael Green with such help from the Council's paid labour as was required from time to time with the removal of major obstacles. One result of this work was to reveal an internal tower about halfway between the west gateway (WFG5) and the south-west angle of the fort (WFG9). The tower (known in the GLA as 'Rybot's turret'), smaller than that at the south-west angle, added another feature to the defences and made it necessary to explore the possibility that a similar tower existed at the corresponding point to the north of the fort gateway.

The location in question lay within the area of the half-cellars of Windsor Court, just north of Bastion 14 (WFG4; Fig 5; Fig 20; Chapter 5.5). However, although the wall itself had survived here there was no trace of an internal tower. It must be assumed, therefore, that although the distance between the west gate and the north-west corner would have allowed for two towers north of the gate, there could not in fact have been more than one, and this must have been destroyed by deep cellars.

In 1959 the greater part of the work was in the nature of a final examination prior to the major rebuilding of the Barbican development, followed by the construction of the Museum of London, due to commence there. At Falcon Square (WFG5; Fig 5; Fig 20; Chapter 5.6), further work on the services of the new London Wall enabled Grimes to examine the area to the south of the north tower of the gate, revealed a few years previously. As a result, the south roadway of the gate was uncovered, together with the north-west angle of the south tower that was seen to be of the same type of construction as that to the north. The Roman remains were much reduced in height, and the outer fort wall carried a later city wall, post-Roman in date. The south roadway had also been blocked with masonry (still *in situ* today), so that the whole gateway, and not merely the northern half of it, had at some time been put out of action. Unfortunately no evidence was available as to the date of this blocking. It is unlikely, however, that the total blocking of this gateway occurred during the Roman period, suggesting that it remained partially open during the period when the west wall of the fort had been incorporated into the city wall. Unfortunately the south tower could not be preserved although the sandstone foundation stones have been retained, in a fashion, in the gardens behind Bastion 14.

Renewed building work in the late 1950s in the area of the Barber-Surgeons' Hall and Bastion 13 (WFG2; Fig 5; Fig 20; Chapter 5.3) enabled Grimes to return to this site for a reinvestigation of the deposits behind the city wall in the light of knowledge attained since his first work in 1947–8. A short length of the fort bank was uncovered and it was possible to see for the first time how the accumulations against this bank related to the internal addition to the fort wall, which equated with the city wall proper. The interior of Bastion 13, immediately west of the new Barber-Surgeons' Hall, was also cleared at this time. Sadly modern foundations had destroyed the significant points of contact with the city wall. However, part of the bottom of the Roman ditch had survived the digging out of the cellar and the base of the bastion had sunk into its filling. There was no datable material and, apart from shedding light on the character of the bastion itself, including much work by Inigo Jones (Milne 2001), the results were disappointing. Once again, it must be emphasised that in 1959 and before the discovery of the datable Bastion 11A (WFG1a; Chapter 5.2), it was still generally believed that these bastions were of late Roman date.

Work complementary to that at the Barber-Surgeons' Hall site was undertaken in the churchyard of St Giles Cripplegate, in particular the examination of the exterior of the city wall, Bastion 12 (WFG1; Fig 5; Fig 20; Chapter 5.1) and Bastion 13 (WFG2) and the related deposits. Here also, churchyard disturbance had penetrated very deeply in the parts examined. The wall itself had been completely refaced in medieval and later periods and the Roman facing was preserved to a height of only four or five courses above the plinth at the south end, where the projecting bastion protected it.

In the area of the southern angle of the Addle Street–Wood Street junction (WFG21; Fig 5; Fig 20; Chapter 9.3), the RMLEC was able to examine another Cripplegate site in the hope of discovering more details about the interior layout of the fort and also of learning something of the Anglo-Saxon occupation, which was, according to documentary sources, to be expected in this area. Once again destruction of the higher deposits by the modern cellars had removed the Roman levels and only very scanty traces of Roman road metalling (part of the *via principalis*) had survived. Some parts of the area, however, were taken up by deeper pits and, amongst the later rubbish pits of ordinary character, was part of a deep, hut pit with large postholes along its sides and angles and, in addition, another big square 'cellar'. Once again, at the time it was believed that these buildings might have been early Anglo-Saxon sunken buildings but subsequent analysis of finds from the site proved them to be 11th- or 12th-century in date (Milne 2001).

3.6 The RMLEC's final years in the City

As the number of available derelict sites rapidly became exhausted, so the field activities of the RMLEC, limited as they were to small-scale excavation, began to wane. Only two sites of significance were examined during this period, both church sites in the Cripplegate area.

St Alban's church, Wood Street (WFG22; Fig 5; Fig 20; Chapter 9.4) was examined between 1962 and 1964 in advance of the Corporation's need to widen Wood Street itself and the construction of a police station. The remains of the church were to be demolished leaving just the tower (a proposal to move the tower physically westwards was not successful); but before this was carried out, Grimes had another opportunity to excavate the interior of a City church. Unfortunately, the removal of the burials in the interior by unsupervised labourers destroyed much of the earlier medieval fabric. However, a sequence was recorded which revealed an early two-cell building that expanded into the late medieval church, destroyed in the Great Fire of 1666 and rebuilt by Wren (Milne 2001). Beneath the church sequence there were traces of Roman masonry buildings that could be identified as barrack blocks, due to their date and orientation rather than architectural plans, belonging to the Cripplegate fort. One intriguing detail, however, was the alignment of earlier Roman gullies and postholes that appear to have been reproduced by these later masonry buildings. It was suggested as a possibility that these represent an earlier timber phase of the fort, but this cannot be confirmed with any certainty from within the GLA. Indeed, subsequent work in the area by MOLA (ie Daiwa House, 84–89 Wood Street (DWA92); Shelley House, 3 Noble Street (NST94); Garrard House, Gresham Street and Haberdashers' Hall, Staining Lane (GAH95); 90–92 and 100 Wood Street and St Albans Court (WOO97); and Barrington House, 59–67 Gresham Street, 27–34 Wood Street and 1–6 Love Lane (LVL97) (Howe and Lakin 2004)) has also failed to identify a timber precursor to the masonry fort. It is possible that, even if they did belong to a military phase of the area, they could simply represent the temporary quarters of the personnel engaged in building the stone fort and not a functioning garrison.

The second church, St Mary Aldermanbury, was examined in 1968 and again a Roman sequence similar to that recorded at St Alban's church was recovered (WFG22a; Fig 5; Fig 20; Chapter 9.5). The remains of the medieval church on the site were also recorded but the presence of brick vaults severely hampered this effort (Milne 2001). The site attracted a great deal of press interest at the time because the remains of the infamous Judge Jefferies were said to be buried there. Much to the relief of the press-shy Grimes, they were not discovered.

Grimes's 1968 publication, *The excavation of Roman and mediaeval London*, brought together much of the information about the fort and other sites and still stands as a valid account of his work in the Cripplegate area (Fig 28). Subsequent analysis of his records allows the following accounts of each of his sites to be presented. However, whereas it has been possible to publish a consistent and detailed account of the temple of Mithras (Shepherd 1998a), it has not proved to be as easy for the Roman fort sites. Before examining the sequences Grimes recorded on the Cripplegate sites, a few comments are necessary to describe the methodologies employed by Grimes and his team on site, as well as the chequered history of the archive itself.

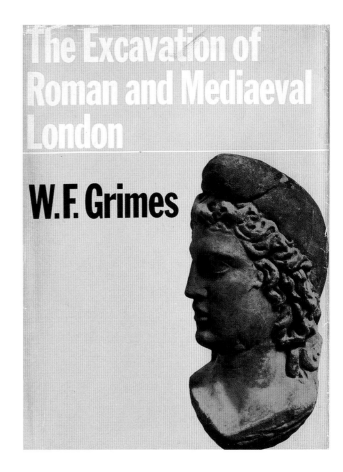

Fig 28 The cover of Grimes's 1968 account of his fieldwork in London

4 Studying the RMLEC Cripplegate archive

4.1 The recording system used by Grimes and the RMLEC

It has been mentioned that there is a frustrating degree of variability in the quality of some of the surviving archives for these sites, due in part to the methods of recording Grimes used (methods which evolved over time), but also due to the incompleteness of a number of them (Chapter 1). Before describing the results of the RMLEC's work in the Cripplegate area (Chapters 5–9), it needs to be reported here that during the analysis phase of the GLA, there proved to be poor correlation between the finds assemblages for these Cripplegate sites and the contents of the written archive. For obvious reasons, the loss of material on site as described in Chapter 3.1 – namely the unscrupulous selling of finds to onlookers by one of the workmen employed by Grimes – cannot help, but as this material never entered the archaeological record the real impact of its loss can never be calculated. Of more significance here is the loss of material, especially fine and coarse wares and animal bone, collected by Grimes and recorded in his notebooks but which can no longer be located or studied. The site notes for the fort gate site at Falcon Square (WFG5) highlight just one example of the problems that confront the researcher. It was recorded in the notes that 'Bags of pottery etc [were] disturbed during Sunday 9 Sept 1956. Strewn over hut floor and on outside ground. Sent to Guildhall in one carton 10/9/56. Returned and scrapped on prof's order'. This loss of information is most frustrating. Furthermore, the finds from a number of the Cripplegate sites, especially WFG2, WFG3 and WFG5 were damaged during flooding in the Guildhall Museum's stores in the late 1960s. Therefore, and unfortunately, detailed dating evidence for these sites is lacking although some key groups do exist. For example, there are good assemblages from the dumps on the internal bank of both the fort and the city wall in Noble Street (WFG6 and WFG7; Chapter 6.1), and good assemblages survive from the fort ditch in both the south-west (WFG9; Chapter 6.3) and south-east corners of the fort (WFG14; Chapter 7.5).

The methods used by the RMLEC to record the stratigraphy on the site focused upon the presence or otherwise of retained finds assemblages. This was the same as used on the temple of Mithras site. Indeed there was no variation in the methodologies applied by Grimes between the two areas from 1952 onwards. It is likely that we see here the influence of Audrey Williams who joined him around this time. Her handwriting can be seen again in many of the notebooks consulted for this report.

As elsewhere throughout the City, modern foundations and intrusions caused considerable problems to Grimes and his team. They were not well equipped for heavy breaking-out work, as George Falkner's recollections explain (Chapter 3.1). The limited funds available to the RMLEC did not extend to the hiring of compressors or drills so, at Bucklersbury House (WFG44/45), the breaking of the concrete basement slabs had to be carried out with 14lb hammers and cold chisel points. All of this day-to-day excavation work was carried out by his team of hired, skilled labourers. Fortunately, unlike at the Mithraeum in the Walbrook valley, there were no groundwater problems here.

In the course of each excavation, notebooks were filled with context and feature details including sketches (Fig 29). The handwriting in the notebooks varies from one site to another, and includes more than just Grimes's handwriting. Once again, from about 1952 onwards, the majority of the recording in these notebooks was by Audrey Williams with numerous annotations, observations and comments by Grimes.

Finds from specific layers were placed in paper bags with the context information written, while still on site, on to them. At the end of each working day the bags were collected and the context information entered into a finds log book. At this stage each group of finds was given a unique number, which became known as its 'bag number'. This method meant that associated bags of finds might become separated but each group within each bag would remain a closed unit. Unfortunately, this system is responsible for the confusing scatter of bag numbers with high numbers appearing stratigraphically higher than some bags with low numbers.

There are two significant disadvantages to this system for any modern researcher dealing with Grimes's records. First, unless the information placed in the finds log book was precise and specific, giving relationships to known features or other bags and with an appropriate annotation of the whereabouts of the 'context' of the bag on a plan or section drawing, because of the considerable period of time since their excavation in the 40s and 50s and the present day, a number of inconsistencies can occur. Sadly, as a result, any bag group which has the slightest ambiguity associated with it, or surrounding its origin on the site, must be regarded as unstratified. Unfortunately this accounts for a large amount of material from the Cripplegate area. The archive contains a large quantity of material simply labelled as Cripplegate 'A', 'B' or 'C'. Grimes originally used an alphabetic system to identify his sites before using a numeric identifying system. Also, at WFG1 – the Cripplegate Bastion site – he also labelled some of the trenches monitored on the interior which were dug by contractors in advance of the pouring of the foundations of the Barbican wall walk. It is unclear whether this material is from his

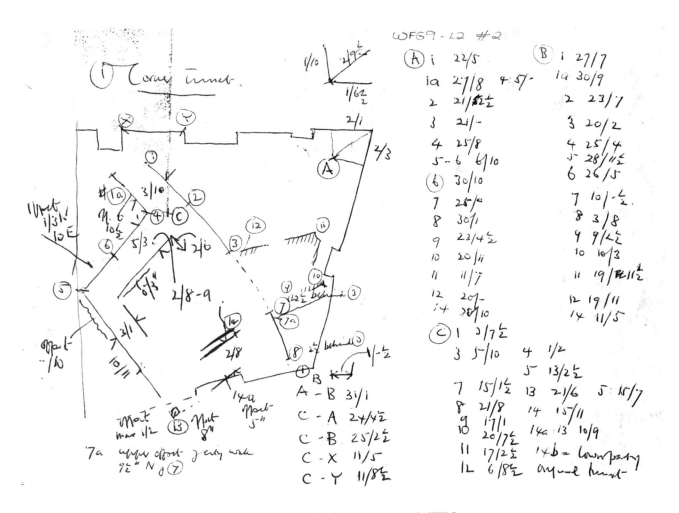

Fig 29 Example from Grimes's notebooks: survey notes for the corner tower in WFG9

early sites (for example Gresham Street or Gutter Lane, sites not included in the current study) or from the wall walk foundation trenches. In either case, the lack of other identifying numbers suggests that, whatever their origins, this material was unstratified. Sadly, it is now both unstratified and unprovenanced.

The second disadvantage is that the amount of recording for individual contexts is dependent upon whether finds were recovered from them or not. If no finds were retained from a particular context then a description of that context might never have been made. In some cases there are context descriptions, without a corresponding bag number, on the section drawings, but this appears to be the case for only a small percentage of the total number of contexts visible on these drawings.

Again, as elsewhere on his sites, Grimes would personally carry out the photographic work as well as all of the section and plan drawing. He placed a lot of emphasis upon the creation of a detailed photographic record but, not surprisingly, the intervening 40 years have seen a marked deterioration in the quality of many of his negatives. The reader is asked to be tolerant about the quality of their reproduction in this report.

The sections were drawn at a scale of 1:12, 1:24 and

1:48 and recorded the detail in the section as he saw it on the day (Fig 30). He was averse to the system of selecting interpreted stratigraphic blocks, and representing them by some sort of stylistic convention, as encouraged by Wheeler. Sections were, to some extent, an arbitrary record – and if the face of the section was cleaned back by a few inches the picture was likely to be quite different (W F Grimes, pers comm). He much preferred to produce a near photographic representation of the section that existed in the trench after the work had been completed. As his published work elsewhere attests (eg Shepherd 1998a), he was a gifted draughtsman with the ability to draw in miniature. It has proved remarkable the amount of information he was able to put on an individual section drawing at such a scale. As has been mentioned, Grimes gave the present author quite specific instruction about the use of his original artwork (Chapter 1.2). As explained, however, these have been cleaned and enhanced by our illustrators, sometimes digitally, but they remain, essentially, Grimes's own work.

Once a section had been drawn, the numbers of the individual finds bags, which had of course been recovered in plan in the trench itself, were projected

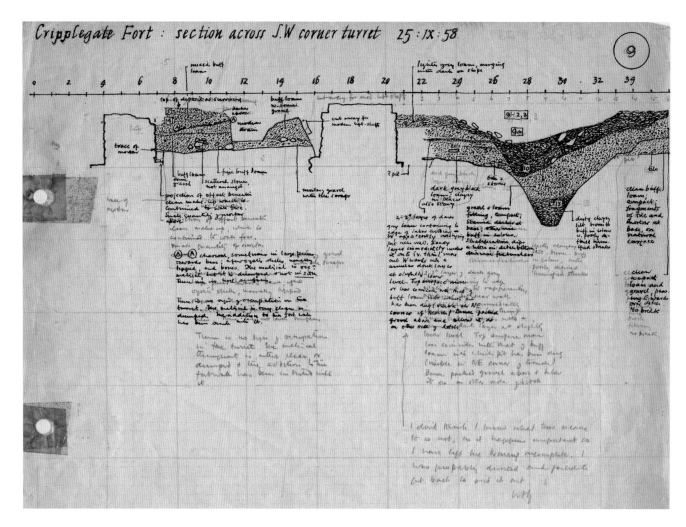

Fig 30 Specimen of Grimes section drawing: the main section across the corner tower and ditch in WFG9

horizontally from their find-spot on to the section, corresponding with the layer in which they were found. This works reasonably well for narrow trenches, but is less successful for large, open areas as encountered at Cripplegate. For the sections included below (Chapters 5–9), the majority of the layer numbers are identified corresponding to the context numbers of the catalogued objects, but not in every case. However, the section drawings are one of the most important components of the GLA.

4.2 About the finds

The post-excavation work on the large body of finds and documents from this excavation appears to have begun almost immediately the excavation had been completed. Finds were washed by RMLEC and Guildhall Museum staff, dried and rebagged. Research on these and other finds, including the bulk finds such as pottery and animal bone, was carried out intermittently from the mid 1950s onwards. This was consolidated in the mid 1990s when specialists from the Museum of London and the Museum of London's

Specialist Services re-examined much of the finds from Cripplegate and many others of Grimes's sites. The identifications in the sections below are largely the result of their work, in particular Nina Crummy and Hella Eckardt (small finds), Martin Henig (intaglio), Jenny Hall (coins), Joanna Bird (samian ware), Jo Groves, Fiona Seeley and Louise Rayner (pottery), and Ian Betts (building material). Jane Sidell carried out initial assessments of the surviving animal bone from these sites, but the material she examined proved to be largely unstratified or from post-medieval contexts and so has not been included in this report. Several categories of finds are separately numbered in consecutive sequences and these catalogues are included in Chapters 5–9. A prefix denoting the category appears inside angled brackets. For example, <MI1> refers to (M)ilitary (I)nscription fragment no. 1, <P2> refers to (P)ottery vessel no. 2, <S3> refers to accessioned (S)mall find no. 3, and <SAM4> refers to (SAM)ian vessel no. 4. Complete lists of the codes for the pottery forms, fabrics and decoration and their expansions are available from the LAARC as part of the research archive and also are posted on the website: http://www.museumoflondonarchaeology.

org.uk/English/ArchiveResearch/ArchiveOnline. Other abbreviations used in the catalogues are as follows: Diam – diameter; L – length; W – width.

In summary, the surviving pottery from the Grimes Cripplegate sites is almost entirely composed of small groups – and it is evident that there has been a lot of selection of material for retention. Diagnostic sherds predominate over plain body sherds. In many instances such assemblages from Grimes's Cripplegate sites have been given a broad late Roman date because of their small size and uncertainty about this period. The samian assemblages are by far the most productive with regard to dating evidence, and more attention has been given to them in the following chapters than the other fine and coarse wares.

The material from the two ditch profiles, at Noble Street (WFG9) and Aldermanbury (WFG14) is of interest in that there is an absence of Oxfordshire red/brown colour-coated ware (OXRC), Portchester ware D (PORD), Roman late 'calcite-tempered' ware (CALC) and Alice Holt/Farnham ware (AHFA) in the late Roman groups. These groups, however, do contain late black-burnished ware 1 (BB1) forms, black-burnished ware 2 (BB2) indented jars, Nene Valley colour-coated wares (NVCC), and Camulodunum form 306 bowls. The likely implication of all this being that these groups are in fact 3rd century AD in date and that OXRC should be dated later than its present start date of *c* AD 270. Symonds noticed a similar pattern with the material from the basilica site at Leadenhall Court (LCT84), City of London (R Symonds, pers comm).

As far as the building material is concerned, the finds retained by Grimes from each site seem to represent the results of a highly biased collection policy. No assemblage can be said to be a representative sample of the building material found during excavation. On many of the sites from which material survived for study, not more than one or two fragments were retained from each context. Often these are curved Roman imbrex tiles which were collected in the apparent belief that they were amphora or mortarium sherds. Other types of tile were especially collected because of their individual interest. In this category are flue tiles with keying and a stamped tile from WFG22 (in this case, the sole tile retained from the entire site; Chapter 9.4, 'Period 3').

Unfortunately, as mentioned above, there was not a large amount of animal bone from any of the Cripplegate sites. It is possible that such material was discarded at the time of excavation. However, a large quantity of animal bone – loose and unstratified – does exist within the GLA. It is possible that this, now unlabelled, material was once the stratified finds from these excavations. The material was scanned, but nothing of interest was noted.

The small finds too are lacking good documentary information to locate their find-spots accurately on their respective sites. In the site summaries in Chapters 5–9, individual finds are placed in their relevant

periods where possible, but the remainder – including any known at the time to be unstratified – are listed at the end of each summary.

With such weak finds assemblages, therefore, the search for potential dating evidence rests upon the examination of material from certain key deposits. For example, material sealed by the dumping of material to make up the fort bank (especially at WFG3, WFG4, WFG6 and WFG7) is of significance, as this would supply a *terminus post quem* for the construction. Material derived from the earliest dumps of the fort banks is also included here, as these dumps would include material that was in circulation at the time of the fort construction. Likewise, material from the infilling of the fort ditch on the south side of the fort, at WFG9 and WFG14, should indicate the date at which the fort ditch was backfilled. Although this activity by no means necessarily equates with an abandonment of the fort, the likelihood is that if the defences of the fort were being neglected in this fashion then the use of the area of the fort itself might have changed.

Summary of land use

Essentially, Grimes's work focused upon the western and southern defences of the fort, with just a couple of areas observed in the centre (Fig 20), and the Roman sequence he recorded on many of these sites followed a similar pattern. This takes the form of just four main periods of activity. These compare with the main periods of Roman activity recorded by Howe and Lakin (2004), but with an emphasis here upon the construction of the city wall during period 4. They can be summarised as follows.

Period 1 – natural surface and prehistoric

This is represented by a natural brickearth surface throughout the Cripplegate area. No evidence survived for a sealed land surface above the brickearth. Some evidence of prehistoric activity is represented by the sherds of Bronze Age pottery at the west gate (WFG5; Chapter 5.6) and, possibly, by the enigmatic ditch recorded at the Cripplegate Bastion (WFG1; Chapter 5.1).

Period 2 – late 1st- and early 2nd-century activity (*c* AD 70–120)

The absence of any surviving land surface, other than perhaps the possible turf layer seen under the fort gate (WFG5; Chapter 5.6), suggests that the area had been remodelled, the brickearth therefore truncated, prior to it being used. The earliest layers on top of this natural surface comprise redeposited dumps of brickearth containing Roman material. Pottery in these layers can be broadly dated to *c* AD 40–100. These dumps are sealed by the lowest layers of the internal bank of the fort and at Windsor Court (WFG3; Chapter 5.4), a mortar-mixing pit cut through these dumped layers.

Period 3 – the 2nd-century fort (*c* AD 120–200)

Any late 1st-century buildings on the site, of which the remains of only a couple could be tentatively identified, were cleared away during the first quarter of the 2nd century AD and the fort was laid out, *de novo.* It needs to be emphasised that there is no reliable evidence in the GLA to support any theory that there was a timber precursor to the masonry fort. This is now supported by the results from more recent excavations (Howe and Lakin 2004, 24). Pottery, especially samian ware, from beneath the fort bank and from the lower levels of the fort bank, is consistently Flavian with a few Trajanic and Hadrianic sherds. Material contemporary with the fort defences ranges from Flavian through to late Antonine. This implies a Hadrianic construction date at the earliest, a date confirmed by the MOLA work on the buildings in the centre of the fort and along its south wall (ibid, 37–9; Lyon 2004, 158).

Detail related to the construction phase of the fort was scarce. As mentioned above, a mortar-mixing pit sealed by the bank of the fort was recorded at Windsor Court (WFG3; Chapter 5.4).

The greater part of the record in the following chapters describes the fort defences, consisting of the wall, its internal bank, parts of the intervallum road and some details about the internal buildings. The fort wall was only properly seen at Bastion 14 (WFG4; Chapter 5.5) and Falcon Square, the west gate site (WFG5; Chapter 5.6). Elsewhere it was either severely truncated by post-medieval activity or obscured by the medieval City wall or by post-medieval brickwork. Grimes was able to record a number of sections through the fort bank, which contained pottery dating from the late 1st and 2nd centuries AD. Sadly little datable material came from the internal buildings. The fort ditch seen in the south-west corner at Noble Street (WFG9; Chapter 6.3) and on the south side at Wood Street (WFG12; Chapter 7.3) contained good assemblages associated with the backfilling of the ditch.

Period 4 – the city wall construction and fort abandonment

It can be argued that the addition of the city wall thickening on the west side of the fort either coincided with the abandonment of the fort or was the cause of its abandonment. Post-medieval encroachment into the fabric of the north–south line of the city wall from the east had severely truncated the city wall portion of the defences. As a result Grimes was able to record the city wall thickening in section in a number of places, especially around the Barber-Surgeons' Hall (WFG2; Chapter 5.3). He was able also to record the internal bank to the city wall. A coin from beneath the fabric of the city wall thickening, dated to AD 183–4, supplies a very reliable *terminus post quem* for the construction date of the landward wall. These defences also included an internal bank, which sealed the fort bank beneath it.

A number of contexts were identified within the fort, on those few sites examined by Grimes which post-date the use of the 2nd-century barracks, such as at 15–17 Silver Street (WFG 20; Chapter 9.2) and St Alban's church, Wood Street (WFG22; Chapter 9.4).

Chapters 5–9, therefore, present the Roman data from the archive of the work of the RMLEC on the Cripplegate sites. They are, in effect, brief texts expanded from the descriptions of Grimes's work that he presented in the interim account of his work (Grimes 1968), and seek to replicate some of the specific data he refers to. In an edited format, they also appear as the entries published in the Museum of London Gazetteer series (Shepherd 1998b). The aim is to present the key stratigraphic units on each site relevant to the history and development of the Cripplegate area during the Roman period. It is evident from many of the section drawings that Grimes recorded a great amount of stratigraphic detail. This has not been reproduced here because, in many instances, it is largely superfluous and repetitive. It is also difficult to relate many of Grimes's finds groups to this data. This additional detail can, of course, be consulted in the GLA within the LAARC.

Each site presented in the following chapters is accompanied by a summary of the datable finds. Apart from a couple of well-stratified coins, the main material from the site, which is of interest from the point of view of supplying dating information, is the pottery. As mentioned above, many of the coarse ware assemblages appear to comprise selections of material. Detailed quantification, therefore, was not attempted. Some assemblages appear to be complete, such as those from the fort ditch on its south side at Noble Street (WFG9; Chapter 6.3) and Aldermanbury (WFG14; Chapter 7.5), but these are an exception. Samian ware represents by far the best dating evidence, and the small size of many of the sherds suggests that a total retention policy was in place and, because it has survived well in the archive, must have been separated early during the post-excavation process from the remainder of the pottery. Wherever possible, or relevant, all information about the samian ware is reproduced here.

5 Excavations in the north-west corner of Cripplegate

These sites include the excavation of Cripplegate Bastion (WFG1), Barber-Surgeons' Hall and Bastion 13 (WFG2), Windsor Court (WFG3), Bastion 14 (WFG4) and Falcon Square (WFG5). These were amongst the earliest excavations carried out by the RMLEC during its entire work programme and, as described in Chapter 3.1, were intended to examine the course of the city wall from Bastion 12 southwards towards Falcon Square (now under London Wall).

5.1 WFG1, Cripplegate Bastion (Bastion 12)

1947 (Grimes 1968, 66–7, 76, 84; Fig 5; Fig 6; Fig 31).
NGR: TQ 32300 81678

Other than St Giles Cripplegate itself, the Cripplegate Bastion (Bastion 12) was the most prominent historic monument visible in this vicinity of the City. Horseshoe-shaped in plan and projecting into the graveyard of the church, it marked the position of a right-angled turn in the course of the city wall. A postcard image from the early 20th century shows warehouses at the rear of the bastion, which appears to be clear of structures, at least above the level of the stonework (Fig 8). During the medieval and early post-medieval period, however, the bastion had been used as housing and once the bastion had been cleared of rubble from the destroyed warehouses referred to

above, the interior displayed a great deal of remodelling. None of the standing fabric, however, was recorded by the RMLEC. Grimes was more interested in examining the buried features of the bastion rather than any of its standing masonry.

The surviving records for this site, which unfortunately represent an obviously incomplete account, indicate that at least three trenches (not labelled in any particular manner by Grimes) were excavated (Fig 31). The first of these was aligned along the radius of the bastion (Fig 32). A surviving sketch section of this trench in the site notebook, not reproduced here, describes the natural surface as a thin layer of brickearth on gravel, approximately 600mm beneath the modern-day surface. Above this natural surface was an accumulation of gravel deposits intermixed with layers of sand and clay. Unfortunately no pottery survives to be able to date these layers and it is most likely that the gravel represented floor surfaces in the bastion itself.

The second trench was to the immediate east of the bastion and perpendicular to the east–west aligned city wall. No records survive for this second trench other than another small sketch section approximately locating its position.

The third was a long contractor's trench perpendicular to the north–south line of the city wall. It appears to have been dug along the same alignment, probably as a foundation trench, as the location for the Barbican wall walk. Grimes appears to have carried out

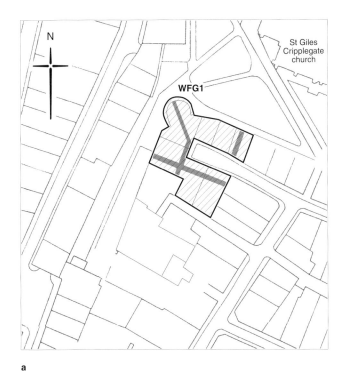

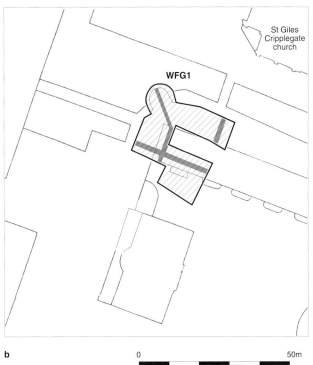

a   b   0   50m

Fig 31 WFG1, the site and trenches: a – located on a contemporary street plan; b – located on a modern street plan (scale 1:1200)

Fig 32 WFG1, view of the trench in Bastion 12 in 1947, looking north-west

a watching brief here – probably during the 1960s (the records are not dated). The only point of interest among the few notes that survive is the line of a curving ditch which appears to run inside the line of the 2nd-century fort (Fig 33). It was seen in section in the long contractor's trench and appeared to be *c* 1m wide and 1.20m deep. It was round-bottomed (Fig 34) and filled at the base with fine gravel and silt. Above this was a layer of fine silt, much compressed in turn by coarser gravel and silt. Grimes, in correspondence, notes that it was the earliest feature on the site but otherwise it could not be dated. Considering the presence of Late Bronze Age pottery on the site of the west gate of the fort (WFG5; below, 5.6) to the south, it is possible that this represents a pre-Roman feature.

The examination of the Cripplegate Bastion, therefore, proved to be most inconclusive with regards to the Roman origins of the city wall – and even the medieval sequence appears to be slight and extremely

Fig 33 WFG1, the ditch seen in a trench adjacent to WFG1, view looking south

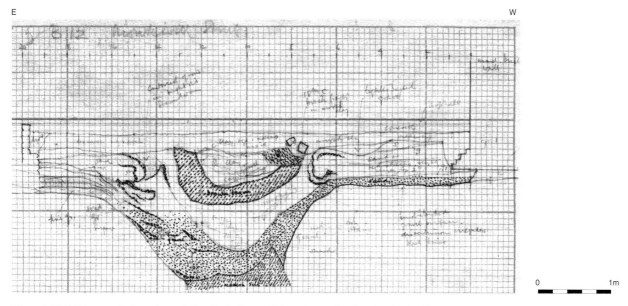

Fig 34 WFG1, pencil drawing of the ditch from Grimes's notebooks (scale 1:50)

poorly dated. No finds can be identified as coming from this site, although some boxes in the archive marked up as 'Cripplegate fort, unstratified' probably come from watching brief work during the course of the construction of the Barbican walkway during the 1960s.

5.2 WFG1a, Bastion 11A

1965 (Grimes 1968, 27; Fig 5; Fig 6; Fig 35). NGR: TQ 32343 81666–TQ 32373 81653

This medieval bastion (Fig 36) does not appear on any of the published post-medieval maps of the City of London and so its discovery during the foundation and underpinning work for the present wall walk was a complete surprise. It was excavated in plan with a single section, parallel to the line of the city wall, cut back from the north (Fig 37). It is situated midway between Cripplegate and the north-western corner of the fort area (Bastion 12) and survives as only two curving stretches of wall. The front of the bastion had been cut away by a 17th-century drain (Terry 1906; Chapter 2.2).

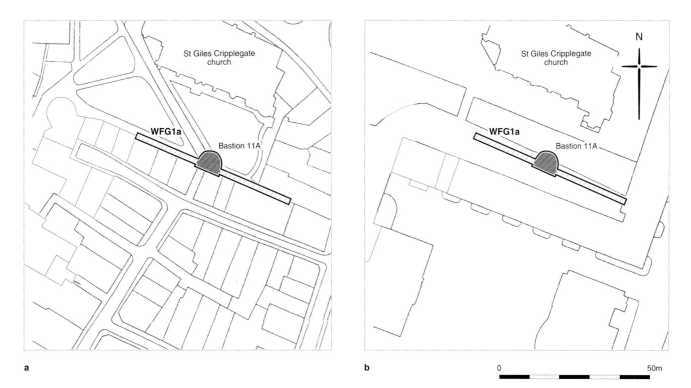

Fig 35 WFG1a, site and trenches: a – located on a contemporary street plan; b – located on a modern street plan (scale 1:1200)

Fig 36 WFG1a, Bastion 11A in 1968, viewed looking south (3ft (0.91m) scale)

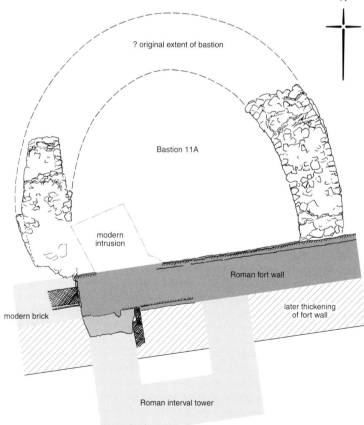

Fig 37 WFG1a, plan of the bastion (after Grimes 1968) (scale 1:100)

Only the foundations of the bastion survived. These had been butted against the line of the Roman and medieval city wall. A modern intrusion damaged the western side of the bastion. It was hoped that traces of the Roman berm would be found here. Although a hard gravel surface was found it could not be accurately dated. On the interior of the city wall, traces of possible Roman stonework projecting beyond the line of the city wall locate the position of an interval tower. It is interesting to note that, based upon this slim piece of evidence, archaeologists from MOLA digging in 2000 were able to predict the position of a corresponding tower on the south side at Gresham Street prior to redevelopment (Howe and Lakin 2004, 36; Lyon 2004, 159). A small trench located the interval tower and ensured its preservation beneath the subsequent redevelopment.

It is important to note here that the bastion foundations had been cut into underlying made-up ground, including a 13th-century pit. This was the first opportunity to date any of the bastions in the Cripplegate area. Based upon the similarity in design Grimes suggested that they all belonged to the medieval period, and not to the late Roman period as was previously believed.

5.3 WFG2, Barber-Surgeons' Hall (Bastion 13)

1947–59 (Grimes 1968, 20, 28; Fig 5; Fig 6; Fig 38). NGR: wall TQ 32278 81637–TQ 32290 81662

Work first began on the Barber-Surgeons' Hall site in 1947–8 and Grimes returned to it on a number of occasions in the 1950s. The main reason for this was the well-preserved depth of archaeological deposits that he encountered there, a phenomenon shared also by the Windsor Court site (WFG3; below, 5.4) to the immediate south. Fortunately, these sites had escaped the construction of deep basements during the Victorian redevelopment of the area. It would appear also that, as his ideas and understanding of the Roman and medieval topography in the Cripplegate area became that much clearer, he would return to these deep deposits hopefully to retrieve additional data that was lacking elsewhere. For example, because of the depth of deposits here the city bank survived to a significant height, including not only the internal bank of the fort wall but also the bank built up against the interior face of the city wall thickening.

The site was located in the bomb-destroyed ruins of the Victorian Barber-Surgeons' Hall. This had originally been part of a larger hall built in the early 17th century, which included Bastion 13 and the three warehouses to the south. These were located between the later hall and Windsor Court and were still in the freehold of the Barber-Surgeons' Company. The earliest work took place in three trenches in the basement of the hall. These revealed two complete sections through the defences on the interior of the city wall and included also the west end of the Barber-Surgeons' Hall. Fig 40a, an edited version of a Grimes original drawing, shows the sloping deposits of the fort

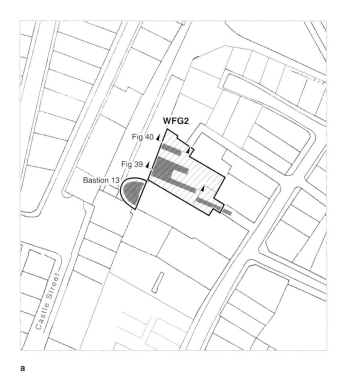

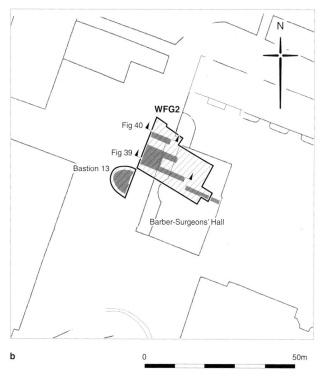

Fig 38 WFG2, site and trenches: a – located on a contemporary street plan; b – located on a modern street plan (scale 1:1200)

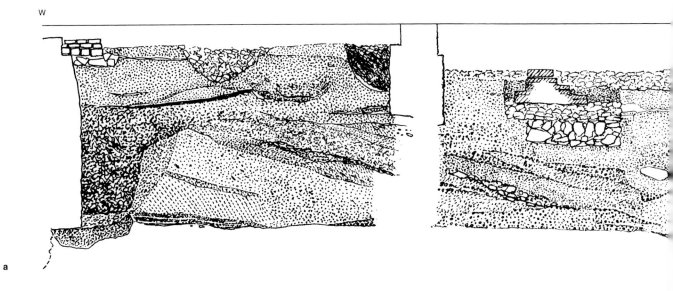

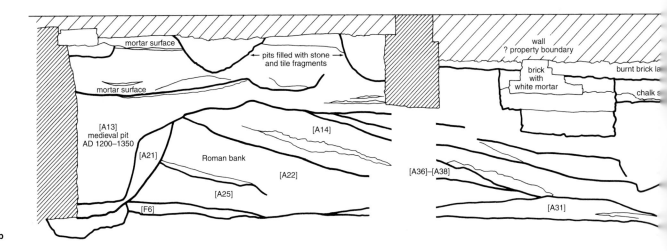

Fig 39 (above and facing) WFG2, the central south-facing section through the defences: a – edited Grimes original; b – interpretive section (scale 1:50)

and city wall banks, raised against the wall to the west, in the cutting at the north end of the site, and Fig 39a shows the section through the centre of the site. The corresponding interpretive drawings (Fig 39b; Fig 40b) locate the finds groups described below. As for a number of his sites, especially the earliest excavations, the finds survival for this site is poor. The fine and coarse wares are missing or at least they can no longer be identified by context (there is a large amount of unmarked material for this site). The samian ware, separated at an early stage in the excavations, does survive for study. This is included, for key layers, below (Fig 41). The results of these trenches can be summarised as follows.

Period 1

Natural soil consisted of brickearth. There were no recorded traces of any pre-Roman activity.

Period 2

This natural layer was covered with a thin mortary layer, presumably from the construction of the fort wall. No dating material came from beneath or within this mortary layer. At the extreme west end of the site there were a number of thin, dumped and made-up brickearth layers immediately above the mortary layer (eg layer [F6]; Fig 40), all of which are sealed by a *c* 30mm thick black 'charcoaly' layer. This, in turn, was sealed by the first dumps of material for the fort wall bank, and therefore probably pre-dates the construction of the bank of the fort. The dumped layers contained a little Roman material, the pottery being broadly dated to the period *c* AD 40–100.

LAYER [F6] (SEALED BY FORT BANK)
Pottery summary:
Small-sized assemblage.

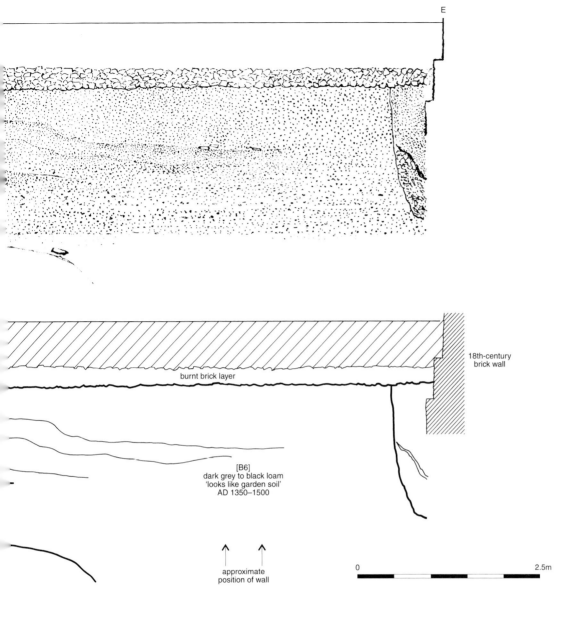

E

18th-century
brick wall

burnt brick layer

[B6]
dark grey to black loam
'looks like garden soil'
AD 1350–1500

approximate
position of wall

0   2.5m

Earliest date *c* AD 70; latest date *c* AD 100.
Samian ware catalogue:
<SAM1> South Gaul (SAMLG 5DR36)
Flavian.
Other wares:
Now missing.

Period 3

The construction of the fort wall was the first major activity on the site – and the mortar seen above probably represents this phase of activity. Unfortunately it was not possible to examine a section through the wall or its foundations so specifications for its build at this point in the circuit are not available. A bank of redeposited brickearth, described as brown loamy clay in the records, with a few lenses of mixed material, had been thrown up against the interior face of the fort wall. Grimes believed that the cleaner material might have come from the cutting of the fort ditch. Little datable material has survived from this bank but, according to the archive notes, it included coarse ceramics that could be broadly dated to the late 1st or early 2nd century AD. The surviving material is all samian dated from the Flavian period to the Hadrianic. The composition of the small assemblage from [A25], from a lens of material deep down in the bank, is significant (Fig 39b). It includes an early 2nd-century Dragendorff form 18/31 dish fragment from les Martres-de-Veyre and a Hadrianic Dragendorff form 33 cup fragment from central Gaul (layer [A25], <SAM4> and <SAM5>, below).

At the foot of the bank was a shallow gully that ran alongside an expanse of tightly packed gravel in a clayey matrix with a slight camber. This was seen in both of the trenches and was evidently an intervallum road. It was also seen in WFG3, WFG5–WFG7 and WFG9 to the south. It is interesting to note that this gravel road lay directly upon the mortary layer described

W

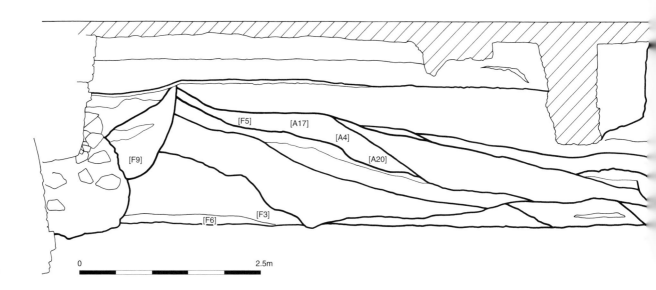

Fig 40 (above and facing) WFG2, the northernmost south-facing section through the defences: a – edited Grimes original; b – interpretive section (scale 1:50)

above as resting directly upon the natural surface. The width of the road could not be recorded as the eastern side was disturbed by post-Roman pit digging.

Both the tops of the bank and the road had received additional dumps of gravelly material. Layer [A31], a thin layer from the surface of the road, contained samian dated to the 2nd century AD (<SAM9> and <SAM10>, below; Fig 39b).

The fort bank

LAYER [A25] (BOTTOM OF BANK)
Pottery summary:
Small-sized assemblage.

Earliest date *c* AD 40; latest date *c* AD 100.
Samian ware catalogue:
<SAM2> South Gaul (SAMLG 5DR15/17)
With part of an illegible stamp.
Neronian–Flavian.
<SAM3> Two sherds, south Gaul (SAMLG 5DR18)
Flavian.
<SAM4> Les Martres-de-Veyre (SAMMV 5DR18/31)
Early 2nd century AD.
<SAM5> Central Gaul (SAMCG 6DR33)
Hadrianic.
Other wares:
Now missing.

E

LAYER [F3]
Pottery summary:
Small-sized assemblage.
Earliest date *c* AD 40; latest date *c* AD 100.
Samian ware catalogue:
<SAM6> Central Gaul (SAMCG 6DR27)
Early to mid 2nd century AD.
<SAM7> South Gaul (SAMLG 5WA81)
Small bowl, probably a variant of Hermet's plain form
24 (1934), with an overhang instead of a groove.
Second half of 1st century AD.
Other wares:
Now missing.

LAYER [A22] (TOP OF BANK)
Pottery summary:
Small-sized assemblage.
Earliest date *c* AD 40; latest date *c* AD 100.
Samian ware catalogue:
<SAM8> South Gaul (SAMLG 5DR15/17)
Neronian–early Flavian.
Other wares:
Now missing.

On surface of intervallum road (sealed by city wall bank)

LAYER [A31]
Pottery summary:
Small-sized assemblage.
Earliest date *c* AD 120; latest date *c* AD 160.
Samian ware catalogue:
<SAM9> Central Gaul (SAMCG 5DR18/31)
Hadrianic–early Antonine.
<SAM10> Les Martres-de-Veyre (SAMMV 5DR18/31)
Early 2nd century AD.
<SAM11> South Gaulish sherd (SAMLG)
Other wares:
Now missing.

Period 4

The next significant phase of activity was represented by the cutting of a straight-sided foundation trench in the top of the fort bank against the internal face of the fort wall. The backfill of this construction trench contained mainly early 2nd-century material, suggesting that it comprised the redeposited material cut out of the top of the early 2nd-century fort bank. A new wall was built in this foundation and would appear to have risen up against the fort wall. Both, therefore, were in use at the same time. This new wall became known as the 'city wall thickening' and can be equated with the construction of the city wall around the rest of the landward side of the city. New dumps of material were thrown up against the inside face of this new wall, consisting of more mixed material containing much fine charcoal and burnt clay, but the extent of these was severely disturbed by post-Roman intrusions. Extant deposits (eg layers [A4], [A14], [A17], [A20], [A36], [A37], [A38], [F5]; Fig 39; Fig 40) contained predominantly 2nd-century material, with a few smaller 1st-century sherds.

A large concentration of medieval pits cut into the eastern edge of the bank and over the road, in some places penetrating deep into the road surface. A line of superimposed foundations aligned north–south, 6.1m distant and parallel with the city wall, would appear to correspond with the western side of the medieval Barber-Surgeons' Hall. Floor surfaces related to the early 17th-century hall extended across the entire site up against the city wall (Bastion 13 was incorporated into the hall at this date). These were covered by burnt rubble, presumably levelled debris from the Great Fire of 1666, which was in turn sealed by later floor surfaces. The contemporary basement floor was the latest of these floors. The presence of the hall appears to have been influential in preserving the Roman deposits beneath.

In the bastion itself, excavation revealed part of a flat-bottomed Roman ditch that ran parallel with the line of the city defences. No dating material came from it but comparison with the ditch sequence elsewhere (WFG4; below, 5.5) would suggest that it was the late Roman ditch contemporary with the city wall. It had removed all trace of the fort ditch in this area. The foundations of the bastion were seen to cut into the fills of this ditch.

From the backfill of the construction trench of the city wall

LAYER [F9]
Pottery summary:
Small-sized assemblage.
Earliest date *c* AD 120; latest date *c* AD 160.
Samian ware catalogue:
<SAM12> In the style of Donnaucus of les Martres-de-Veyre (SAMMV 4DR37) (Fig 41)
Stanfield and Simpson 1958, pl 45 no. 517 is identical, except for the short bead row coming from the acanthus in the lower frieze.
c AD 100–25.
<SAM13> Les Martres-de-Veyre (SAMMV 4DR37)
Early 2nd century AD.
<SAM14> South Gaul (SAMLG 5DR18/31)
Trajanic.
<SAM15> Les Martres-de-Veyre (SAMMV 5DR18/31)
Trajanic–Antonine.
<SAM16> Central Gaul (SAMCG 5DR18/31)
Hadrianic.
<SAM17> South Gaul (SAMLG 4CU11)
Flavian–Trajanic.
Other wares:
Now missing.

LAYER [A21]
Pottery summary:
Small-sized assemblage.
Earliest date *c* AD 40; latest date *c* AD 100.
Samian ware catalogue:
<SAM18> South Gaul (SAMLG 5DR18/31)
Neronian–Flavian.
<SAM19> South Gaul (SAMLG 5DR15/17)
Neronian–early Flavian.
<SAM20> South Gaul (SAMLG 4DR37)
Flavian.
Other wares:
Now missing.

Fig 41 Selected samian vessels <SAM12>, <SAM31>, <SAM42> and <SAM48> from period 4 at the Barber-Surgeons' Hall (WFG2) (scale 1:1)

The city wall bank

LAYER [A14] (TOP OF BANK)
Pottery summary:
Small-sized assemblage.
Earliest date *c* AD 120; latest date *c* AD 250.
Samian ware catalogue:
<SAM21> Lezoux (SAMCG 4DR37)
Panel border of ovoid beads.
Hadrianic to early Antonine.
<SAM22> South Gaul (SAMLG 4CU11)
Flavian.
<SAM23> South Gaul (SAMLG 5DR18)
Early Flavian.
<SAM24> South Gaul (SAMLG 5R18)
Flavian.
Other wares:
Now missing.

LAYER [A4]
Pottery summary:
Small-sized assemblage.
Earliest date *c* AD 120; latest date *c* AD 250.
Samian ware catalogue:
<SAM25> South Gaul (SAMLG 5DR15/17)
Pre-Flavian.
<SAM26> South Gaul (SAMLG 4DR37)
Flavian.
<SAM27> Platter sherd, south Gaul (SAMLG 5)
1st century AD.
<SAM28> Central Gaul (SAMCG 5DR18/31)
Hadrianic–early Antonine.
<SAM29> South Gaul (SAMCG 5DR18)
Neronian–Flavian.
<SAM30> Central Gaul (SAMCG 5DR31)
Mid–late Antonine.
Other wares:
Now missing.

LAYER [A20]
Pottery summary:
Small-sized assemblage.
Earliest date *c* AD 40; latest date *c* AD 140.
Samian ware catalogue:
<SAM31> South Gaul (SAMLG 4DR37) (Fig 41)
Hare (Oswald 1936–7, no. 2113) with vines; Knorr 1952, table 6, c, by Biragillus, has the hare, ovolo, grapes, vine stem and style of branches, and is a closely similar arrangement.
c AD 85–105.
<SAM32> South Gaul (SAMLG 6DR27)
Late 1st century AD.
<SAM33> South Gaul (SAMLG 5DR35)
Late 1st century AD.
<SAM34> Les Martres-de-Veyre (SAMMV 5DR18/13)
Early 2nd century AD.
<SAM35> Central Gaul (SAMCG 5DR18/31)
Hadrianic.
<SAM36> Four south Gaulish sherds (SAMLG)

Other wares:
Now missing

LAYER [A17]
Pottery summary:
Small-sized assemblage.
Earliest date *c* AD 120; latest date *c* AD 250.
Samian ware catalogue:
<SAM37> Central Gaul (SAMCG 5DR18/31)
Hadrianic–Antonine.
Other wares:
Now missing.

LAYER [A36]
Pottery summary:
Small-sized assemblage.
Earliest date *c* AD 120; latest date *c* AD 250.
Samian ware catalogue:
<SAM38> Central Gaul (SAMCG 4DR37)
Hadrianic–Antonine.
<SAM39> Central Gaul (SAMCG 5DR18/31)
Hadrianic.
<SAM40> Probably central Gaulish but heavily over fired (SAMCG 6DR33)
Mid 2nd century AD.
Other wares:
Now missing.

LAYER [A37]
Pottery summary:
Small-sized assemblage.
Earliest date *c* AD 120; latest date *c* AD 200.
Samian ware catalogue:
<SAM41> Central Gaul; the ovolo is broken (SAMCG 4DR37)
Hadrianic–Antonine.
<SAM42> In the style of the Quintilianus group at Lezoux (SAMCG 4DR37) (Fig 41)
The deer (Oswald 1936–7, no. 1752A) in the panel is on Stanfield and Simpson 1958, pl 69 no.15, the borders and rosette terminals on pl 71 no. 27, and the basal wreath between guidelines on pl 70 no. 21.
c AD 125–45.
<SAM43> Central Gaul (SAMCG 5DR36)
Hadrianic.
<SAM44> Central Gaul (SAMCG 5DR18/31)
Antonine.
<SAM45> Central Gaul (SAMCG 5DR31)
Antonine.
<SAM46> Central Gaul (SAMCG 6DR33)
Antonine.
Other wares:
Now missing.

LAYER [A38]
Pottery summary:
Small-sized assemblage.
Earliest date *c* AD 120; latest date *c* AD 200.

Samian ware catalogue:

<SAM47> Les Martres-de-Veyre (SAMMV 4DR37)
The broken ovolo may be that used by Drusus I.
c AD 100–25.

<SAM48> In the style of Valens of Lezoux (SAMCG 4DR37) (Fig 41)
The pigmy, trifid motif, tier of cups, saltire and ovoid beads are all on Stanfield and Simpson 1958, pl 81 no. 32, and the next figure is probably the nymph shown here.
c AD 125–45.

<SAM49> South Gaul (SAMLG 4DR37)
Flavian.

<SAM50> South Gaul (SAMLG 4DR30)
Flavian.

<SAM51> South Gaul (SAMLG 4CU11)
Flavian.

<SAM52> South Gaul (SAMLG 5DR18)
Neronian–Flavian.

<SAM53> Central Gaul (SAMCG 5DR36)
Hadrianic.

<SAM54> Central Gaul (SAMCG 6DR33)
Hadrianic–Antonine.

<SAM55> South Gaul (SAMLG 5DR18)
Flavian.

Other wares:
Now missing.

LAYER [F5]
Pottery summary:
Small-sized assemblage.
Earliest date *c* AD 120; latest date *c* AD 250.

Samian ware catalogue:

<SAM56> Les Martres-de-Veyre (SAMMV 4DR37)
Trajanic–Hadrianic.

<SAM57> Central Gaul (SAMCG 5DR31)
Antonine.

<SAM58> Central Gaul (SAMCG 5DR18/31)
Hadrianic–Antonine.

Other wares:
Now missing.

Building material

Very little survived for study; most building material comprises very small fragments, which cannot be accurately identified. The only items of interest are a small fragment of roofing slate (layer [A1], not illustrated) and plain white wall plaster (layer [A20]; Fig 40b).

5.4 WFG3, Windsor Court and Castle Street

1947, 1953, 1958–9 (Grimes 1968, 17, 19, 28, 64–5, 79, 164–7; Fig 5; Fig 6; Fig 42). NGR: city wall – TQ 32266 81603–TQ 32249 81564

Grimes returned to this site on a number of occasions too, as he did to the site of the Barber-Surgeons' Hall to the immediate north (WFG2; above, 5.3), to re-examine the complex sequence of Roman remains he

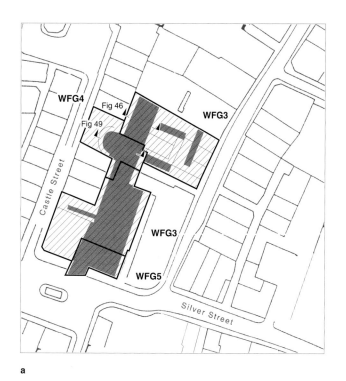

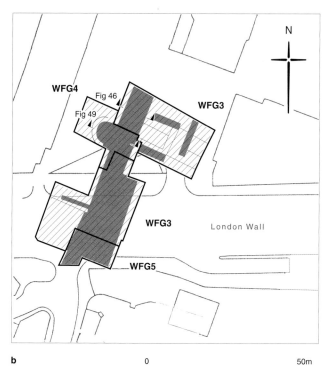

Fig 42 WFG3–WFG5, the sites and trenches: a – located on a contemporary street plan; b – located on a modern street plan (scale 1:1200)

discovered there. Before summarising these below, it should be pointed out that medieval pit cutting had penetrated deep into natural soil across much of the site on the east side of the city defences. In only a few places were natural and overlying Roman deposits seen. Even though they were poorly truncated, their significance was such that Grimes examined them as thoroughly as possible. On the western side of the site, against the city defences, modern foundation stanchions had severely reduced the area available for study (Fig 43).

Period 1

Natural soil consisted of brickearth with no obvious traces of pre-Roman activity.

Period 2

Immediately above natural surface, and underneath the

bank of the fort, it was possible to discern horizontal layers (eg layers [5], [346], not illustrated) similar to those at WFG2, which appear to represent pre-fort activity of an unspecified character.

LAYER [5]
Pottery summary:
Small-sized assemblage.
Earliest date *c* AD 60; latest date *c* AD 100.
Samian ware catalogue:
<SAM59> South Gaul (SAMLG 6DR27)
Flavian.
<SAM60> South Gaulish sherd (SAMLG)
Flavian.
Other fine and coarse wares:
AMPH; HWB 4F; OXID abraded; HOO abraded; AMPH RIM abraded.
<S1> Copper-alloy coin
WFG3 <8>, [5]
Domitian dupondius, AD 87 (*BMC*, ii, 398)

Fig 43 WFG3, view of the southern site in 1948 towards the location, beneath the spoil dump, of the fort gate, looking south-west: the wall on the right follows the line of the city wall

Fig 44 Selected samian vessels <SAM61>, <SAM64>, <SAM68> and <SAM82> from Windsor Court (WFG3) (scale 1:1, stamp detail 2:1)

Fig 45 WFG3, the mortar pits beneath the fort bank at the north end of the site, view looking west

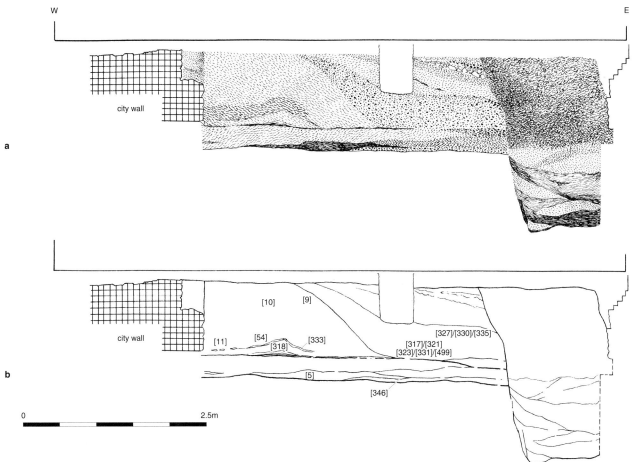

Fig 46 WFG3, a south-facing section through the defences from the centre of the site: a – edited Grimes original; b – interpretive section (scale 1:50)

LAYER [346]
Pottery summary:
Small-sized assemblage.
Earliest date *c* AD 60; latest date *c* AD 85.
Samian ware catalogue:
<SAM61> South Gaul (SAMLG 4DR29) (Fig 44)
Fine scrollery with palmette and ?draped figure, smudged on removal from the mould.
c AD 45–60.
Other fine and coarse wares:
HWB/C.

Period 3

In the north-west part of the site, the horizontal layers beneath the bank of the fort had been cut by three rectangular pits, which were lined with mortar (Fig 45). These mixing pits were backfilled with the lowest dumps of material that made up the fort bank and so were probably employed for the mixing of mortar for use in the construction of the fort wall itself (Fig 46a). The latter could not be seen owing to the presence of the city wall thickening and modern foundations. The fort bank consisted of redeposited brickearth with some mixed material. The latter contained a few finds, in particular coarse wares and

samian ware, broadly dated to the late 1st or early 2nd century AD. A deposit low down in the fort bank, either pre-dating the raising of the bank or one of its earliest dumped components, contained a stamped sherd of samian ware dating to the Trajanic period (area A, cut 1, 3).

As at WFG2, at the foot of the internal bank was a gully alongside a gravel, metalled surface with a slight camber (Fig 47). Layer [356], containing late 1st-century material, was sealed by the first gravel make-up layer for this road. Other make-up layers for remetallings of this road contained 2nd-century material (layers [338], [345], [347]). The gully alongside had evidently been lined with wicker or horizontal planks: a great many stakeholes from vertically driven posts were found along either side of the gully (Fig 48; this gully or drain connected with that seen in WFG5, below 5.6; cf Fig 63). Material from the fill of the gully was also 2nd century AD in date (layers [51], [316], [322]). On the eastern side of the road, at the north and south ends of the site, short sections of ragstone wall were recorded aligned parallel with the line of the fort wall. At the south end, gravel metallings ran across the projected line of this wall, suggesting a turn eastwards of the wall. Stakeholes in the natural may record the line of drainage gullies

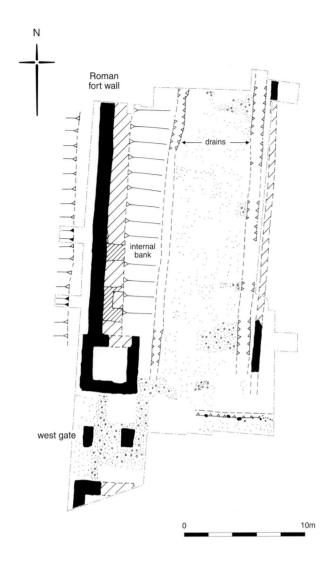

N

Roman
fort wall

← drains →

internal
bank

west gate

0   10m

Fig 47 WFG3, general plan of the main Roman features on WFG3 and WFG5 (scale 1:300)

aligned east–west across this part of the site, but the gullies themselves had been backfilled with gravel and were not seen in plan. No floor levels or accompanying dating evidence is available for these features.

Low in fort bank

AREA A, CUT 1, [4]
Pottery summary:
Small-sized assemblage.
Earliest date *c* AD 40; latest date *c* AD 100.
Samian ware catalogue:
<SAM62>South Gaulish sherd (SAMLG)
1st century AD.
Other wares:
Now missing.

LAYER [11] (1957)
Pottery summary:
Medium-sized assemblage.

Earliest date *c* AD 100; latest date *c* AD 120.
Fine and coarse wares:
VRW 1; VRW 7 HOF; VRW; VRW 4A burnt rim; LOMI; HWC 9A; HWC 2T; HWC 2T slip no dec; HWC 3 BDD; AHSU 2T abraded; AHSU 2A; HWB; DR20.

LAYER [54]
Pottery summary:
Small-sized assemblage.
Earliest date *c* AD 70; latest date *c* AD 120.
Fine and coarse wares:
VRW; VRW 2T burnt rim; VCWS; HWC; AHSU 2T; SAND.

LAYER [318]
Pottery summary:
Small-sized assemblage.
Earliest date *c* AD 70; latest date *c* AD 160.
Fine and coarse wares:
VRW; HWC; AHSU; SAND.

LAYER [333]
<S2> Copper-alloy coin
WFG3 <25>, [333]
Vespasian, as.

Fort bank

AREA A, CUT 1, [1]
Pottery summary:
Small-sized assemblage.
Earliest date *c* AD 70; latest date *c* AD 100.
Samian ware catalogue:
<SAM63> DR37, south Gaul (SAMLG)
Flavian.
Other wares:
Now missing.

AREA A, CUT 1, [3]
Pottery summary:
Small-sized assemblage.
Earliest date *c* AD 100; latest date *c* AD 120.
Samian ware catalogue:
<SAM64> Les Martres-de-Veyre (SAMMV 5DR18/31)
(Fig 44)
With stamp of Biracius.
Trajanic.
<SAM65> South Gaul (SAMLG 4DR37)
Flavian.
Other wares:
Now missing.

LAYER [10] (1957)
Pottery summary:
Small-sized assemblage.
Earliest date *c* AD 50; latest date *c* AD 130.
Samian ware catalogue:
<SAM66> Sherd of the Montans (Tarn) area (SAMMT)

Fig 48 WFG3, view of stake-lined gully, looking north

Other fine and coarse wares:
GAUL1; VRW 7; VRW; VRW 1B; LOMI; ERSB 2A;
HWC 2; HWC 2E BUD; HWC; HWC 2T; HWC 9A;
AHSU; RHOD; VRW 2K.
<S3> Copper-alloy coin
WFG3 <7>, [10] (1957)
Trajan dupondius.
AD 98–117.

Dumps on fort bank

LAYER [9] (1957)
Pottery summary:
Small-sized assemblage.
Earliest date *c* AD 120; latest date *c* AD 160.
Samian ware catalogue:
<SAM67> South Gaulish sherd (SAMLG).
Flavian.
Fine and coarse wares:
VRW; GAUL1; VCWS; SAND; OXID 9A; OXID;
KOLN 3 RC; AHSU; HWC 2E BUD; BB2 2 AL;
HWC.

Make-up for intervallum road

LAYER [345]
Pottery summary:
Small-sized assemblage.
Earliest date *c* AD 70; latest date *c* AD 120.
Samian ware catalogue:
<SAM68> South Gaul (SAMLG 4DR37) (Fig 44)
The wreath festoons, large rosette and astralagus were
used by Meddillus (Knorr 1919, table 55, K), and the
rosette and festoon are on a bowl assigned to him from
199 Borough High Street, Southwark (Bird 1988, 255
no. 580, fig 107). The frieze beneath is a scroll with
large-toothed leaves, winding over a crane (O.2206:
Oswald 1936–7). The ovolo may have a rosette tongue.
c AD 70–90.
<SAM69> Two sherds, south Gaul (SAMLG 6DR27)
Neronian–Flavian.
<SAM70> South Gaul (SAMLG 5DR15/17)
Neronian–early Flavian.
Other fine and coarse wares:
VRW 7; NFSE 7; GAUL1; VRW; HWB 4F abraded;
HWC 4F; HWC 2C; HWC; FMIC; AHSU 2A; SAND.

LAYER [347]
Pottery summary:
Small-sized assemblage.
Earliest date *c* AD 40; latest date *c* AD 160.
Samian ware catalogue:
<SAM71> South Gaul (SAMLG 4DR37)
Flavian.
Other fine and coarse wares:
VRW 9D; HWC 3F.

LAYER [338]
Pottery summary:
Small-sized assemblage.
Earliest date *c* AD 70; latest date *c* AD 160.
Fine and coarse wares:
GAUL1; HWC; OXID.

LAYER [356]
Pottery summary:
Small-sized assemblage.
Earliest date *c* AD 50; latest date *c* AD 160.
Samian ware catalogue:
<SAM72> South Gaul (SAMLG 5DR18)
Neronian–early Flavian.
Other fine and coarse wares:
FMIC.

Fill of intervallum road gully

LAYER [51]
Pottery summary:
Small-sized assemblage.
Earliest date *c* AD 120; latest date *c* AD 160.
Fine and coarse wares:
HWC 9A; HWC 3.

LAYER [316]
Pottery summary:
Small-sized assemblage.
Earliest date *c* AD 70; latest date *c* AD 160.
Other fine and coarse wares:
HWC; HWC 3 BDD; SAND; VCWS 1; KOAN; ?BB2
?2F; SAND.

LAYER [322]
Pottery summary:
Small-sized assemblage.
Earliest date *c* AD 70; latest date *c* AD 120.
Fine and coarse wares:
VRW 1; VRW; VRMA; BHWS; NFSE 1; HWC 3
BDD; AHSU 2C; AHSU; ERSB; ERMS; HWC 4.

Other small finds

FASTENINGS AND FITTINGS
<S4> Iron loop
WFG3 <15>, layer [59]
Double-spiked loop with the lower parts of both points
missing. L 54mm.

METALWORKING
<S5> Copper-alloy slag
WFG3 <56>, layer [521]
A small lump. Max dimensions 16 × 19mm.

MISCELLANEOUS OBJECT
<S6> Copper-alloy disc
WFG3 <54>, layer [521]
Fragment with slight marginal wall housing a tiny
fragment of a second disc. Probably part of a composite
brooch, such as the *Adlocutio* series (Hattatt 1987,
191). The underside is very corroded, and the
accretions may mask a hinge fitting. Diam 27.5mm.

Summary of building material

Late 2nd-/3rd-century, rare late Roman shelly fabric
flue tile, Harrold kiln, Bedfordshire (from layer [106],
a dump on the city wall bank)
Rare ferruginous sandstone from a number of contexts
([311], [313], [314], [322], [343], [375], [377], [381],
[382], [518], [519])
Purbeck marble moulding ([386])

Period 4

A straight-sided foundation trench was cut into
the top of the fort bank. This made up the foundation
of the city wall thickening, which was built against the
internal face of the fort wall. The lower fills of the
bank (layers [317], [321], [323], [331], [499]; Fig 46)
contain predominantly 2nd-century material. Pottery
from layer [499] could be dated as late as *c* AD 180.
It is perhaps interesting to note that the material
found within the upper layers of the bank is earlier
than those below, suggesting that the soil had been
excavated from elsewhere for dumping on to the bank
(layers [327], [330], [335]; Fig 46). New road
surfaces were laid but it is not certain if the Roman
building on the east side of the fort road continued in
use. A late 3rd-century coin (<S7>, layer [93]) comes
from the gully at the foot of the bank, alongside the
intervallum road.

Dumps of mixed soil, truncated by post-medieval
features, suggest an addition to the city wall bank
(layer [106]). This contains exclusively 4th-century
pottery. Horizontal layers to the east of the wall and
bank, and sealing the intervallum road, contain 3rd-
and 4th-century material (layers [M.12.1], [M.8.2],
[372], [397]). Their presence suggests that the road
had gone out of commission at this time, or at least
it was no longer being maintained as a gravelled
surface.

Lower fill of city wall bank

LAYER [317]
Pottery summary:
Small-sized assemblage.

Earliest date *c* AD 70; latest date *c* AD 160.
Fine and coarse wares:
VRW burnt base; VRW; HWC 2 AL; GAUL1.

LAYER [321]
Pottery summary:
Small-sized assemblage.
Earliest date *c* AD 50; latest date *c* AD 160.
Samian ware catalogue:
<SAM73> South Gaul (SAMLG 5DR18)
Flavian.
Other fine and coarse wares:
VRW.

LAYER [323]
Pottery summary:
Small-sized assemblage.
Earliest date *c* AD 70; latest date *c* AD 160.
Other fine and coarse wares:
VRW 1; VRW; HWC.

LAYER [331]
Pottery summary:
Small-sized assemblage.
Earliest date *c* AD 120; latest date *c* AD 160.
Samian ware catalogue:
<SAM74> South Gaul (SAMLG 6DR27)
Flavian.
<SAM75> South Gaul (SAMLG 4DR29)
Pre- or early Flavian.
Other fine and coarse wares:
AMPH; VRW; BHWS; HWC; BB2 4; BB2 2F; VRW
burnt; HWC 2 BUD; ERSB 2; SAND 5.

LAYER [499]
Pottery summary:
Small-sized assemblage.
Earliest date *c* AD 120; latest date *c* AD 180.
Samian ware catalogue:
<SAM76> South Gaul (SAMLG 6DR27)
Flavian.
Other fine and coarse wares:
VRW 2; VRR/VCWS; VRW; OXID; SAND ?9A; BB2 2
AL; SAND; ?HWC.

Upper fill of city wall bank

LAYER [327]
Pottery summary:
Small-sized assemblage.
Earliest date *c* AD 70; latest date *c* AD 120.
Samian ware catalogue:
<SAM77> South Gaul (SAMLG 4DR29)
Neronian–Flavian.
<SAM78> South Gaulish ware sherd (SAMLG)
Flavian.
Other fine and coarse wares:
HWC; ERSB; AHSU 2A; AHSU; SAND 4F; NFSE;
RDBK.

LAYER [330]
Pottery summary:
Small-sized assemblage.
Earliest date *c* AD 60; latest date *c* AD 160.
Fine and coarse wares:
VRW1; AHSU; ERSB 2; SAND; SAND ?4.

LAYER [335]
Pottery summary:
Small-sized assemblage.
Earliest date *c* AD 120; latest date *c* AD 140.
Samian ware catalogue:
<SAM79> South Gaul (SAMLG 5DR18/31)
Flavian.
Fine and coarse wares:
VRW; OXID; LOEG 3; BB1 4 AL; HWC; HWC 3
BDD; HWC ?4.

Gully associated with city wall bank

LAYER [93]
<S7> Copper-alloy coin
WFG3 <45>, [93]
Radiate copy.
c AD 270–80.

LAYER [319]
Pottery summary:
Small-sized assemblage.
Earliest date *c* AD 120; latest date *c* AD 160.
Samian ware catalogue:
<SAM80> Lezoux (SAMCG 4DR37)
Hadrianic–Antonine.
<SAM81> Central Gaul (SAMCG 5DR187/31)
Hadrianic–Antonine.
Other fine and coarse wares:
VRW; GAUL1; NFSE ?1; LOMI 5J; VCWS 1B; VRW;
BB2 2; AHSU; HWC+ 2 AL; BB2 2F; SAND 3 BDD;
NKGW; COAR 2; HWC 4.
Comments:
All the pottery from this assemblage is very abraded.

Dumps on city wall bank

LAYER [106]
Pottery summary:
Large-sized assemblage.
Earliest date *c* AD 300; latest date *c* AD 350.
Fine and coarse wares:
SAND 2 NCD; SAND 2T; SAND 4; 4C306; SAND
4C306; CALC 2; AHFA 5J; AHFA 4; AHFA 4 BUD;
BB1 4; BB1 2FX; OXWW 7M22; OXID; OXWW
7M17; OXID 7; NVCC 3 ROD; NVCC; CC ROD;
OXID 4.
Comments:
A very large assemblage of closely dated 4th-century
material. Evidently part of a single dump. The group
includes some complete profiles.

Horizontal layers at rear of city wall bank

LAYER [M.12.1]
Pottery summary:
Small-sized assemblage.
Earliest date *c* AD 270; latest date *c* AD 400.
Fine and coarse wares:
RWS; VRW 1; VCWS 1B7–9; OXRC 4; OXRC DR36
WPD; NVCC 3 BAD; GAUL1; NFSE 1; DR20;
AHFA 4M; AHFA 2FX; BB1 4M; AHFA 1 NCD; BB2
4H; ?AHFA 2/3; SAND 2T burnt; BB2 5J; HWC 9A;
HWC; BBS 2 BUD; ERSB; HWC 4 BUD; VRW 7;
BB1 5.

LAYER [M.8.2]
Pottery summary:
Small-sized assemblage.
Earliest date *c* AD 250; latest date *c* AD 400.
Fine and coarse wares:
AHFA 2.

LAYER [372]
Pottery summary:
Small-sized assemblage.
Earliest date *c* AD 160; latest date *c* AD 300.

Samian ware catalogue:
<SAM82> Central Gaul (SAMCG 4DR37) (Fig 44)
The ovolo (Rogers 1974, B145) was used by Illixo,
Carantinus II and occasionally by Cinnamus. The leaf
is a small version of Rogers 1974, J153, the acanthus
has no precise parallel.
c AD 150–80.
Other fine and coarse wares:
GAUL1; BB1 4G226 AL; HWC.

LAYER [397]
Pottery summary:
Small-sized assemblage.
Earliest date *c* AD 200; latest date *c* AD 400.
Samian ware catalogue:
<SAM83> Central Gaul (SAMCG 5DR18/31)
Hadrianic.
Other fine and coarse wares:
HWC; AMPH; LRRA; OXID.

5.5 WFG4, Bastion 14

1948–9 (Grimes 1968, 17–20, 64–6, 68–9, 76, 79, 84;
Fig 5; Fig 6; Fig 42). NGR: TQ 32258 81591

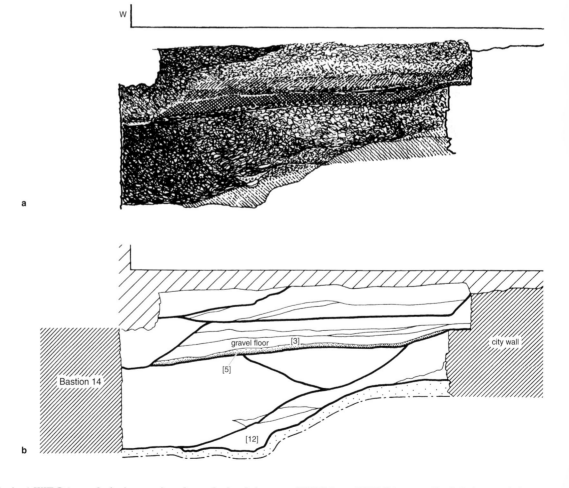

*Fig 49 (above and facing) WFG4, south-facing section through the defences at WFG3 and WFG4: a – edited Grimes original;
b – interpretive section (scale 1:50)*

Bastion 14 was exposed during the demolition of post-medieval brickwork of buildings, which fronted on to Castle Street to the west and Windsor Court to the east. It had previously been revealed in 1865 when the buildings were constructed (Fig 9). The removal of this brickwork revealed an open bastion with the city wall itself reduced to the level of the basements. When the slab of these basements was removed, this revealed that the city wall had been built of two parallel walls (Fig 18). As described in Chapter 3.3, it was first believed that the inner wall was the rebuild of the outer wall but in a slightly different position. However, subsequent excavation in the area to the north and south of the bastion revealed that the outer inner wall (the city wall thickening) was added to the outer wall (the fort wall).

The primary aim of the excavation, however, was to attempt to date the construction of the bastion itself. The excavation revealed a sequence of ditches outside the city defences (Fig 49a and b). The earliest was a broad, flat-bottomed ditch with steep sides, which contained exclusively Roman pottery, a coin of Constans (AD 346–50) and building material (layer [12]; Fig 49b; Grimes 1968, 70). Tumbled debris had accumulated in the base of the ditch and on its east side. This material probably came from the city wall itself. The western side of the ditch had been cut by a broad ditch, much deeper and with a less steep profile. Little material was kept from this feature on this site but it included 12th- or 13th-century pottery, which, at the time of excavation, was regarded as intrusive. This material is likely to come from the backfill of a medieval ditch sealed by the foundations of the bastion and its floor.

The foundations of the bastion butted against the outer face of the foundation and the first few courses of what has survived of the fort wall. Above this it appeared to butt against medieval stonework raised on the Roman fort wall. This relationship with the underlying ditch and the city wall would appear to suggest a medieval date for the bastion but, for reasons unknown, it was not until the discovery of Bastion 11A in 1963, the foundations of which cut a medieval pit, that these open bastions in the area of Cripplegate were dated as medieval (above, 5.2).

Above the ditch fills, and sealing them, were horizontal layers of gravel, which would appear to represent floor surfaces in the sealing medieval material dated c 1200–50. The superstructure of the bastion was not recorded in any detail.

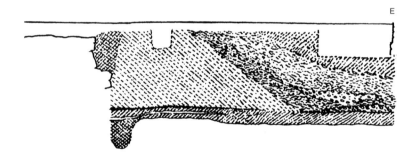

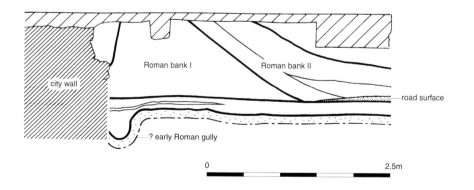

Backfill of flat-bottomed ditch (probably period 4) sealed by gravel floor of bastion

LAYER [12]
Pottery summary:
Small-sized assemblage.
Earliest date *c* AD 120; latest date *c* AD 400.
Fine and coarse wares:
GAUL1; AMPH; OXID 9A; AHSU 2C; AHSU; VRW CC; GROG; HWC; SAND; ?BB1 ?2F.

Small finds

BELT FITTING
<S8> Copper-alloy buckle plate
WFG4 <1>, layer [3] from above the gravel floor (layer [5]) of Bastion 14
Severely corroded, with traces of the hinge fitting and one rivet visible. L 38mm, W 19.5mm. Possibly military.

CRESCENTIC PENDANT
Nina Crummy

<S9> Copper-alloy crescentic pendant (Fig 50)
WFG4 (no acc no.), layer [5], out of the gravel floor of Bastion 14 on the north side of the main cutting, *c* 3m from the internal face of the bastion wall itself
On each side is a hare biting (swallowing) a dog. Published by Grimes as 8th or 9th century in date (Grimes 1968, fig 16), this pendant was found in a gravel surface close to a coin of Constans (AD 346–50). The object is now lost, and the drawing shows no section, making interpretation difficult. The object appears to have been cast, with many of the features of the animals, such as the haunches of the hares and the dogs' eyes, delineated by grooves. Some of the detail may have been worked after casting on the cold metal.

The reason for Grimes's attribution of an 8th- to 9th-century date to the pendant from Bastion 14 is unclear. The animals cannot be attributed to any particular style of the period, whether Celtic, Anglo-Saxon or Viking, while they could easily be accommodated in the Roman period. The motif of a hound chasing and biting the rump of a hare is found in the late Roman period, most notably on openwork

Fig 50 WFG4, copper-alloy crescent-shaped pendant <S9> showing a hare biting a dog to each side of the centre (scale 1:1)

copper-alloy knife handles of probable 4th-century date (Hattatt 1989, fig 36, 242–3; Rees et al 2008, 149, cat no. 661 SF VR701 fig 79, SF HA72). Were the pendant also of late Roman date, the reversal here of the hare-coursing theme could be perhaps interpreted as, subversively, showing the sacred Celtic hare turning to rend the Roman dog. The crescentic form of the pendant could link it to lunula pendants, suggesting an alternative interpretation with the hare as a female icon.

5.6 WFG5, Falcon Square

1956, 1959 (Grimes 1968, 29–30, 33; Fig 5; Fig 6; Fig 42). NGR: fort west gate – TQ 32246 81556

In 1956 the proposed line of the new London Wall (Route 11) ran diagonally across the medieval street pattern in the north-west corner of the City, from Moorgate in the east to the junction of Aldersgate and St Martin's le Grand in the west (Fig 15). In this area, where Silver Street joined Falcon Square, Grimes had the opportunity to examine the site of the west gate of the fort. This was carried out in the course of two campaigns. The first, in 1956, exposed the greater part of the gate, the north tower, north roadway, *spina* and part of the south roadway (Fig 51; Fig 52). In 1959, during the removal of the Falcon Square public conveniences, Grimes was able to locate more of the south roadway and part of the south tower. The pottery from this site is very poorly preserved. Some good assemblages of the post-medieval period survive but, in general, contexts became mixed as a result of disturbance by vandals at the time of the excavation and subsequent flood damage while the material was in the care of the Guildhall Museum. Some samian survives, and this is listed below for a few relevant contexts, but as can be seen their existence tells us little except to confirm a 2nd-century date for the use of the gate and its associated road surfaces. Unfortunately, therefore, it is not possible whatsoever to date any of the individual elements of the site. The coin of Commodus (<S14>, layer [4] <51>) is of importance. It came from the mortar of the city wall thickening and gives the *terminus post quem* for the construction of the city wall at this point in the circuit of the city's defences.

Grimes produced a number of detailed section drawings through the fort gate and of the defences immediately to the north of the gate. However, he did not annotate these drawings with any of the finds bag numbers and the precise significance of some of the labelling cannot be ascertained. Two sections, however, are reproduced here as they are clearer to understand. One shows a north–south section across the west gateway itself (Fig 53), the second shows a section through the defences to the immediate north of the north tower of the gate structure (Fig 54). As a result,

Fig 51 WFG5, general view of the site in 1956 with the west gate of the fort in the foreground and Bastion 14 behind on the left, looking north-east

any surviving finds cannot be satisfactorily located on the site. However, as mentioned above, the surviving finds do little to add any stratigraphic detail other than emphasising the 2nd-century date of the use of the structure.

Period 1

A north–south section through the north entrance to the west gate and part of the south illustrates a brief sequence of activity prior to the construction of the

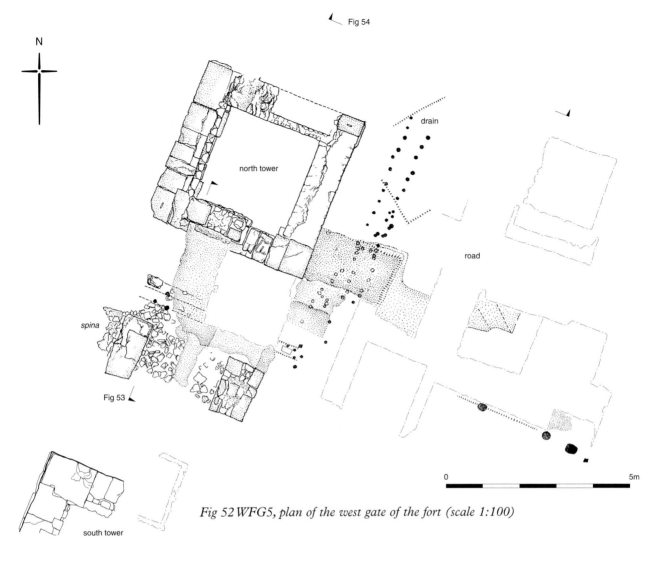

Fig 52 WFG5, plan of the west gate of the fort (scale 1:100)

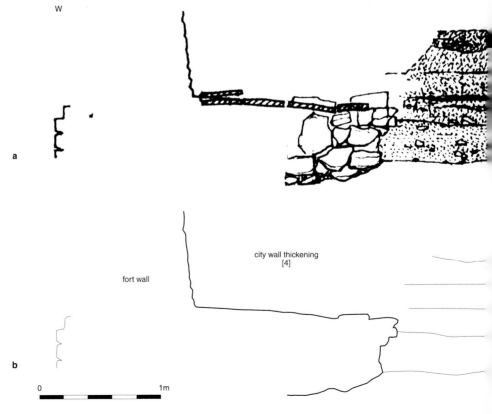

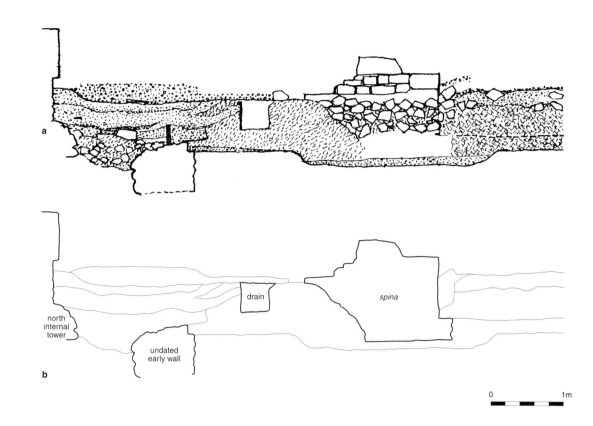

Fig 53 WFG5, west-facing section across the north gateway of the west gate: a – edited Grimes original; b – interpretive section (scale 1:50)

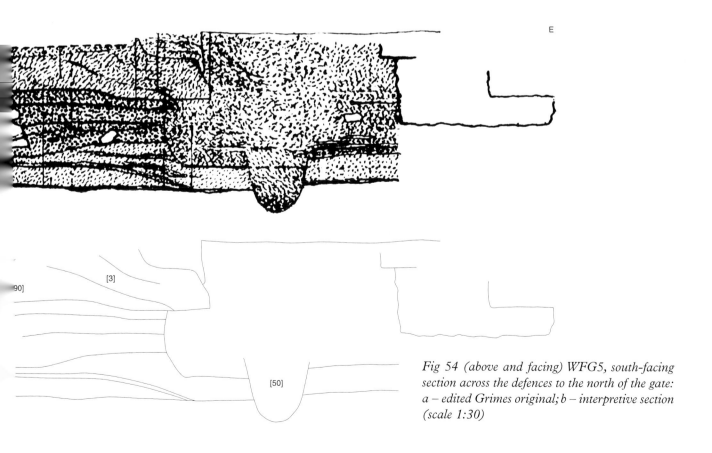

Fig 54 (above and facing) WFG5, south-facing section across the defences to the north of the gate: a – edited Grimes original; b – interpretive section (scale 1:30)

gate (Fig 53). The natural soil on this site was brickearth. Two fragments of Late Bronze Age pottery were recovered from its surface under the north roadway, indicating the presence of prehistoric activity nearby.

Period 2

The earliest Roman occupation was represented by a small portion (c 0.8m) of ragstone wall (Fig 53), also under the north roadway (see also Fig 52 for the position of this wall in plan), which was on the same east–west alignment of the south wall of the north tower. Its square cut, trench-built foundation was cut into the natural brickearth. Only two courses of the wall survived above natural surface. A thin layer of 'hummified' material (Fig 53) lay over a slight offset on the south side of the wall; however, Grimes remarked in his notes that this appeared to be natural material. It might possibly be redeposited turf. No floor surfaces associated with the small wall were noted. Too little of the wall survived to allow an interpretation to be made, but it should be noted that this is the only masonry pre-fort feature in any of Grimes's work in the fort. The absence of a deep foundation suggests a lightly made structure. To the south of this wall, and underneath the line of the later *spina*, was a shallow scoop filled with mixed fine sandy gravels (Fig 53). A thick, c 0.5m, layer of redeposited brickearth, containing quantities of oyster shell, was laid across the site and appeared to butt against the wall. Unfortunately, the precise relationship of this redeposited layer and the wall coincided with the construction cut for the building of the north tower of the gate. A coin of Domitian came from the top of this redeposited layer, immediately under the south side of the *spina*. The wall, redeposited humic material, shallow scoop and redeposited brickearth are the sum, therefore, of pre-gate activity on this site. All the remaining stratigraphy recorded in this section relate to the construction and use of the fort gate itself.

Some traces of pre-fort bank stratigraphy, perhaps contemporary with this wall, were noted just to the north of the gate (Fig 54), and were similar to those mixed layers which either pre-dated or were the lowest layers of the fort bank at Barber-Surgeons' Hall (WFG2) and Windsor Court (WFG3) (above, 5.3, 5.4).

Sealed by first road gravel in fort gate entrance

LAYER [44]
Pottery summary:
Small-sized assemblage.
Earliest date c AD 100; latest date c AD 130
Samian ware catalogue:
<SAM84> Central Gaul (SAMCG 5DR36)
Trajanic–Hadrianic.

<SAM85> Central Gaul (SAMCG 4DR37)
Trajanic–Hadrianic.
<SAM86> Central Gaul (SAMCG 2DE67)
Trajanic–Hadrianic.
Other fine and coarse wares:
Now missing.

Period 3

A broad construction trench, extending c 1.5m to the south of the north tower's south wall, had been cut into this redeposited material and appeared to have truncated the top of the small wall described above. The north tower of the gate itself (Fig 55; Fig 56) was constructed on a foundation of large, ferruginous sandstone blocks (Fig 57). Some coarse mortared ragstone rubble was noted as underpinning these stones under the south wall of the tower (Fig 53).

Many of large ferruginous sandstone blocks had lewis holes and coarse rustication (Fig 58). The fact that this rustication was obscured, since these particular stones were placed within the foundation trench of the gate and did not protrude above the contemporary construction level, indicates that the stones had been reused from a dismantled structure. The identification and whereabouts of this structure are not known (Chapter 4.2, 'Summary of land use', 'Period 3'). The construction trench had been backfilled with a variety of mixed building rubble. The lowest dumps contained ferruginous sandstone fragments in a buff clay with a sandy layer over it. This extended over the remains of the older small wall. The remainder of the construction trench was backfilled with an assortment of layers, such as mixed sandy loam and gravel.

It would appear that the large sandstone blocks in the north tower and, perhaps on the *spina* of the gate (see below), originally continued above the foundation on the exterior of the building, now robbed, but the interior of the north tower was lined with small, squared ragstone blocks. An entrance way into the tower was found in the east end of the south wall of the tower (Fig 59; Fig 60). Reused sandstone blocks here had worn down through use and a curvilinear groove indicated the position of a door bolt, which had repeatedly dragged over the door sill. No floor surfaces were found inside the tower apart from layers of trampled brickearth and some gravel patches. It would appear that the tower had been kept clear throughout its life and may even have had the floors excavated out at a later date. Unfortunately no finds from these layers inside the tower survive for study.

A shallower construction trench was cut c 2.4m to the south of the north tower. This was just over 1.5m wide and c 0.4m deep. It was entirely filled with rough ragstones in a grey-buff clay (Fig 53). On top of this was built the *spina* support, comprising square dressed ragstone and, once again, reused ferruginous ragstone blocks. On the west side, on the north-west corner of

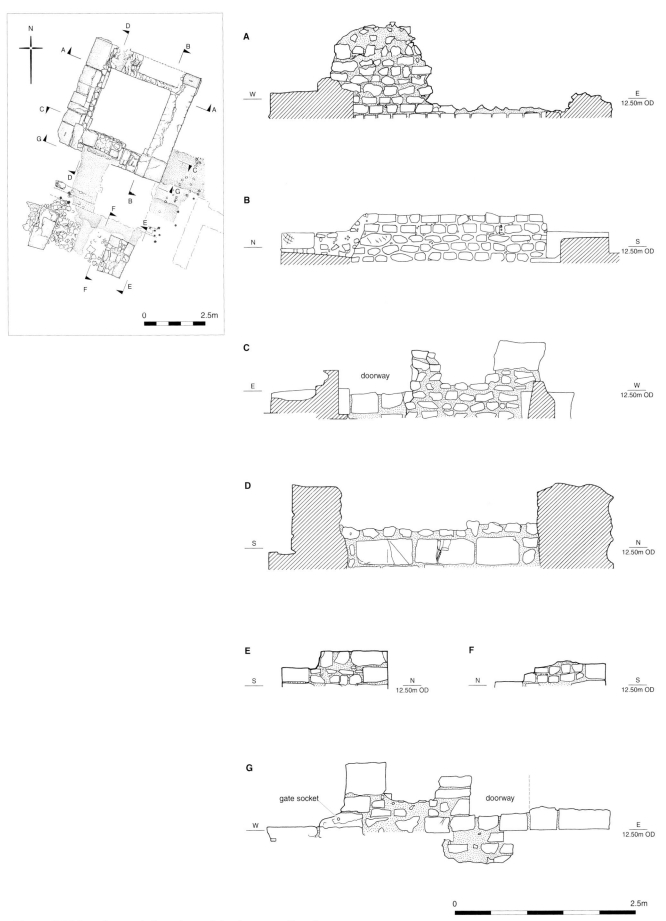

Fig 55 WFG5, plan and elevations of the fort gate (London Archaeological Research Facility) (scale 1:50; inset 1:150)

Fig 56 WFG5, view of the north tower and north passageway of the gate, looking north-east (4ft (1.22m) scale)

Fig 57 WFG5, view showing the foundation of the north tower on the left and the later (medieval) blocking of the north passageway in the foreground, looking north (1ft (0.31m) scale)

Fig 58 WFG5, example of lewis hole (upper block) and coarse rustication (lower block) on the foundation stones of the north tower (1ft (0.31m) scale)

Fig 59 WFG5, the doorway to the north tower of the west gate of the fort (1ft (0.31m) scale)

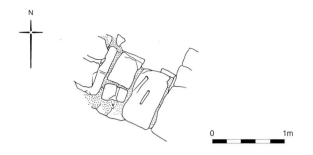

Fig 60 WFG5, plan of the doorway to the north tower of the west gate of the fort (scale 1:50)

the easternmost of the piers and on the south-west corner of the north tower, irregularly shaped rebates cut into the sandstone blocks indicated the positions of the door sockets (Fig 61). Similar features were found for the gate for the south roadway. The south tower was only partially seen: only its north-west corner could be excavated (Fig 52; Fig 62). This was of similar construction to the north tower.

At the time of construction, the surface between the towers and the *spina* had been levelled flat, so that the top of the earlier thick brickearth dump was truncated and was level with the latest fills of the construction trench for the north tower. A timber-lined box drain, *c* 0.25m square and filled with silt

and gravel, was cut into this surface. Two parallel lines of stakeholes indicated its position and it would appear to connect with the drain at the rear of the tower (Fig 52; Fig 63). The drain connected with those seen in WFG3 (above, 5.4; cf Fig 48) and presumably drained out of the fort into the fort ditch. An imbrex seen in one of the sections may have been used as an additional aid to cap this drain. Above this levelled surface with the drain was laid the first of the road surfaces, the clean gravel making direct contact with the levelled surface. This roadway passing through the north entrance of this two-gate structure was made up of *c* 0.25m of gravel. No features cut through this road surface at this point. This is significant because Grimes's notes for layers [44] and [45] are of importance here. Layer [45] is described as the 'pottery etc coming from the gully running west–east through the gateway (towards the baulk at the east end of the excavation). It contained sandy grey silt and small pieces of sandstone, with a little gravel'. Importantly, Grimes describes the depth of the gully as 4ft 11in (1.5m) below his site datum. Adjacent to this, and also at 1.5m below his site datum, was layer [44], described as pottery from a very sandy layer with some smooth clay and oyster shell. This layer does not appear on any section, but it too is below the base of the first road gravels described above. It is significant to note that the

Fig 61 WFG5, detail of the door sockets next to the north tower (1ft (0.31m) scale)

Fig 62 WFG5, the south tower in 1957, view looking south-west (1ft (0.31m) scale)

Fig 63 WFG5, view of the rear of the north tower (left) and the stake-lined gully behind, looking north; note the city wall thickening butting against the fort wall (top left); the chalk wall (right) belongs to the medieval phase (Neville's Inn) (4ft (1.22m) scales)

Fig 64 WFG5, view of the latest road surface in the fort gate entrance, looking east; note that the level of the road is the same as the threshold at the rear (1ft (0.31m) scale)

samian from layer [44], although only three sherds, is exclusively Trajanic or Hadrianic in date. Other samian sherds from road gravels, which can no longer be accurately located, are listed below.

As far as Grimes was able to discern, the foundation cut of the fort wall and the gate were contemporary. Indeed, the top level of the lowest course of sandstone blocks, buried in their foundation trench, was the same as the level for the offset of the fort wall, at the top of its foundation, to the north and there was no recorded indication of the fort gate structure being butted up against the fort wall – in fact, the dressed ragstone blocks and the core of the wall demonstrates that they were built at the same time.

Inside the fort wall, redeposited brickearth, interleaved with some layers made of mixed material, was heaped up against the internal face. The north–south gully seen at Windsor Court (WFG3) was also recorded here at the foot of this bank. Recent features had severely truncated the Roman stratigraphy but this gully, identified as two parallel rows of stakeholes, was seen to skirt around the back, the

eastern side, of the north tower and curve towards the north roadway. These rows probably joined up with the gully, also with vertical stakeholes and described above (containing layer [45]), under this road (Fig 52). The gravel metalling of the road outside the tower and in the entrance sealed Flavian and early 2nd-century material (period 2, layer [44], from under the road and period 3, layer [23], from within the lower gravels of the road). During its lifetime, the roadway had only slightly been built up with additional layers of gravel (eg layers [18], [19], [28], [29]). Pottery contained within these later road layers includes sherds that can be dated to the middle of the 2nd century AD. The new road surfaces, however, respected the existing structure, especially the level of the threshold of the doorway into the tower, and did not encroach upon it (Fig 64).

Coins from beneath the *spina* of the fort gate

Grimes's notes describe a coin of Domitian as coming from beneath the *spina* foundation in the fort gate entrance. Three coins of Domitian were recorded on this site. However, the layer numbers, layers [3] and [6], do not correspond with the location of the *spina*. Layer [3] comes from a deposit of mixed material visible on the outside of the north wall of the tower, and is likely to be residual in its context. This layer corresponds with the position of dumps of material on top of the city wall bank at this point (cf Fig 54). This layer contained 2nd- to mid 3rd-century samian ware. Layer [6], with two coins of Domitian, comes from a pit *c* 2.5m to the east of the eastern wall of the north tower.

<S10> Copper-alloy coin
WFG5 <48>, layer [3]
Domitian, as.
AD 87 (*BMC*, ii, 401).
<S11> Copper-alloy coin
WFG5 <47>, layer [6]
Domitian, as.
AD 87 (*BMC*, ii, 402–3).
<S12> Copper-alloy coin
WFG5 <56>, layer [6]
Domitian, as.
AD 84–96.

Layers from within the road gravels to the east of the tower and in the entrance of the gate

LAYER [23] (FIRST ROAD GRAVEL IN GATEWAY ENTRANCE, SOUTH OF *SPINA*)
Pottery summary:
Small-sized assemblage.
Earliest date *c* AD 70; latest date *c* AD 85.
Samian ware catalogue:
<SAM87> South Gaul (SAMLG 5DR18)
Early–mid Flavian.
<SAM88> South Gaul (SAMLG 6DR27)
Early–mid Flavian.
Other fine and coarse wares:
Now missing.

LAYER [24] (FILL OF POSSIBLE GULLY OF ROAD AGAINST SOUTH WALL OF NORTH TOWER)
Pottery summary:
Small-sized assemblage.
Earliest date *c* AD 100; latest date *c* AD 125.
Samian ware catalogue:
<SAM89> (SAMMV 4DR37)
The ovolo is probably one attributed to Ioenalis of les Martres-de-Veyre (Stanfield and Simpson 1958, pl 35 no. 416). The rosette is on Stanfield and Simpson 1958, pl 37 no. 436, the ovoid beads on pl 36 no. 417. There is apparently no exact parallel for the stag.
c AD 100–25.
Other fine and coarse wares:
Now missing.

LAYER [18] (UPPER ROAD GRAVEL IN GATEWAY ENTRANCE, NORTH OF *SPINA*)
Pottery summary:
Small-sized assemblage.
Earliest date *c* AD 110; latest date *c* AD 140.
Samian ware catalogue:
<SAM90> (SAMMV 5DR18/31)
With stamp of Medtus of les Martres-de-Veyre (die 3a).
c AD 110–25.
<SAM91> Probably Lezoux (SAMCG 2DE68)
Rouletted above the moulded section. The trophy is Rogers 1974, Q43, noted on a jar of this form by Campanus (Bémont 1977, 194–6, where he is dated after AD 140).
This form is usually to be dated to the Antonine period, but it was also made by Butrio (ibid, 10 and 12) and the fabric of this sherd would suggest a Hadrianic–early Antonine date.
<SAM92> Central Gaul (SAMCG 2DE68/72)
Hadrianic.
<SAM93> Central Gaul (SAMCG 6DR33)
Hadrianic.
Other fine and coarse wares:
Now missing.

LAYER [47] (AS FOR LAYER [18])
Pottery summary:
Small-sized assemblage.
Earliest date *c* AD 100; latest date *c* AD 125.
Samian ware catalogue:
<SAM94> In the style of Donnaucus of les Martres-de-Veyre (SAMMV 4DR37)
The ovolo is on Stanfield and Simpson 1958, pl 48 no. 562, the ovoid beads above and below it on pl 48 no. 574, the large beaded rosette and the astralagus on pl. 48 no. 573. The figure may be a warrior, but there is apparently no exact parallel.
c AD 100–25.
Other fine and coarse wares:
Now missing.

LAYER [19] (UPPER ROAD GRAVEL TO THE EAST OF NORTH TOWER)
Pottery summary:
Small-sized assemblage.
Earliest date *c* AD 100; latest date *c* AD 125.
Samian ware catalogue:
<SAM95> In the style of Igocatus of les Martres-de-Veyre (SAMMV 4DR37)
His characteristic wavy line border, with a small vine scroll (Stanfield and Simpson 1958, pl 17 no. 219), wreath (ibid, pl 18 no. 233) and curly scroll (ibid, pl 18 no. 231).
c AD 100–25.
Other fine and coarse wares:
Now missing.

LAYERS [28] AND [29] (UPPER ROAD GRAVEL TO EAST AND SOUTH-EAST OF TOWER)

Pottery summary:
Small-sized assemblage.
Earliest date *c* AD 100: latest date *c* AD 160.
Samian ware catalogue:
<SAM96> Central Gaul (SAMCG 5DR31R)
Later Antonine.
<SAM97> Central Gaulish sherd (SAMCG)
Early 2nd century AD.
Other fine and coarse wares:
Now missing.

Toilet, surgical or pharmaceutical instrument

<S13> Copper-alloy mirror
WFG5 <14>, layer [30]; from the surface of the road gravels to the immediate east and south-east of the north tower of the gate structure
Corner fragment of square copper-alloy (presumably speculum) mirror, with severe corrosion on both surfaces. Max surviving dimensions 36 × 28mm. Probably 1st or 2nd century AD in date.

Period 4

At the north end of the site, in the top of the fort bank, a foundation cut for the city wall thickening was recorded. This was the best-preserved section of this feature and gave the full width of the city wall, made up of the fort wall and the city wall thickening. A worn coin <S14> from the mortar of this section of the thickening (layer [4]) was dated to AD 183–5. It is important here to note that, at the time of the construction of the city wall, there was no attempt at this stage to block the gateway itself. It would appear, therefore, that the gateway remained in use throughout the Roman period. The small patches of blocking in the two gateways are likely to be medieval in date (Milne 2001, 45). Some traces of the dumps on the city wall bank were also revealed (eg layer [3]; Fig 54). This material was being discarded during the 3rd century AD.

Coins

<S14> Copper-alloy coin
WFG5 <51>, layer [4] – the city wall thickening to the north of the tower
Commodus, sestertius.
AD 183–4.
<S15> Copper-alloy coin
WFG5 <49>, layer [50] – small gully at foot of city wall bank

?Tetricus I, radiate copy.
c AD 270–80.
<S16> Copper-alloy coin
WFG5 <50>, layer [90] – a layer *c* 2.5m east of the inside face of the fort wall; probably from over the city wall bank
Unidentified, radiate copy.
c AD 270–80.

Dumps on city wall bank

LAYER [3]
Pottery summary:
Small-sized assemblage.
Earliest date *c* AD 120; latest date *c* AD 250.
Samian ware catalogue:
<SAM98> Central Gaul (SAMCG 4DR37)
Vine scroll; the leaf is incomplete and not certainly identifiable. Similar leaves were used by a number of Lezoux potters; the fabric and moulding of this group would indicate the Sacre-Attianus group (cf Stanfield and Simpson 1958, pl 83 no. 8, pl 87 no. 26).
Hadrianic–early Antonine.
<SAM99> (SAMEG 5DR31R/LUD Sb)
Unidentified stamp. Rheinzabern by fabric.
Late 2nd to mid 3rd century AD.
<SAM100> Trier (SAMEG 5DR31/ LUD Sa)
Late 2nd–mid 3rd century AD.
Other fine and coarse wares:
Now missing.

Coins from unstratified and post-Roman contexts

<S17> Copper-alloy coin
WFG5 <52>, unstratified
Magnentius/Decentius, Diam 16mm.
AD 351–3.
<S18> Copper-alloy coin
WFG5 <46>, layer [1] – residual in post-medieval cesspit no. 1
Unidentified, Diam 17mm.
?Late 3rd century AD.
<S19> Copper-alloy coin
WFG5 <55>, layer [9] – residual in post-medieval cesspit no. 6
Magnentius, Diam 18mm.
AD 351–3 (*LRBCII*, nos 5–6).
<S20> Copper-alloy coin
WFG5 <45>, layer [338] – no record survives
Vespasian, as.
AD 69–79.

6 Excavations in the south-west corner of Cripplegate

6.1 WFG6 and WFG7, Noble Street, north end

1958–9 (Grimes 1956, 127–9; 1968, 20, 27–8, 33–4, 79; Fig 5; Fig 6; Fig 65). NGR: city wall – TQ 32236 81532 to TQ 32215 81470

With the identification of the fort in the Cripplegate area in 1949–50 and the discovery of the fort gate in 1956, the basements between the fort gate site (WFG5; Chapter 5.6) and the corner tower site (WFG9; below, 6.3) took on a new importance. Previously, Grimes had not considered examining these areas because he felt that the depth of the basements would have removed the greater part of the archaeology. However, his work there discovered a truncated section through the Roman defences as well as an internal tower. This was one site examined by George Rybot and Michael Green throughout the later 1950s, with the aid of a number of volunteers, including students. Throughout the archive, Grimes refers to this site as 'Rybot's turret'.

This particular site was re-examined in 1973 by the DUA of the Museum of London. A single trench was cut and the archive report describing the sequence recorded there is reproduced, with a facsimile of the section drawing (Fig 129), in Chapter 11.1. This gives a more complete description of the make-up of the fort

and city wall banks, as well as some detail relating to the intervallum roads.

Grimes and Rybot located three trenches perpendicular to the line of the city defences, recording the line of the fort wall, city wall thickening, the internal banks and the intervallum roads (Fig 66a and b). Section drawings for the three trenches survive (Fig 67; Fig 68). As Grimes expected, the archaeological sequence had been severely truncated leaving only the lowest part of the Roman sequence. Finds survival from this site was reasonably good; one is illustrated on Fig 71.

Period 1

The natural surface was brickearth. This appeared to have been truncated.

Period 2

There was only a little pre-bank stratigraphy. Two layers, [12] and [13], were identified (Fig 67). These were mainly redeposited brickearth layers, containing some small sherds of pottery. Layer [12], with a date extending into the middle of the 2nd century AD, cannot be securely dated and could easily date from much earlier in the Roman period – for example Flavian (F Seeley, pers comm).

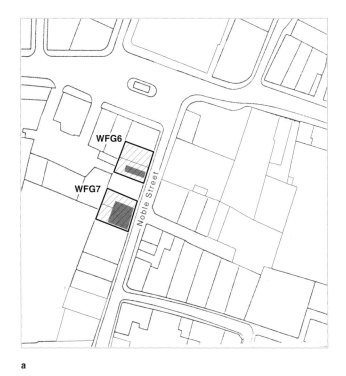

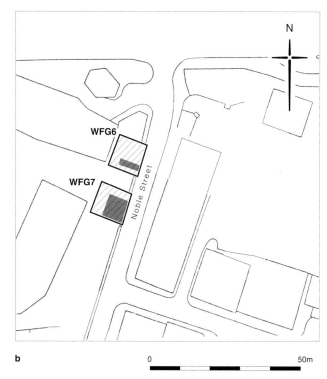

Fig 65 WFG6 and WFG7, the sites and trenches: a – located on a contemporary street plan; b – located on a modern street plan (scale 1:1200)

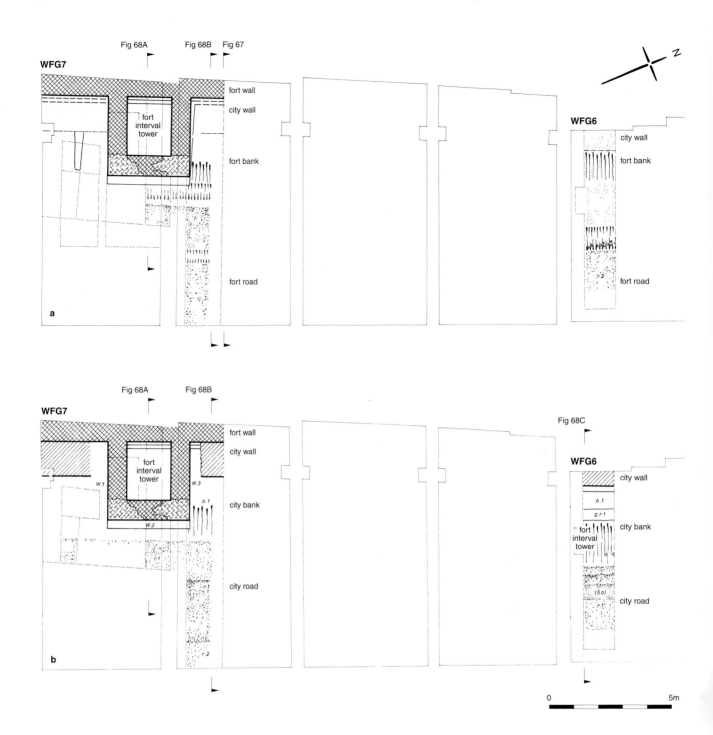

Fig 66 WFG6 and WFG7, plans of the site trenches: a – showing the fort phase; b – showing the city wall phase (scale 1:150)

Pre-fort dumped layers over the natural surface

LAYER [12], BAG 20
Pottery summary:
Small-sized assemblage.
Earliest date *c* AD 70; latest date *c* AD 160.
Fine and coarse ware types present:
VRW 9A; AHSU; HWC; FMIC 3B.
Pottery catalogue:
<P1> Verulamium region white ware lid (VRW 9A);
(WFG6 and WFG7 P1)

Comments:
This small context is dated on the presence of Highgate Wood ware C (HWC). The sherds are not very diagnostic and the context cannot be closely dated.

LAYER [13], BAG 12A
Pottery summary:
Small-sized assemblage.
Earliest date *c* AD 90; latest date *c* AD 120.
Samian ware catalogue:
<SAM101> South Gaulish sherd
Flavian.

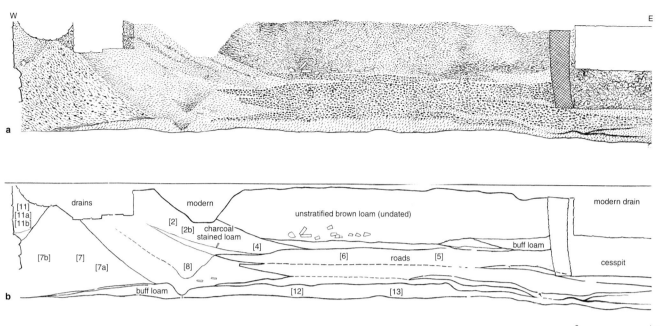

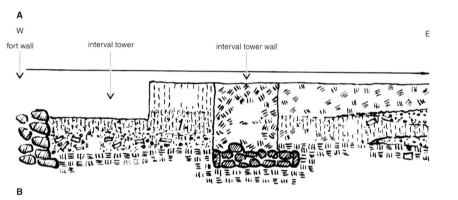

Fig 67 WFG6 and WFG7, south-facing section through the defences: a – edited original by Grimes and Green; b – interpretive section (scale 1:50)

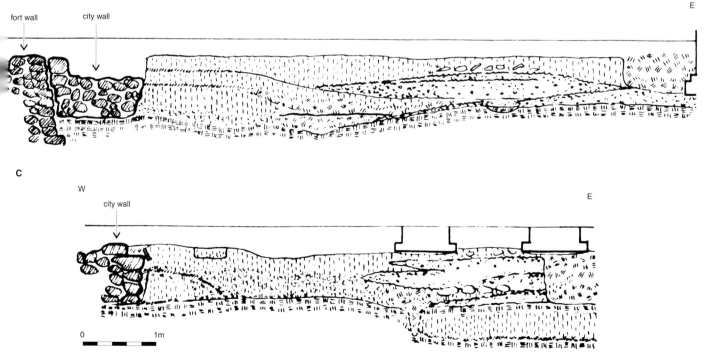

Fig 68 WFG6 and WFG7, south-facing sections through the tower and defences: section A – showing fort wall and tower; section B – showing fort wall, city wall and defences; section C – showing city wall and defences (scale 1:50)

Other fine and coarse ware types present:
VRW; AHSU 2A; HWC 9A; HWC 4F; FMIC 4 NCD; HWC; FMIC 3 BDD; FMIC; AHSU.
Pottery catalogue:
<P2> Alice Holt/Surrey ware bead-rimmed jar (AHSU 2A); (WFG6 and WFG7 P2)
Comments:
The dating of this context is based on the presence of a fine micaceous reduced ware bowl with incised decoration (FMIC 4 NCD), probably in the form of an imitation Dragendorff form 37 bowl. The remainder of the coarse wares and the samian date from the Flavian period.

Period 3

The fort wall was not seen, although the fort bank was seen (layer [7] and its sub-components listed below; Fig 67). These dumps are more mixed than those seen at the Barber-Surgeons' Hall (WFG2; Chapter 5.3) and Windsor Court (WFG3; Chapter 5.4) to the north. Some of the later dumps contain material that could come from the middle of the 2nd century AD. This probably indicates additions being made to the fort bank at this time. Road surfaces contemporary with this bank were recorded on the east side of the site. Layer [8], containing 2nd-century material, comes from a gully alongside this road.

Of particular interest was a small rectangular tower found in the southernmost trench (Fig 69). This was built of squared ragstone blocks that appeared to butt against the inner face of the fort wall. This suggested that it was an addition to the original scheme. However, no trace of a foundation cut later than the fort bank was noted implying that, although the tower was not built at the same time as the fort wall, it was constructed before the bank was raised. The tower is now incorporated in the preserved section in Noble Street (Fig 70; note the restoration on the eastern wall).

Dumped material on fort bank

LAYER [7], BAG 13
Pottery summary:
Small-sized assemblage.
Earliest date *c* AD 100; latest date *c* AD 120.
Fine and coarse ware types present:
LOMI 5J; LOMI; OXID 9A; LOXI 9A; KOLN; CGOF 9LA; HWC 4F; HWC; HWC 2T; HWC 3F BDD; HWC 9A; FMIC 4 NCD; AHSU; AHSU 2T; AHSU 2C; FMIC.
Pottery catalogue:
<P3> London mica-dusted ware plain-rimmed dish (LOMI 5J); (WFG6 and WFG7 P3)
<P4> Highgate Wood ware C flat-rimmed bowl (HWC 4F); (WFG6 and WFG7 P4)

Fig 69 WFG6 and WFG7, the rectangular tower butting against the inner face of the fort wall, view looking south (3ft (0.91m) scales)

Fig 70 WFG6 and WFG7, the restored tower, view looking west

<P5> Highgate Wood ware C lid (HWC 9A); (WFG6 and WFG7 P5)
<P6> London oxidised ware lid (LOXI 9A); (WFG6 and WFG7 P6)
<P7> Unsourced fine reduced ware poppy-head beaker (FINE 3F); (WFG6 and WFG7 P7)
Comments:
The latest component of this context is Cologne colour-coated ware (KOLN).

LAYER [7], BAG 13A
Pottery summary:
Small-sized assemblage.
Earliest date *c* AD 70; latest date *c* AD 110.
Samian ware catalogue:
<SAM102> South Gaul (SAMLG 6DR27)
Flavian to Trajanic.
Other fine and coarse ware types present:
VRW 1; VRW; LOMI 1; VRMI 4; OXID 9A; VRW; OXID; HWC 4A; HWC; HWC 9A; AHSU; SAND 9A; SAND; VRG.
Pottery catalogue:
<P8> Highgate Wood ware C reed-rimmed bowl (HWC 4A); (WFG6 and WFG7 P8)
Comments:
The latest components of this context are Highgate Wood ware C (HWC) and London mica-dusted ware (LOMI). The samian is from south Gaul, also dating

from the Flavian to Trajanic period.

LAYER [7], BAG 7
Pottery summary:
Small-sized assemblage.
Earliest date *c* AD 70; latest date *c* AD 160.
Fine and coarse ware types present:
VRW; ? BB2 2F; SAND 9A; HWC; HWC 2T.
Comments:
This context is dated on the presence of Highgate Wood ware C (HWC), despite the presence of ? blackware-burnished ware 2 (BB2).

LAYER [7A], BAG 15
Pottery summary:
Large-sized assemblage.
Earliest date *c* AD 120; latest date *c* AD 140.
Samian ware catalogue:
<SAM103> South Gaul (SAMLG 6DR27)
Flavian.
<SAM104> Three sherds, south Gaul (SAMLG 5DR18)
Flavian to Trajanic.
<SAM105> South Gaulish sherd (SAMLG)
Other fine and coarse ware types present:
AHSU 2T; AHSU 2; AHSU 2D; FMIC 4E; ROD; FMIC 4 NCD; FMIC; NKGW 3; FMIC 3B BDD; HWB; BB1 9A BUD; BB1 2 BUD; BB1 2F BUD; HWC+2F AL; BB1 3E; NKSH; SAND; SAND 2/3;

SAND 9A; HWC 3F; HWC 3 BDD; HWC; FINE ROD; CGOF 3 RCD; CC SCD; LOMA; LOMI; LOMI 3; RDBK; OXID 4; VCWS; LOXI 9A; OXID; 8DR2–4; LOXI 9A; VRW 9A; VRW 7; VRW; VRW 1; VRW 9S; VRW 1C; VRW 4; AHSU 2A; HWC 9A; HWC 2A; HWC 4A; HWC 4F; HWC 2T; HWC 2E.

Pottery catalogue:
<P9> Highgate Wood ware C reed-rimmed bowl (HWC 4A); (WFG6 and WFG7 P9)
<P10> Verulamium region white ware unguentarium (VRW 9S); (WFG6 and WFG7 P10)
<P11> Fine micaceous reduced ware bowl (FMIC 4); (WFG6 and WFG7 P11)
<P12> Cologne colour-coated ware beaker with scale decoration (KOLN 3 SCD); (WFG6 and WFG7 P12)
<P13> Black-burnished ware 1 lid (BB1 9A); (WFG6 and WFG7 P13)
<P14> Highgate Wood ware C lid (HWC 9A); (WFG6 and WFG7 P14)
<P15> Alice Holt/Surrey ware bead-rimmed jar (AHSU 2A); (WFG6 and WFG7 P15)
<P16> Alice Holt/Surrey ware round-bodied necked jar with figure 7 rim (AHSU 2D); (WFG6 and WFG7 P16)
<P17> Highgate Wood ware C bead-rimmed jar (HWC 2A); (WFG6 and WFG7 P17)
<P18> Highgate Wood ware C bowl with curved walls and flat rim (HWC 4F); (WFG6 and WFG7 P18)
<P19> Highgate Wood ware C bowl with curved walls and flat rim (HWC 4F); (WFG6 and WFG7 P19)
<P20> Black-burnished-style ware everted-rimmed jar (BBS 2F); (WFG6 and WFG7 P20)
<P21> Highgate Wood ware C round-bodied necked jar with decorated shoulder (HWC 2E); (WFG6 and WFG7 P21)
<P22> Unsourced fine reduced ware round-bodied necked jar with decorated shoulder (FINE 2E); (WFG6 and WFG7 P22)
<P23> Verulamium region white ware lid (VRW 9A); (WFG6 and WFG7 P23)
<P24> London oxidised ware lid (LOXI 9A); (WFG6 and WFG7 P24)
<P25> London oxidised ware lid (LOXI 9A); (WFG6 and WFG7 P25)
<P26> London oxidised ware lid (LOXI 9A); (WFG6 and WFG7 P26)

Comments:
The latest components of this context are vessels in black-burnished ware 1 (BB1) and also imitation black-burnished types in Highgate Wood ware with added coarse sand C+ (HWC+). A number of mica-dusted (LOMI) and marbled (LOMA) fine wares are present and also colour-coated ware from Cologne (KOLN).

LAYER [7B], BAG 17
Pottery summary:
Small-sized assemblage.
Earliest date *c* AD 100; latest date *c* AD 160.
Samian ware catalogue:
<SAM106> DR37, south Gaul (SAMLG 4DR37)

Large foliage motif shared by several potters, notably the Crucuro-M Crestio group.
c AD 75–95.
<SAM107> South Gaul (SAMLG 4/5)
Dish/bowl sherd.
Flavian.
Other fine and coarse ware types present:
VRW; VRW1; OXID; HWC; AHSU; HWC ?2E; HWC3 BDD.
Comments:
The latest element in this context is a round-bodied necked jar with decorated shoulder in Highgate Wood ware C (HWC 2E). The samian is all from south Gaul and dated to the Flavian period.

LAYER [7B], BAG 17A
Pottery summary.
Small-sized assemblage.
Earliest date *c* AD 120; latest date *c* AD 160.
Fine and coarse ware types present:
VRW; BB1 2; AHSU 2; HWC; HWB; HWC 3 BDD; FMIC.
Comments:
The date of this context is based on the presence of black-burnished ware 1 (BB1).

The fill of the roadside gully above layer [7]

LAYER [8], BAG 14
Pottery summary:
Medium-sized assemblage.
Earliest date *c* AD 120; latest date *c* AD 160.
Samian ware catalogue:
<SAM108> Central Gaul (SAMCG 5DR18/31)
Early 2nd century AD.
<SAM109> South Gaul (SAMLG 4DR37)
Flavian.
<SAM110> South Gaul (SAMLG 5DR35/36)
Flavian.
<SAM111> South Gaulish sherd (SAMLG)
Other fine and coarse ware types present:
C186; VRW; VRW 2T; VRW 1; VRW 1B2; VRW 1C; LOMI 5J; OXID 9A; 0XID ?9A; OXID; OXID 4; VCWS; CGOF 3 HPD; CGOF 3 ROD; FMIC 3 BAD; AHSU ?2D; AHSU 2T; AHSU 4K; SAND; SAND 4F; SAND 4; SAND 9A; HWC 4F; HWC ?2E; HWC 3 BDD; HWC 2T; BB1 2; BB1 2 AL; HWC+ 2F; HWC+ 2AL.
Comments:
The latest elements of this context are black-burnished wares 1 and 2 (BB1; BB2) and central Gaulish samian. A colour-coated ware beaker with hairpin decoration (CGOF 3 HPD) from central Gaul has also been identified.

BROOCH
<S21> Copper-alloy ?brooch pin
WFG6 <8>, layer [8]
Remains of rivet in flattened terminal. L 23mm.

Period 4

The fort bank had been cut against the fort wall by a foundation trench for the city wall. Backfilling into this contained 2nd-century material, the latest being *c* AD 160 (layers [11] and its sub-components; Fig 67). Further dumped deposits had been piled up against this new wall (layers [2], [4]), containing 2nd-century material. A road surface contemporary with this bank was recorded, sealing pottery dated to the 2nd century AD, and possibly into the 3rd (layers [5], [6]). However, this later date is based upon a single sherd of a long-lived pottery type (layer [6], bag 6). The gully at the foot of this bank was not as well defined as that seen further to the north at Barber-Surgeons' Hall (WFG2) and Windsor Court (WFG3; Chapter 5.3 and 5.4).

The building of the city wall thickening appeared to respect the position of this tower. It butted against its external faces where it met the fort wall but was not built inside the tower itself. It would appear, therefore, that the tower was retained for use when the city wall was in existence. A gravel surface inside the tower suggested the presence of a floor. This was overlain by dark soil, unlike any of the bank deposits. Unfortunately, no datable material was retained from this floor. The rear wall of the tower had been robbed following the build-up of this soil.

Fill of construction trench of city wall thickening

LAYER [11], BAG 18
Pottery summary:
Small-sized assemblage.
Earliest date *c* AD 120; latest date *c* AD 150.
Samian ware catalogue:
<SAM112> Central Gaul (SAMCG 5DR36)
Early 2nd century AD.
Other fine and coarse ware types present:
VRW; VRW 4A; NKSH; VRW 2T; OXID 9A; AHSU.
Comments:
The latest component of this context is the Dragendorff form 36 plate from central Gaul. The remainder of the assemblage dates from the mid 1st century AD onwards.

LAYER [11A], BAG 19
Pottery summary:
Small-sized assemblage.
Earliest date *c* AD 120; latest date *c* AD 160.
Samian ware catalogue:
<SAM113> South Gaul (SAMLG 4DR37)
Flavian.
Other fine and coarse ware types present:
VRW; HWC2 AL; FMIC; HWC 9A.
Comments:
The date of this context is based on Highgate Wood ware C jars with acute lattice decoration (HWC 2 AL). The samian is from south Gaul (SAMLG) and dates from the Flavian period.

LAYER [11B], BAG 22
Pottery summary:
Small-sized assemblage.
Earliest date *c* AD 70; latest date *c* AD 160.
Samian ware catalogue:
<SAM114> South Gaulish sherd (SAMLG)
1st century AD.
Other fine and coarse ware types present:
VRW; HWC; ?AHSU.
Comments:
The date of this context is based on Highgate Wood ware C (HWC).

Dumped material making up the road contemporary with the city wall

LAYER [5], BAG 10
Pottery summary:
Small-sized assemblage.
Earliest date *c* AD 120; latest date *c* AD 160.
Samian ware catalogue:
<SAM115> Two central Gaulish sherds (SAMCG)
1st century AD.
Other fine and coarse ware types present:
AMPH; VRW; KOLN 3 RCD; ?LOEG; OXID; TNIM 5; HWC; HWC+; BB1.
Comments:
The presence of black-burnished ware 1 (BB1) and samian from central Gaul give this context a date of *c* AD 120–60. Sherds of Cologne colour-coated ware with rough cast decoration (KOLN 3 RCD) and eggshell wares are also present (LOEG).
Small find:
<S22> Copper-alloy loop
WFG6 and WFG7 <9>, 6 (II), [5], bag 10
Fragment of the top of a copper-alloy split-spike loop. Max surviving L 15mm.

LAYER [6], BAG 13
Pottery summary:
Small-sized assemblage.
Earliest date *c* AD 120; latest date *c* AD 160.
Samian ware catalogue:
<SAM116> Two south Gaulish sherds (SAMLG)
1st century AD.
Other fine and coarse ware types present:
VRW 7HOF; VRW 9C; BAET 8DR20; VRW; CGOF 3 RCD; ERMS; FMIC 4 NCD; FMIC; SAND 9A; HWC 3 BDD; HWC; SAND; HWC 2T; SAND 4A; BB1 2F; LOMA; OXID.
Comments:
The latest element of this context is the black-burnished ware 1 (BB1) everted-rimmed jar. The remainder of the assemblage dates from the Flavian to Trajanic period; colour-coated wares from central Gaul with rough cast decoration (CGOF 3 RCD) are also present.

LAYER [6], BAG 6
Pottery summary:
Small-sized assemblage.

Earliest date *c* AD 120; latest date *c* AD 250.
Samian ware catalogue:
<SAM117> Central Gaulish sherd (SAMCG)
Hadrianic–Antonine.
Other fine and coarse ware types present:
SAND 9a.
Comments:
Central Gaulish samian ware from this layer is the closest datable item.

Dumps on the city wall bank

LAYER [2], BAG 3
Pottery summary:
Medium-sized assemblage.
Earliest date *c* AD 120; latest date *c* AD 160.
Samian ware catalogue:
<SAM118> South Gaul (SAMLG 4DR37)
Basal wreath of trifid leaves, below band with foliage, hound and grass.
c AD 75–100.
<SAM119> Cup, south Gaul (SAMLG 5DR42)
Flavian.
<SAM120> South Gaul (SAMLG 4DR37)
Flavian.
Other fine and coarse ware types present:
VRW; VRW 4A; VRW 1; VRW 7; LOMI 5J; AMPH; OXID; RWS; HWC 2E; HWC 9A; AHSU 2; HWC; HWC 3 BDD; AHSU; FINE AL; SAND 2; BB1 2F; SAND 9A; BBS 2F; LOMI 5.
Pottery catalogue:
<P27> Verulamium region white ware reed-rimmed bowl (VRW 4A); (WFG6 and WFG7 P27)
<P28> London mica-dusted ware bowl (Marsh 37) (LOMI 4); (WFG6 and WFG7 P28)
<P29> Highgate Wood ware C lid (HWC 9A); (WFG6 and WFG7 P29)
Comments:
This context has been dated on the presence of black-burnished ware 1 (BB1) and black-burnished-style vessels (BBS). The samian is all from south Gaul and Flavian in date.

LAYER [2B], BAG 9
Pottery summary:
Small-sized assemblage.
Earliest date *c* AD 70; latest date *c* AD 160.
Fine and coarse ware types present:
VRW; OXID ?3; OXID; HWC; NKSH; AHSU; GAUL1 8G4; SAND; VCWS 1.
Comments:
This context has been dated on the presence of Highgate Wood ware C (HWC) and Verulamium region coarse white-slipped ware (VCWS). Also present is a rim sherd from a flat-bottomed Gaulish amphora (GAUL1).

LAYER [4], BAG 5
Pottery summary:
Small-sized assemblage.

Earliest date *c* AD 120; latest date *c* AD 160.
Samian ware catalogue:
<SAM121> Central Gaul (SAMCG 6DR33)
Antonine.
Other fine and coarse ware types present:
VRW; VRW 2T; AMPH; NFSE 7; ?RWS; OXID; OXID 9A; RWS; VRW 1 C; BB2 4H; BB2 2 AL; AHSU 2A; SAND 4; RWS 1B; SAND.
Pottery catalogue:
<P30> Verulamium region white ware necked jar (VRW 2T); (WFG6 and WFG7 P31)
<P31> Black-burnished ware 2 round-rimmed bowl (BB2 4H); (WFG6 and WFG7 P32)
Comments:
The dating for this context is based on the presence of black-burnished ware 2, from a jar with acute lattice decoration and a round-rimmed bowl (BB2 AL; BB2 4H). The samian is from central Gaul.

Building material

A moderate-sized wall plaster assemblage (2950g) is of considerable interest. There are areas of plain maroon, probably part of a panel, and border areas in white, maroon and yellow. One fragment has a decorative design in pink on maroon. All the plaster has a pock-marked surface for attachment of another plaster layer (as observed on the Winchester Palace (Southwark) plaster; Yule 2005, 128). These came from a number of layers within the city wall bank.

Unstratified small finds

Unfortunately, although these are labelled as coming from WFG6 or WFG7, the specific labelling does not appear to match any of either Grimes's or Rybot's recording. It appears that some renumbering of contexts occurred during the post-excavation phase, but an explanatory concordance no longer survives in the archive.

Jet hairpin

<S23> Jet hairpin shaft
WFG6 and WFG7 <31>, unstratified
Two joining fragments. L 47mm.

Gaming pieces

Price suggests that plain glass counters, in general accepted as gaming pieces, may also have been used in reckoning (1995, 129–30). There is no evidence for this, while two groups of plain glass counters have been found in post-conquest Celtic graves at Stanway, Colchester (Essex): one with copper-alloy fittings for a wooden board and one with the pieces laid out on a board (Crummy 1997, 68–9).

<S24> Glass gaming piece (Fig 71)
WFG6 and WFG7 <13>, layer [1]

Fig 71 Glass gaming piece or counter *<S24> from the north end of Noble Street (WFG6 and WFG7) (scale 1:1)*

Small gaming piece or counter of dark green opaque glass. Underside slightly rough, with air bubbles. Diam 11mm; Th 6mm.
<S25> Glass gaming piece
WFG6 and WFG7 <5>, unstratified
Small gaming piece or counter of dark green opaque glass. Underside slightly rough, with air bubbles. Diam 11mm; Th 6mm.
<S26> Glass gaming piece
WFG6 and WFG7 <6>, unstratified
Small gaming piece or counter of dark green opaque glass. Underside slightly rough, with air bubbles. Diam 11mm; Th 6mm.

Fastenings and fittings

<S27> Copper-alloy nail
WFG6 and WFG7 <1>, layer [11] bag 2
The head and a short part of the circular section shaft. Surviving L 10mm; Diam of head 7mm.
<S28> Copper-alloy stud
WFG6 and WFG7 <7>, layer [2A]
Domed head, square section shaft and remains of washer.

L with shaft 10mm; Diam 14mm.
<S29> Copper-alloy stud
WFG6 and WFG7 <2>, layer [2] bag 3
Dome-headed, shaft broken close to the head. Diam 15mm.

Military equipment

<S30> Copper-alloy hook and plate
WFG6 and WFG7 <22>, layer [14]
The hook and a short length of the plate from a girdle-plate tie-hook from *lorica segmentata*. Surviving L 19mm.

Miscellaneous objects

<S31> Pottery graffito
WFG6 and WFG7 <->, layer [1] bag 1
Graffito M on the rim of a Verulamium region red ware (VRR) vessel.
<S32> Mortarium stamp
WFG6 and WFG7 <36>, layers [7], [8] bag 12
Stamp on a rim fragment from a Verulamium region red ware (VRR) mortarium.

6.2 WFG8, Bastion 15

1949–50 (Grimes 1968, 67, 76–7, pls 14 and 23; Fig 5; Fig 6; Fig 72). NGR: TQ 32212 81474

At the southern end of Noble Street, the main area examined by Grimes when he located the corner

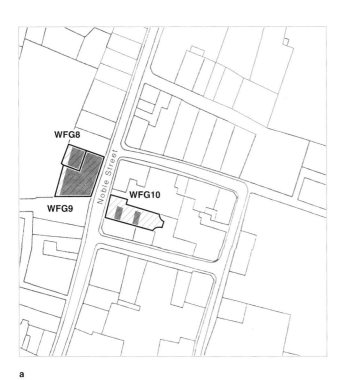

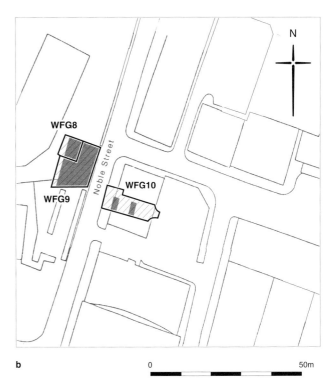

Fig 72 WFG8–WFG10, the sites and trenches: a – located on a contemporary street plan; b – located on a modern street plan (scale 1:1200)

tower of the fort (WFG9; below, 6.3) was on the east side of the line of the city defences. In this area, however, the Victorian property line, which superseded the line of the city wall, diverged westwards from the original Roman and medieval alignments. The result was that the basement of 31 Noble Street included the full width of the line of the city defences and a small part of the exterior of the city – in effect, part of the berm of the city ditches. The area for study was too cramped to enable a full and detailed excavation to the natural surface, and this area was even more reduced by the presence of a large masonry foundation.

This foundation, *c* 1m wide, butted against the exterior face of the Roman wall. Its relationship with any medieval masonry could not be seen. It appeared to curve to the south-west. This coincided with the presence on 16th-century maps of a bastion, which filled the re-entrant corner at Aldersgate, and was identified by Merrifield (1965) as Bastion 13. Being hollow, rather than a solid bastion, it belongs to the Cripplegate group of bastions which Grimes dated to the medieval period.

6.3 WFG9, 31–32 Noble Street, south end (south-west tower)

1949–50 (Grimes 1956, 127, 129; 1968, 20–1; Fig 5; Fig 6; Fig 72). NGR: tower – TQ 32220 81470

In 1949 Grimes had been working in the Cripplegate area at Cripplegate Bastion (WFG1; Chapter 5.1), around Barber-Surgeons' Hall (WFG2; Chapter 5.3), at Windsor Court (WFG3; Chapter 5.4) and Bastion 14 (WFG4; Chapter 5.5). On the south side of Falcon Square, since removed by the line of the new London Wall, a line of basements, once the properties which fronted on to Noble Street, ran as far as St Anne and St Agnes church. He resolved to examine the southernmost of these basements to compare the evidence he recovered there with the data already retrieved from the sites further to the north. This selection proved to be most fortunate as his discoveries there helped him to understand the real significance of the complex sequence of city wall features he had recorded to the north (Fig 73).

Periods 1 and 2

The natural soil was brickearth. There was no evidence of any pre-fort activity, either prehistoric or early Roman.

Period 3

The earliest recorded features on the site were related to the fort. This evidence was made up of five main components:

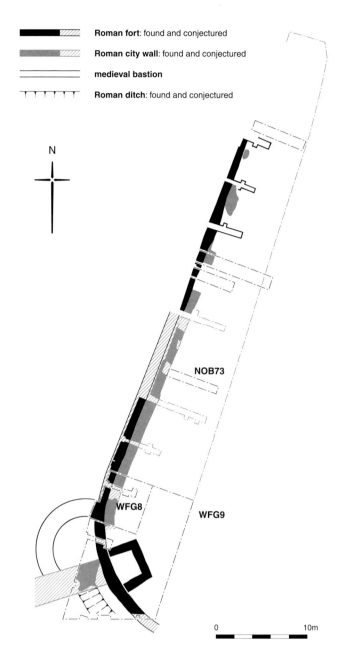

Fig 73 WFG9, *plan of the fort and city walls at the south end of Noble Street, including location of DUA trench excavated in 1973 (NOB73) (scale 1:400)*

1) The fort wall
2) The fort ditch
3) The internal tower
4) The fort bank
5) The intervallum road.

At the north end of the site (Fig 74), the fort wall was seen to diverge eastwards from the line of the modern property boundary so that the full width of the top of the wall, measuring 0.80m wide, could be seen. As the wall ran southwards, it curved in a 90° angle towards the east. It was this dramatic realignment of the wall which led Grimes to resolve the problems of interpretation with the double wall thicknesses down this, the west

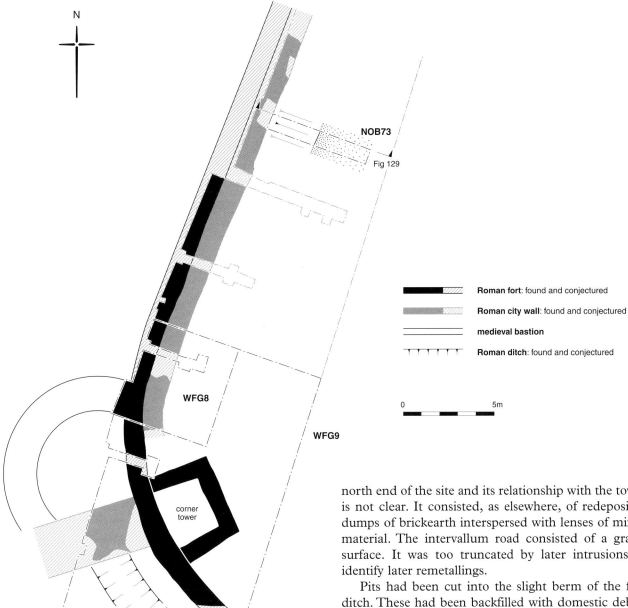

Fig 74 WFG9, plan showing detail of Fig 73 (scale 1:200)

side, and the north side of what he realised was a Roman fort. On the west side of the site, and outside the fort, a V-shaped ditch was seen to follow the curve of the wall. The upper fills of this had been cut by the later drain (below, 'Period 4'), but material from its lowest fills dated to the 2nd century AD (Fig 75).

Inside the fort wall, the full plan of a rectangular tower was recorded (Fig 76; Fig 77). Unlike the small internal tower to the north (WFG6 and WFG7, above 6.1), the walls of this corner tower were bonded into the fort wall. Excavations in the interior of the tower revealed traces of an insubstantial gravel floor. As with the internal tower, it would appear that the floor level was never raised during the life of the tower.

The bank of the fort was only partially seen at the

north end of the site and its relationship with the tower is not clear. It consisted, as elsewhere, of redeposited dumps of brickearth interspersed with lenses of mixed material. The intervallum road consisted of a gravel surface. It was too truncated by later intrusions to identify later remetallings.

Pits had been cut into the slight berm of the fort ditch. These had been backfilled with domestic debris and their proximity to the fort wall might suggest that they had been dug when the fort ditch was no longer in use. Significant finds from period 3 are illustrated on Fig 78 and Fig 79.

From the lowest levels of the fort bank

LAYER [15]
Pottery summary:
Medium-sized assemblage.
Earliest date *c* AD 100; latest date *c* AD 160.
Samian ware catalogue:
<SAM122> Two sherds, south Gaul (SAMLG DR35)
Flavian.
<SAM123> South Gaul (SAMLG 4DR37)
Flavian.
<SAM124> Three worn south Gaulish sherds (SAMLG)
Flavian.
Other fine and coarse wares:
OXID; RWS; AMPH; GAUL1; NKSH; AHSU 2; VRG;

SW

N

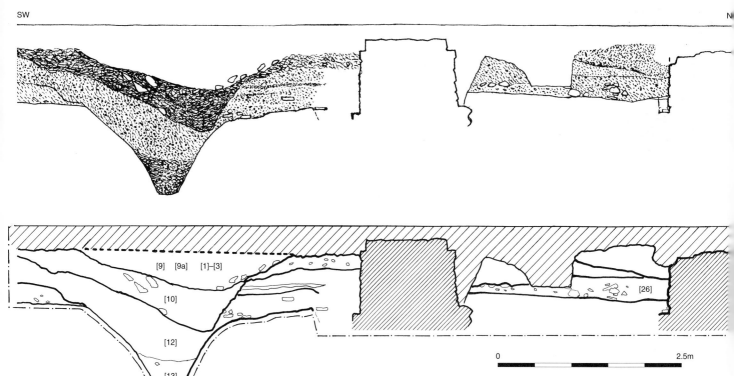

*Fig 75 WFG9, south-east-facing section through the ditch, wall and south-west tower:
a – edited Grimes original; b – interpretive section (scale 1:50)*

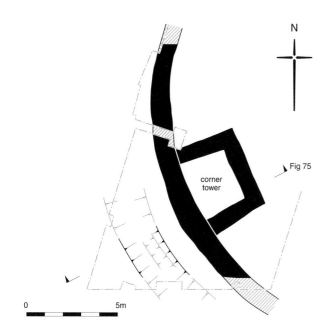

Fig 76 WFG9, plan of the period 3 ditch, wall and south-west tower (scale 1:200)

HWC ?2E BUD; SAND; HWC 3 BDD; KOLN 3 RCD.
Comments:
The latest elements of this assemblage are a round-bodied necked jar with burnished decorated shoulder in Highgate Wood ware C (HWC 2E), dated *c* AD 100–60 and a Cologne colour-coated ware beaker with

rough cast decoration (KOLN 3), dated *c* AD 100–40. The samian is all south Gaulish and Flavian in date.

Dump of material making up first intervallum road

LAYER [25]
Pottery summary:
Small-sized assemblage.
Earliest date *c* AD 100; latest date *c* AD 160
Samian ware catalogue:
<SAM125> (SAMLG 5DR15/17/18)
Stamped. Die 1a, Frontinus of la Graufesenque.
c AD 70–90.
<SAM126> South Gaul (SAMLG 5DR15/17)
Neronian–Flavian.
<SAM127> South Gaul (SAMLG 5DR15/17r)
Neronian–Flavian.
<SAM128> South Gaul (SAMLG 5DR18)
Flavian.
<SAM129> Three south Gaulish sherds (SAMLG)
Later Flavian–Trajanic.
Other fine and coarse wares:
LOMI 5J; VRW; OXID; AMPH; SAND; HWC ?2E
BUD; HWB/C; AHSU; FMIC; HWC 3 BDD; VRG.
Comments:
The latest component of this context is a round-bodied necked jar with burnished decorated shoulder in Highgate Wood ware C (HWC 2E), dated *c* AD 100–60. The remainder of the assemblage dates from the Flavian period onwards. The samian is all south

Fig 77 WFG9, view of the south-west tower in the course of excavation, looking south-west

Gaulish and dates to the Neronian–Flavian period.

Floor of tower

LAYER [26]
Pottery summary:
Medium-sized assemblage.
Earliest date *c* AD 120; latest date *c* AD 140.
Samian ware catalogue:
<SAM130> South Gaul (SAMLG 6DR33)
Later Flavian–Trajanic.
<SAM131> South Gaul (SAMLG 5DR15/17)
Flavian–Trajanic.
<SAM132> South Gaul (SAM 5DR18)
Flavian–Trajanic.
Other fine and coarse wares:
SAND; FINE 3 ROD; VRW 5J; VRW; VRW 1B2; AMPH; GAUL1; DR2–4; LOMI 4; OXID 4; CC 3 RCD; OXID 5J; VRG 4A; HWC 2T; HWC; HWC 3F; HWC 9A; HWC 2E BUD; FMIC 3C; FMIC 3 BDD; BB1 5J; AHSU 2; SAND 9A.
Pottery catalogue:
<P32> Black-burnished ware 1 shallow simple dish (BB1 5J); (WFG9 P1)
<P33> Verulamium region grey ware reed-rimmed bowl (VRG 4A); (WFG9 P2) (Fig 78)
<P34> Highgate Wood ware C necked jar (HWC 2T); (WFG9 P3)
<P35> Highgate Wood ware C poppy-head beaker (HWC 3F); (WFG9 P4)
<P36> Unsourced sand-tempered ware necked jar (SAND 2T); (WFG9 P5)
<P37> Unsourced sand-tempered ware lid (SAND (A)); (WFG9 P6)
<P38> Verulamium region white ware ring-necked flagon with flared mouth (VRW 1B2); (WFG9 P7)
<P39> Verulamium region white ware shallow simple dish (VRW 5J); (WFG9 P8)
<P40> London oxidised ware bowl (LOXI 4); (WFG9 P9)
<P41> Unsourced white-slipped ware amphora (? RWS 8); (WFG9 P10)
Comments:
This context contains larger sherds, some of them joining to form profiles. The latest vessel present is a black-burnished ware 1 shallow simple dish (BB1 5J); the majority of the assemblage can be dated to the Flavian–Trajanic period. The samian is all south Gaulish and dates to the Flavian–Trajanic period.

From top of first road and subsequent road make-ups and surfaces

LAYER [22]
Pottery summary:
Small-sized assemblage.
Earliest date *c* AD 120; latest date *c* AD 160.
Samian ware catalogue:
<SAM133> Early east Gaul (SAMEG 5DR36)
Hadrianic–early Antonine.
<SAM134> South Gaulish platter with the tip of a stamp (SMLG 5)
1st century AD.

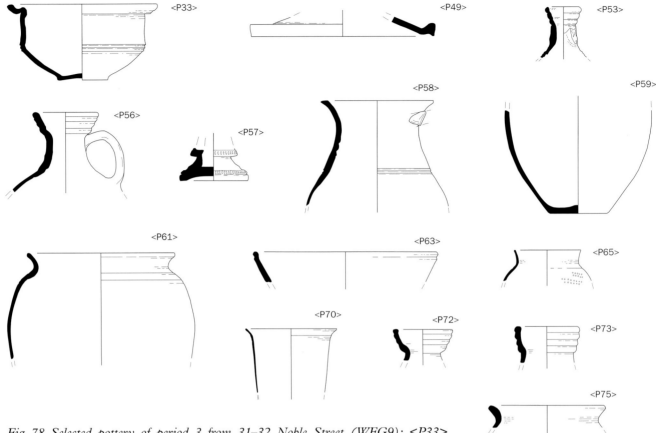

Fig 78 Selected pottery of period 3 from 31–32 Noble Street (WFG9): <P33>, <P49>, <P53>, <P56>–<P59>, <P61>, <P63>, <P65>, <P70>, <P72>, <P73> and <P75> (scale 1:4)

<SAM135> Central Gaulish sherd (SAMCG)
Flavian–Trajanic.
Other fine and coarse wares:
HWC 2E BUD; HWC 4F; NFSE 1; NFSE 7; LOMI 1; OXID; SAND 9A; VCWS 1; VCWS; VRW 1; VRW; HWC; BB2 2 AL; BB2 4H1; BB2 4 AL; BB1 9A BUD; AHSU 2; HWC 3 BDD.
Pottery catalogue:
<P42> Black-burnished ware 1 lid (BB1 9A); (WFG9 P11)
<P43> Black-burnished ware 2 round-rimmed bowl (BB2 4H); (WFG9 P12)
<P44> Highgate Wood ware C bowl with curved walls and flat rim (HWC 4F); (WFG9 P13)
<P45> Unsourced sand-tempered ware lid (SAND 9A); (WFG9 P14)
Comments:
The presence of black-burnished ware 2 (BB2), samian from central Gaul (SAMCG) and an early east Gaulish (SAMEG) factory give this context a date of *c* AD 120–60. Some of the assemblage may be earlier in date from the Flavian to Trajanic period.

LAYER [23]
Pottery summary:
Large-sized assemblage.
Earliest date *c* AD 135; latest date *c* AD 160.

Samian ware catalogue:
<SAM136> South Gaul (SAMLG 4DR37) (Fig 79)
Large rosette ovolo, wreath festoons with small birds and poppy-head pendants between.
c AD 110–45.
<SAM137> South Gaul (SAMLG 4DR37) (Fig 79)
Grape clusters and vine stem: cf Knorr 1952, table 6, c, by Biragillus.
Flavian–Trajanic.
<SAM138> South Gaul (SAMLG 4DR37) (Fig 79)
Grapes as pendant between wreath festoons: cf Hermet 1934, pl 100 nos 12, 18, by Germanus.
c AD 75–95.
<SAM139> Les Martres-de-Veyre (SAMMV 4DR37) (Fig 79)
The beaded circle was used as a basal wreath by Donnaucus (Stanfield and Simpson 1958, pl 43 no. 491), Ioenalis (ibid, pl 40 no. 470) and Drusus I (ibid, pl 16 no. 206) and the 'Potter of the Rosette' (Terrisse 1968, pl 18 no. 71).
c AD 100–25.
<SAM140> Central Gaul (SAMCG 6DR27) (Fig 79)
Stamped by Silvanus of Lezoux (die 3c).
c AD 135–60.
<SAM141> Two sherds, south Gaul (SAMLG 5DR18)
Flavian.

Fig 79 Selected samian vessels of period 3 from 31–32 Noble Street (WFG9): <SAM136>–<SAM140>, <SAM143>–<SAM145>, <SAM154>–<SAM156> (scale 1:1, except <SAM145> 1:2, stamp details 2:1)

<SAM142> South Gaul (SAMLG 6DR27) Flavian.

Other fine and coarse wares:
SAND 9A; FMIC; AHSU 2C; AHSU 2T; AHSU 2D; SAND; BB1 4G; HWC+ 2F; BB1 4G; BB1 4; BB2 2 AL; BB2 4 BUD; BBS 2F; BB1 2; HWC 2T; SAND 2; HWC 4; HWC 2T; BBS 2F; HWC 2E BUD; HWC 3 BDD; HWC 9A; HWC 2 AL.

Pottery catalogue:
<P46> Black-burnished ware 1 flat-rimmed bowl with vertical wall (BB1 4G); (WFG9 P15)

<P47> Highgate Wood ware C necked jar (HWC 2T); (WFG9 P16)

<P48> Alice Holt/Surrey ware necked jar with carinated shoulder and figure 7 rim (AHSU 2C); (WFG9 P17)

<P49> Unsourced sand-tempered ware lid (SAND 9A); (WFG9 P18) (Fig 78)

<P50> Unsourced fine reduced ware beaker with short everted rim (FINE 3E); (WFG9 P19)

<P51> Unsourced oxidised ware lid (OXID 9A); (WFG9 P20)

<P52> Verulamium region white ware shallow simple dish (VRW 5J); (WFG9 P21)

<P53> Verulamium region white ware ring-necked flagon with flared mouth (VRW 1B2); (WFG9 P22) (Fig 78)

<P54> Verulamium region white ware bowl (VRW 4); (WFG9 P23)

<P55> Verulamium region white ware bowl (VRW 4); (WFG9 P24)

Comments:

The date for this context is based on a stamped Dragendorff form 27 cup from central Gaul of Silvanus ii dated *c* AD 135–60. The presence of black-burnished wares 1 and 2 (BB1; BB2) and imitation black-burnished-type vessels and Highgate Wood ware C with added coarse sand (HWC+) support this date range. Also present is samian from les Martres-de-Veyre (SAMMV) dating *c* AD 100–20 and south Gaul (SAMLG) dating to the Flavian–Trajanic period; some of the coarse wares also date to this period.

LAYER [24]

Pottery summary:

Small-sized assemblage.

Earliest date *c* AD 120; latest date *c* AD 160.

Fine and coarse wares:

VRW 1B2; VRW; GAUL1; HWC 4F; NKSH; BB1 2; AMPH; OXID 9A.

Comments:

This context has been dated on the presence of a black-burnished ware 1 9A (BB1 9A). The majority of the assemblage dates from the Flavian period.

Latest road surface and primary fill of fort ditch

LAYER [13]

Pottery summary:

Small-sized assemblage.

Earliest date *c* AD 150; latest date *c* AD 200.

Samian ware catalogue:

<SAM143> (SAMEG 4DR37) (Fig 79)

In the style of Janu I of Rheinzabern: his ovolo (Ricken and Fischer 1963, E19) and corded border.

c AD 150–80.

<SAM144> (SAMEG 5DR31) (Fig 79)

Stamped by Secundinus (die 26) of Rheinzabern.

Late 2nd century AD.

<SAM145> East Gaul (probably Trier) (SAMEG 6DR33) (Fig 79)

Unstamped; graffito BII under base.

Later 2nd or early 3rd century AD.

<SAM146> Probably east Gaul (?SAMEG 6DR33)

Later 2nd century AD.

<SAM147> Central Gaul (SAMCG 5DR31)

Antonine.

<SAM148> Central Gaulish sherd (SAMCG)

Other fine and coarse wares:

FMIC 3; HWC; BB2 2F; BB2 2 AL; BB2 4 AL; SAND

2; VCWS 1B7–9; BHWS 1; VCWS 1; VCWS 9C.

Pottery catalogue:

<P56> Verulamium region coarse white-slipped ware ring-necked flagon with cupped mouth (VCWS 1B7–9); (WFG9 P25) (Fig 78)

<P57> Verulamium region white ware tazza (VRW 9C); (WFG9 P26) (Fig 78)

<P58> Brockley Hill white-slipped ware flagon (BHWS 1); (WFG9 P27) (Fig 78)

<P59> Highgate Wood ware C jar with acute lattice (HWC 2 AL); (WFG9 P28) (Fig 78)

<P60> Black-burnished-style everted-rimmed jar (BBS 2F); (WFG9 P29)

Comments:

This assemblage includes some large-sized sherds and an intact rim, neck and handle from a Verulamium region coarse white-slipped ware ring-necked flagon with cupped mouth (VCWS 1B7–9). The context has been dated by the decorated Dragendorff form 37 samian bowl from east Gaul (SAMEG 4DR37), attributed to the style of Janu I of Rheinzabern, *c* AD 150–80. The quantity of black-burnished-type vessels and the cupped-mouth flagon support the date. The absence of 3rd-century colour-coated wares from, for example, the Nene valley or Oxfordshire industries, suggests the group does not extend beyond the end of the 2nd century AD.

LAYER [20]

Pottery assemblage:

Medium-sized assemblage.

Earliest date *c* AD 150; latest date *c* AD 200.

Samian ware catalogue:

<SAM149> Dish, south Gaul (SAMLG 5DR42) Flavian.

<SAM150> Central Gaul (SAMCG 4DR37) Hadrianic–Antonine.

<SAM151> South Gaul, (SAMLG 6DR27) Flavian.

<SAM152> Central Gaul (SAMCG 5DR31) Slightly burnt.

Antonine.

<SAM153> South Gaulish sherd (SAMLG)

Other fine and coarse wares:

LOEG 6C; C186; NFSE 1; GAUL1; VCWS; KOLN 3 UND RCD; VRW 7; VRW 1B; OXID; LOXI 9A; OXID; BB2 2F AL; BB2 4H1; BB2 4; BB1 4 AL; BB1 ?4; HWC 3F; HWC 9A; SAND 9A; SAND 4A; AHSU; HWC 2E BUD; HWC.

Pottery catalogue:

<P61> Black-burnished ware 2 everted-rimmed jar with acute lattice (BB2 2F AL); (WFG9 P30) (Fig 78)

<P62> Black-burnished ware 2 round-rimmed bowl (BB2 4H); (WFG9 P31)

<P63> Black-burnished ware 1 bowl with beaded rim (BB1 4); (WFG9 P32) (Fig 78)

<P64> Black-burnished ware 1 bowl with beaded rim (BB1 4); (WFG9 P33)

<P65> Highgate Wood ware C poppy-head beaker

(HWC 3F); (WFG9 P34) (Fig 78)

<P66> Highgate Wood ware C lid (HWC 9A); (WFG9 P35)

<P67> Unsourced sand-tempered ware lid (SAND 9A); (WFG9 P36)

<P68> Unsourced sand-tempered ware bowl or jar (SAND 2/4); (WFG9 P37)

<P69> Unsourced oxidised ware lid (OXID 9A); (WFG9 P38)

<P70> London eggshell ware cup with narrow foot, carination and concave upper wall (LOEG 6C); (WFG9 P39) (Fig 78)

Comments:

The latest component of this assemblage is the samian Dragendorff form 31 plate from central Gaul (SAMCG 5DR31), dated to the Antonine period. The quantity of black-burnished-type vessels supports a date of *c* AD 150– 200. The cup in a local eggshell ware (LOEG 6C; Marsh type 11) has a date range of *c* AD 90–130, being particularly prominent in Hadrianic groups from the City of London (Arthur and Marsh 1978, 144–5, 199). The vessel is smashed but almost complete.

LAYER [21]

Pottery summary:

Large-sized assemblage.

Earliest date *c* AD 150; latest date *c* AD 200 (but includes one sherd, probably intrusive, of Portchester ware D (PORD); date range *c* AD 350–400).

Samian ware catalogue:

<SAM154> Central Gaul (SAMCG 4DR37) (Fig 79)
With the cockerel (Oswald 1936–7, no. 2348) and small circles used by X-6 (Stanfield and Simpson 1958, pl 74 nos 5, 10); the wreath is not recorded in his work.
c AD 130–50.

<SAM155> (SAMCG 4DR37) (Fig 79)
In the style of Advocisus of Lezoux: the neat ovoid beads and four-armed rosette are on Stansfield and Simpson 1958, pl 114 no. 33. The goat is Oswald 1936–7, no. 1840.
c AD 150–80.

<SAM156> (SAMMT 4DR37) (Fig 79)
In the style of the Malcio group at Montans. The ovolo occurs on bowls stamped inside the base by Malcio i and Nomus (at Montans) and by Felicio iii (Davies Pryce 1945, fig 8 no. 4), and on a bowl from a mould stamped by Malcio (Davies Pryce 1932, pl 29 no. 1). The medallion and roundels are found on stamped Malcio bowls from Agen (Lot-et-Garonne) and Périgueux (Dordogne), and the chevron on a bowl probably stamped by him (Simpson 1976, fig 2 no. 10). The hare is also found on late Montans ware.
c AD 110–45.

<SAM157> South Gaul (SAMLG 4DR37)
Blurred trident ovolo, coarse wavy line borders.
c AD 90–110.

<SAM158> Central Gaul (SAMCG 5DR31)
With an unidentifiable stamp.
Antonine.

<SAM159> East Gaul (SAMEG 4DR38)
Later 2nd to mid 3rd century AD.

<SAM160> Central Gaul (SAMCG 5DR31)
Antonine.

<SAM161> Dish, central Gaul (SAMCG 5DR42)
Hadrianic.

<SAM162> South Gaul (SAMLG 5DR18)
Flavian–Trajanic.

<SAM163> South Gaul (SAMLG 4DR37)

<SAM164> South Gaul (SAMLG 6DR33)
Flavian–Trajanic.

<SAM165> South Gaul (SAMLG 6DR27)
Flavian–Trajanic.

<SAM166> Two sherds, south Gaul (SAMLG 5DR18)
Flavian.

<SAM167> Central Gaul (SAMCG 6DR27)
Hadrianic–early Antonine.

<SAM168> Central Gaul (SAMCG 4DR37)
Hadrianic–early Antonine.

<SAM169> Four south Gaulish sherds (SAMLG)

<SAM170> Five central Gaulish sherds (SAMCG)

Other fine and coarse wares:

PORD; LOEG 6C; VRW; VRW 7; VRW 9C; VRW 4A; VRW 1; VRW ?2F; VRW 1B7–9; VRW 7; KOLN 3 RCD; CGOF 3; VCWS 1; VCWS ?1; VCWS 1B7–9; LOMI 9A; OXID 7; GAUL1; NFSE 1; LOMI 5J; VRW 9A; SAND; ERSB; GROG; HWC; HWC 3 BDD; HWC 9A; HWC 2E; HWC 4F; HWC 2T; NKGW; NKSH 2M; AHSU 2; AHSU 2T; AHSU 2A; SAND 2A; BB2 4H; BB2 4; BB1 4G; BB1 5J; BB2 2F; BB1 4; BB2 2 AL.

Pottery catalogue:

<P71> Verulamium region coarse white-slipped ware ring-necked flagon with cupped mouth (VCWS 1B7–9); (WFG9 P40)

<P72> Verulamium region coarse white-slipped ware ring-necked flagon with cupped mouth (VCWS 1B7–9); (WFG9 P41) (Fig 78)

<P73> Verulamium region coarse white-slipped ware ring-necked flagon with cupped mouth (VCWS 1B7–9); (WFG9 P42) (Fig 78)

<P74> Verulamium region white ware bowl (VRW 4); (WFG9 P43)

<P75> Verulamium region white ware everted-rimmed jar (VRW 2F); (WFG9 P44) (Fig 78)

<P76> Verulamium region white ware tazza (VRW 9C); (WFG9 P45)

<P77> London eggshell ware cup with narrow foot, carination and concave upper wall (LOEG 6C); (WFG9 P46)

<P78> Unsourced oxidised ware lid (OXID 9A); (WFG9 P47)

<P79> London mica-dusted ware shallow simple dish (LOMI 5J); (WFG9 P48)

<P80> Central Gaulish colour-coated ware (other fabric) ovoid beaker (CGOF 3B); (WFG9 P49)

<P81> Black-burnished ware 2 bead-rimmed jar (BB2 2A17); (WFG9 P50)

<P82> Black-burnished ware 2 round-rimmed dish (BB2 4H); (WFG9 P51)
<P83> Black-burnished ware 2 shallow simple dish (BB2 5J); (WFG9 P52)
<P84> Black-burnished ware 1 flat-rimmed bowl with vertical wall (BB1 4G); (WFG9 P53)
<P85> Highgate Wood ware C bowl with curved walls and flat rim (HWC 4F); (WFG9 P54)
<P86> Highgate Wood ware C lid (HWC 9A); (WFG9 P55)
<P87> Alice Holt/Surrey ware bead-rimmed jar (AHSU 2); (WFG9 P56)
<P88> Unsourced sand-tempered ware bead-rimmed jar (SAND 2A); (WFG9 P57)
Comments:
This context is dated on the presence of a single sherd of Portchester ware D (PORD). The remainder of the assemblage dates from the mid 2nd century AD onwards, which may indicate that the sherd of PORD is intrusive. The samian dates to the Flavian–Trajanic period and the Antonine period. If the PORD sherd is intrusive the date of the assemblage would be *c* AD 150–200.

Period 4

The next major phase of activity is represented by the building of the city wall (Fig 73; Fig 74; Fig 80). On this site, both the city wall thickening and the single-width city wall were recorded. The former ran alongside the fort wall and began to curve eastwards until it met with the north-west wall of the internal tower. A block of masonry in the corner of the tower against the fort wall shows that this part of the structure had probably undergone some strengthening.

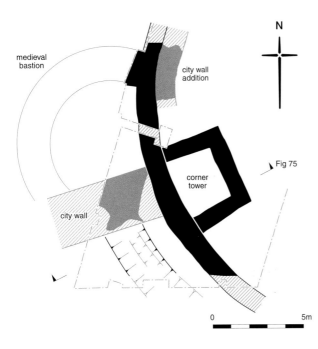

Fig 80 WFG9, plan of the period 4 city wall features (scale 1:200)

It is probable, however, that the tower was incorporated into the city defences as was the small internal tower to the north.

On the west side of the site, the full width of the city wall was recorded heading westwards towards Aldersgate. Through this had been built a tile-lined culvert (Fig 81), a later drainage channel for which was cut into the upper fills of the backfilled fort ditch. It would appear that this culvert was to take water draining out of this particular area. No evidence of a city wall bank was recorded on this site, either inside the area of the fort or outside. Significant finds from these later assemblages are illustrated on Figs 82–4.

Fill of fort ditch/city drain – possibly coming from slumped city wall bank

LAYER [12]
Coins:
<S33> Copper-alloy coin
WFG9 <63>, [12]
?Claudius, ?as.
?1st century AD.
<S34> Copper-alloy coin
WFG9 <61>, [12]
Domitian, as.
AD 86–7.
Pottery summary:
Small-sized assemblage.
Earliest date *c* AD 150; latest date *c* AD 200.
Samian ware catalogue:
<SAM171> Rheinzabern (Fig 82)
Tree motif, cf Ricken and Fischer 1963, P6 and P7 (SAMEG 4DR37).
Later 2nd–mid 3rd century AD.
<SAM172> Stamped by Gnatius (die 7a) of Lezoux (SAMCG 5DR18/31).
c AD 130–60.
<SAM173> Tall-necked beaker, central Gaul (SAMCG 3)
As Stanfield 1929, fig 12 no. 60.
Probably Hadrianic.
<SAM174> South Gaul (SAMLG 5DR18)
Pre- or early Flavian.
<SAM175> Central Gaul (SAMCG 6DR33)
Mid 2nd century AD.
<SAM176> South Gaul (SAMLG 4CU11)
Flavian–Trajanic.
<SAM177> Central Gaul (SAMCG 5DR31)
Antonine.
<SAM178> Central Gaul (SAMCG 3DE68)
Antonine.
<SAM179> South Gaulish sherd (SAMLG)
<SAM180> Three central Gaulish sherds (SAMCG)
Other fine and coarse wares:
SAND; HWC 2/3; HWC 4F; HWC+ 2 AL; HWC; BB2 2 AL; BB2 4; BB2 4H; BB2 4 AL; GAUL1; VCWS 5J; VRW; BATE 8DR20; OXID; VCWS; HOO; OXID 7BEF.

Fig 81 View of the fort ditch and late Roman culvert passing under the east–west city wall, looking north-west (3ft (0.91m) scales)

Fig 82 Selected samian vessels of period 4 from 31–32 Noble Street (WFG9): <SAM171>, <SAM182>, <SAM184>, <SAM187>, <SAM201>, <SAM217>–<SAM219> and <SAM229> (scale 1:1)

Pottery catalogue:

<P89> Unsourced oxidised ware bead and flange mortarium (OXID 7BEF); (WFG9 P58)

<P90> Verulamium region coarse white-slipped ware dish (VCWS 5); (WFG9 P59) (Fig 83)

<P91> Highgate Wood ware C jar or beaker (HWC 2/3); (WFG9 P60) (Fig 83)

<P92> Black-burnished ware 2 round-rimmed bowl (BB2 4H); (WFG9 P61)

<P93> Black-burnished ware 2 bowl or dish (BB2 4/5); (WFG9 P62) (Fig 83)

Comments:

The latest element of this assemblage is a samian decorated bowl from east Gaul (SAMEG 4DR37). The assemblage has other strong indicators of an Antonine date including a bead and flange mortarium (OXID 7BEF), black-burnished-type jars in Highgate Wood ware with added coarse sand with acute lattice (HWC+ 2 AL), quantities of black-burnished wares 1 and 2 (BB1; BB2) and a samian plate Dragendorff form 31 from central Gaul (SAMCG 5DR31).

Silting up and filling of fort ditch/city drain

LAYER [9] UPPER

Pottery summary:

Large-sized assemblage.

Earliest date *c* AD 250; latest date *c* AD 300.

Samian ware catalogue:

<SAM181> By Cettus/Satus of les Martres-de-Veyre (SAMMV 4DR7)

The ovolo and beads are on Stanfield and Simpson 1958, pl 143 no. 40.

c AD 135–65.

<SAM182> Central Gaul, in the style of the Quintilianus group (SAMCG 4DR37) (Fig 82)

The large rosette in a circle, rosettes in the field and the wavy line borders are on Stanfield and Simpson 1958, pl 71 no. 30, pl 71 no. 27 has the vertical band of fringed circles.

c AD 125–45.

<SAM183> Central Gaul. Part of medallion (SAMCG 4DR37)

Burnt.

Antonine.

<SAM184> Central Gaul (SAMCG 4DR37) (Fig 82)

Minerva (Oswald 1936–7, no. 126b) in panel of ovoid beads and double festoon from astragalus.

Antonine.

<SAM185> Rheinzabern (SAMEG 4DR37)

Scrollery probably with ?foliage.

Later 2nd–mid 3rd century AD.

<SAM186> South Gaul (SAMLG 4DR37)

With neat rosette-tongued ovolo and wavy line border.

Flavian.

<SAM187> By the Quintilianus group at Lezoux (SAMCG 4DR37) (Fig 82)

The grapes are on Stanfield and Simpson 1958, pl 69 nos 9, 15 and the bird on pl 69 no. 11. The leaf is

Rogers 1974, J35; the animal is probably a deer.

c AD 125–45.

<SAM188> South Gaul (SAMLG 4DR37)

Flavian.

<SAM189> Three rims, central Gaul (SAMCG 4DR37)

Hadrianic–Antonine.

<SAM190> Rheinzabern (SAMEG 4DR37)

Burnt.

Later 2nd to mid 3rd century AD.

<SAM191> Two sherds, central Gaul (SAMCG 5DR18/31)

Hadrianic–Antonine.

<SAM192> Central Gaul (SAMCG 5DR18/31)

Early 2nd century AD.

<SAM193> Two sherds, central Gaul (SAMCG 5DR31)

Antonine.

<SAM194> South Gaul (SAMLG 5DR18)

Flavian.

<SAM195> Central Gaul (SAMCG 4DR38)

Antonine.

<SAM196> Central Gaul (SAMCG 6DR33)

Antonine.

<SAM197> Central Gaul (SAMCG 5DR36)

Antonine.

<SAM198> Central Gaul (SAMCG 5WA81)

Antonine.

<SAM199> Two south Gaulish sherds (SAMLG)

<SAM200> Ten central Gaulish sherds (SAMCG)

Other fine and coarse wares:

BB1 4M BUD; BB1 4G AL; BB1 2F; BB1 2; BB1 2 OL; BB1 5J; SAND; COAR; ERSB; BB2 3 UND; BB2 2 AL; BB2 2F; BB2 5J; BB2 4; BBS 5J; BB2 2 BUD; BB2 2F6; BB1 4; SAND 4C306; SAND 2T; SAND 9A; AHFA 4; FMIC; SAND 9T; OXID 1; GAUL1; AMPH; LOMI 4; VCWS; VCWS 1; VCWS 1B7–9; RWS; BHWS; NVCC 3; END SCD; KOLN 3 RCD; NVCC; KOLN 3; RCD; NVCC 3 ROD; NVCC HANDLE; NVCC 3 ROD WPD; CC 3 BAD; MOSL 3; CC 3 ROD; NKGW 3 ROD; CC3; LOXI; OXID 2T; CC; OXID 3K; RWS; MOSL 3 UND; NKSH; HWC 2E; HWC 2 BUD; HWC 3F; HWC 2T; HWC+? 4F; FINE ROD; HWC 9A; OXID 9A; IMPT; HOO; MHAD; RDBK?; OXID 1; VRW 2; RWS 9C; VRW 7HOF; VRW 8DR2–4; VRW 2T; VRW 2.

Pottery catalogue:

<P94> Unsourced oxidised ware ring-necked flagon with cupped mouth (OXID 1B7–9); (WFG9 P63) (Fig 83)

<P95> Unsourced oxidised ware necked jar (OXID 2T); (WFG9 P64)

<P96> Verulamium region white ware hook-flanged mortarium (VRW 7HOF); (WFG9 P65) (Fig 83)

<P97> Unsourced white-slipped ware tazza (RWS 9C); (WFG9 P66)

<P98> Verulamium region white ware necked jar (VRW 2T); (WFG9 P67)

<P99> Verulamium region white ware jar (VRW 2); (WFG9 P68) (Fig 83)

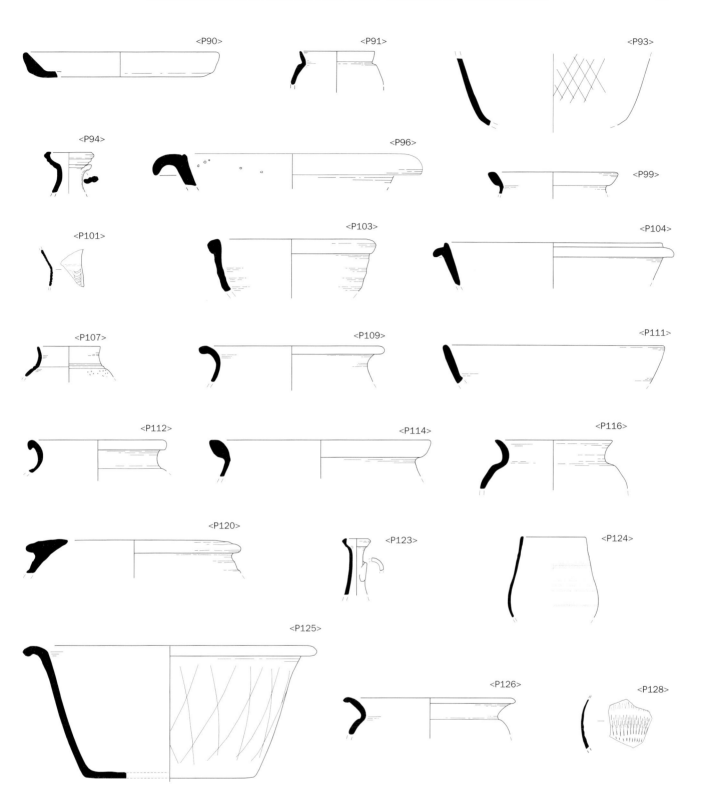

Fig 83 Selected pottery of period 4 from 31–32 Noble Street (WFG9): <P90>, <P91>, <P93>, <P94>, <P96>, <P99>, <P101>, <P103>, <P104>, <P107>, <P109>, <P111>, <P112>, <P114>, <P116>, <P120>, <P123>–<P126> and <P128> (scale 1:4)

<P100> London mica-dusted ware dish (LOMI 5); (WFG9 P69)

<P101> Nene Valley colour-coated ware indented beaker with scale decoration (NVCC 3 END SCD); (WFG9 P70) (Fig 83)

<P102> Unsourced colour-coated ware beaker with rouletted decoration (CC3 ROD); (WFG9 P71)

<P103> Unsourced sand-tempered ware Camulodunum form 306 bowl (SAND 4C306); (WFG9 P72) (Fig 83)

<P104> Black-burnished ware 1 flanged bowl (BB1 4M); (WFG9 P73) (Fig 83)

<P105> Black-burnished ware 1 flanged bowl (BB1 4M); (WFG9 P74)

<P106> Black-burnished ware 1 flat-rimmed bowl with vertical wall (BB1 4G); (WFG9 P75)

<P107> Highgate Wood ware C poppy-head beaker (HWC 3F); (WFG9 P76) (Fig 83)

<P108> Black-burnished ware 2 shallow simple dish (BB2 5J); (WFG9 P77)

<P109> Unsourced sand-tempered ware necked jar (SAND 2T); (WFG9 P78) (Fig 83)

<P110> Black-burnished ware 1 later everted-rimmed jar with cavetto rim (BB1 2F13); (WFG9 P79)

Comments:

This context includes a range of 3rd-century colour-coated wares, both Romano-British and imported wares. The context is dated on the presence of black-burnished ware 1 flanged bowls (BB1 4M) and jars with obtuse lattice (BB1 2 OL), as well as later grey wares from Alice Holt (AHFA). There is a component of earlier material dating from the mid 2nd century AD and possibly earlier. The samian present comes from south, central and east Gaul, and ranges in date from the Flavian to Antonine periods.

LAYER [9] LOWER

Pottery summary:

Small-sized assemblage.

Earliest date *c* AD 250; latest date *c* AD 300.

Samian ware catalogue:

<SAM201> By Reginus I of Rheinzabern (SAMEG 4DR37) (Fig 82)

Double circle (Ricken and Fischer 1963, 0.125) inside a leaf festoon (ibid, 0.139).

Antonine.

<SAM202> Trier (SAMEG 4DR38)

Later 2nd–mid 3rd century AD.

<SAM203> East Gaul (SAMEG 4DR37)

Later 2nd–mid 3rd century AD.

<SAM204> Central Gaul (SAMCG 4DR37)

Antonine jar base, Trier (SAMEG 2/3)

Later 2nd–mid 3rd century AD.

<SAM205> Neck sherd, disk rim flagon (SAMCG 1D)

Antonine.

Other fine and coarse wares:

OXID; NFSE; VRW; MHAD; KOLN 3; NVCC 3; OXID; MICA; CC; BB1 2; BB1 2F OL; HWC; BB1 4 BUD; HWC; SAND 2; BB2 2F6; BB1 5J; ?HWC 4; MOSL 3.

Comments:

This context is dated *c* AD 200–400 due to the presence of obtuse lattice decoration on an everted-rimmed jar in black-burnished ware 1 (BB1 2F OL). The samian includes examples from Trier and Rheinzabern and dates to the later 2nd and 3rd centuries AD. Colour-coated wares such as Moselkeramik (MOSL), Much Hadham red ware (MHAD) and Nene Valley (NVCC) also date to the 3rd century AD. The absence of the later grey ware from Alice Holt is noticeable.

LAYER [9A]

Pottery summary:

Small-sized assemblage

Earliest date *c* AD 250; latest date *c* AD 400.

Samian ware catalogue:

<SAM206> Rheinzabern sherd (SAMEG 5DR31)

Later 2nd–mid 3rd century AD.

<SAM207> Central Gaul (SAMCG 5DR31)

Antonine.

Other fine and coarse wares:

?VRW 2; MICA; NVCC 3 END SCD; NVCC 3; NVCC; MOSL 3; OXID 3; SAND; BB1 2F; SAND 2T; ?AHFA 2F; BBS 2F; ?BB1 2; BB1 2 OL; SAND 2; BB1 5J; BB2 4H.

Pottery catalogue:

<P111> Black-burnished ware 1 shallow simple dish (BB1 5J); (WFG9 P80) (Fig 83)

<P112> Alice Holt/Farnham ware jar (AHFA 2); (WFG9 P81) (Fig 83)

<P113> Nene Valley colour-coated ware pentice beaker with plain rim (NVCC 3K PR); (WFG9 P82)

<P114> Unsourced oxidised ware jar (OXID 2); (WFG9 P83) (Fig 83)

<P115> Black-burnished ware 1 later everted-rimmed jar with cavetto rim (BB1 2F13); (WFG9 P84)

Comments:

This context appears to have sherd links with layer [9], particularly the colour-coated wares. The context is dated on the presence of black-burnished ware 1 jars with obtuse lattice (BB1 2 OL) and later grey wares from Alice Holt (AHFA).

LAYERS [9] AND [9/2] INTERFACE

Pottery summary:

Medium-sized assemblage.

Earliest date *c* AD 250; latest date *c* AD 400.

Samian ware catalogue:

<SAM208> Central Gaul (SAMCG 4DR37)

Antonine.

<SAM209> Central Gaul with tip of ovolo (SAMCG 4DR37)

Antonine.

<SAM210> Central Gaul (SAMCG 4DR37)

Antonine.

<SAM211> Central Gaul (SAMCG 6DR33)

Antonine.

<SAM212> Central Gaul (SAMCG 5DR31)

Antonine.

<SAM213> Central Gaulish mortarium sherd (SAMCG 7)

Later 2nd century AD.

<SAM214> Six central Gaulish sherds (SAMCG)

<SAM215> East Gaulish sherd (SAMEG)

Other fine and coarse wares:

COAR; SAND 3 UND; NVCC 3; VRW; VRW 3 ROD; 8DR2–4; 8DR20; GAUL1; OXID ?1; LOXI 9A; OXID; RWS; BHWS; VCWS; KOLN 3; ?NVCC; BB1 4 BUD; BBI 2; AHFA; SAND; BB1 2 OL; GROG 2V; BB2 4; HWC; BBS 2 AL; BB2 2F6; HWC 2E.

Comments:
The latest components of this context are black-burnished ware 1 jars with obtuse lattice (BB1 2 OL) and later grey wares from Alice Holt (AHFA). The samian is from central and east Gaul, mainly dating to the Antonine period.

LAYER [9/2]
Pottery summary:
Medium-sized assemblage.
Earliest date *c* AD 250; latest date *c* AD 400.
Fine and coarse wares:
BB2 4H1; HWC; AHSU 2; OXID7; SAND BUD; VRW 7; VRW; OXID 1; VRW ?2; LOXI 9A; VCWS 1; MICA; NVCC 2 SCD; KOLN 3 BAD; KOLN 3 CR; NVCC 3 CR BAD; MOSL/CGBL 3 BAD; HWC 2T; BB1 4G226; BB1 2F; AHFA 2 OL; BBS 2F; HWC 9A.
Pottery catalogue:
<P116> Black-burnished-style everted-rimmed jar (BBS 2F); (WFG9 P85) (Fig 83)
<P117> Alice Holt/Farnham ware shallow simple dish (AHFA 5J); (WFG9 P86)
<P118> Alice Holt/Farnham ware necked jar (AHFA 2T); (WFG9 P87)
<P119> Nene Valley colour-coated ware beaker with cornice rim (NVCC 3 CR); (WFG9 P88)
Comments:
This context also has sherd links with context [9], but in addition to the 3rd-century colour-coated wares, also has a number of 2nd-century vessels from Cologne (KOLN). The context is dated by the late grey wares from Alice Holt, including jars with obtuse lattice. The majority of the types present date from the mid–late 2nd century AD.

LAYER [10]
Coins:
<S35> Copper-alloy coin
WFG9 <60>, [10]
Antoninus Pius, sestertius.
AD 145–61 (*BMC*, iv, 1698–704).
<S36> Copper-alloy coin
WFG9 <64>, [10]
Plated denarius.
?Late 2nd–early 3rd century AD.
<S37> Copper-alloy coin
WFG9 <65>, [10]
Denarius.
?Late 2nd–early 3rd century AD.
<S38> Copper-alloy coin
WFG9 <67>, [10]
Tetricus I, Diam 17mm; ?copy.
AD 270–3.
Pottery summary:
Medium-sized assemblage.
Earliest date *c* AD 250; latest date *c* AD 400.
Samian ware catalogue:
<SAM216> Unidentifiable stamp, central Gaulish

(SAMCG 6DR33)
Hadrianic–Antonine.
<SAM217> Central Gaul (SAMCG 4DR37) (Fig 82)
With part of a large vine leaf.
Antonine.
<SAM218> Central Gaul (SAMCG 3DE72) (Fig 82)
Large incised floral motif within a roundel as Oswald and Pryce 1920, pl 77 no. 5 or 6.
Antonine.
<SAM219> Central Gaul (SAMCG 3DE72) (Fig 82)
Incised roundel and (probably) floral motif.
Antonine.
<SAM220> East Gaul (SAMEG LUD V)
With fragmentary incised decoration.
Later 2nd–mid 3rd century AD.
<SAM221> Two sherds, central Gaul (SAMCG 5DR31)
Late Antonine.
<SAM222> Central Gaul (SAMCG 4DR38)
Antonine.
<SAM223> Central Gaul, tip of ovolo (SAMCG 4DR37)
Antonine.
<SAM224> Trier (SAMEG 7DR45)
Later 2nd–mid 3rd century AD.
<SAM225> Central Gaul (SAMCG 6DR33)
Antonine.
<SAM226> Two sherds, central Gaul (SAMCG 5WA79)
Later 2nd century AD.
<SAM227> Central Gaulish (SAMCG 7)
<SAM228> Three central Gaulish sherds (SAMCG)
Other fine and coarse wares:
?CGOF; NVCC 3 ROD; SAND 9T; BB1 4G/4G226; BB1 5J; NVCC 1; MOSL 3 UND; MOSL 3; OXID VRW; OXID ?9A; C186; GAUL1 8G4; AMPH; VRW2; OXID 2T; VCWS 9C; BBS 4; AHFA 2 NCD; BB1 2; BBS 2F; SAND 3 UND; OXID; CC; NVCC 3 END SCD; NVCC 3 CR; NVCC 4; KOLN 3 BFD; NVCC 3 BAD; NVCC 3 ROD; NVCC 9GB ROD; MOSL 3 ROD.
Pottery catalogue:
<P120> Unsourced oxidised ware hammerhead mortarium (OXID 7HAM); (WFG9 P89) (Fig 83)
<P121> Gauloise form 4 amphora (GAUL1 8G4); (WFG9 P90)
<P122> London oxidised ware lid (LOXI 9A) or dish (LOXI 5); (WFG9 P91)
<P123> Nene Valley colour-coated ware flagon (NVCC 1); (WFG9 P92) (Fig 83)
<P124> Nene Valley colour-coated ware beaker (NVCC 3); (WFG9 P93) (Fig 83)
Comments:
This context also has sherd links with layers [9] and [9/2] (above) and is dominated by colour-coated wares. Later grey wares from Alice Holt are also present and are the latest element of the group. The samian is from central and east Gaul, dating mainly to the Antonine period.

Fill of culvert

LAYER [7A]

Coins:

<S39> Copper-alloy coin
WFG9 <59>, [7A]
Hadrian, as.
AD 117–38.

<S40> Coin
WFG9 <66>, [7A]
Antoninus Pius, as.
c AD 152–4.

Pottery summary:

Large-sized assemblage.

Earliest date *c* AD 250; latest date *c* AD 300.

Samian ware catalogue:

<SAM229> Central Gaul (SAMCG 4DR37) (Fig 82)
Large scroll design; the leaf is a small version of one
used by the Paternus II group and others.
Mid–late Antonine.

<SAM230> Central Gaul (SAMCG 5DR31R)
Late Antonine.

<SAM231> Central Gaul (SAMCG 5DR31)
Antonine.

<SAM232> East Gaul (Rheinzabern) (SAMEG
5DR31/LUD Sa)
Later 2nd–mid 3rd century AD.

<SAM233> Central Gaul (SAMCG 5DR36)
Slightly burnt.
Antonine.

<SAM234> Central Gaulish sherd (SAMCG)

<SAM235> Three East Gaulish (Rheinzabern) sherds
(SAMEG)

Other fine and coarse wares:

CGBL3; BAD; VRW 2; VRW; OXID 3 ROD; BB1 4G;
BB1 4G226; BBS 2F; BB1 2F; MICA; MOSL 3 UND;
BB2 4H; SAND 2A; BB1 4G226; SAND 2T; BAET
8DR20; GAUL1 8G; VRW; RWS; BHWS; VCWS;
?MHAD; OXID NCD; SAND; BB1 4; NKSH; BB2 2;
BB2 2F9 SL; BB2 2 UND; BB1 2 OL; BB1 2; BB1 4;
BB2F 4; BB1 4 AL; KOLN 3 BAD; KOLN 3; NVCC;
KOLN 3 ROD; MOSL 3; NVCC 3 END SCD.

Pottery catalogue:

<P125> Black-burnished ware 1 flat-rimmed bowl
with vertical wall (BB1 4G); (WFG9 P94) (Fig 83)

<P126> Black-burnished ware 1 everted-rimmed jar
(BB1 2F); (WFG9 P95) (Fig 83)

<P127> Black-burnished ware 1 Gillam form 226
bowl with lid groove (BB1 4G226); (WFG9 P96)

<P128> Unsourced oxidised ware beaker with
rouletted decoration (OXID 3 ROD); (WFG9 P97)
(Fig 83)

Comments:

The latest element in this context is black-burnished
ware 1 jars with obtuse lattice (BB1 2 OL). There are a
number of colour-coated vessels and again sherd links
with layers [9] and [9/2] (above) can be found. There
are a number of black-burnished types that have been
identified including a flanged bowl with a lid groove

(Gillam 1970, form 226) (BB1 4G226). The samian is
from central and east Gaul, dating mainly to the
Antonine period, although some pieces have been dated
later Antonine and later 2nd–mid 3rd century AD.

Building material

Mostly small and fragmentary tile and stone was
retained. Items of interest include a Roman imbrex with
an unusual ridged outer surface (from the fill of the fort
ditch, layer [9]) and two fragments of imported marble.
One is white, of Carrara type (layer [15]) whilst the other
is a white-veined grey marble (layer [10]).

Wall plaster came from a number of contexts ([14],
[21], [27]). This is plain white or maroon (one part
covered by bluish-green paint).

One tile is of outstanding importance, an imbrex
with part of a Classis Britannia stamp, coming from the
late backfill of the fort ditch [9a]. The stamp would
have read CLBR, although only part of the letters CL
survive. This tile was imported into London,
presumably by ship, from the Classis Britannica tilery,
which is believed to have been situated near the south
coast not far from Hastings (Sussex). This stamp tile,
along with two examples from Winchester Palace, is
discussed in more detail by Crowley and Betts (1992).

Small finds

Military equipment

<S41> Copper-alloy stud
WFG9 <10/1>, layer [21]
Damaged, flat-headed. L 5mm; max Diam 13mm.
Possibly military, as it was associated with a tongue
from a military belt.

<S42> Copper-alloy buckle tongue
WFG9 <10/2>, layer [21]
Fragment of the tongue from a copper-alloy military
buckle, with characteristic moulding just below the
terminal pierced for the hinge bar. The tip is bent. L
20mm; max W 4.5mm. Associated with a flat-headed
stud <S41>.

<S43> Bone plaque fragment
WFG9 <57>, layer [9]
Decayed, with a low ridge along the long side, grooved
for most of its length. Max dimensions 34 × 29mm.
Probably part of the back plate of a military sword
scabbard chape (Oldenstein 1976, tables 25–7,
especially table 26).

Hairpins

There are two complete bone hairpins and four with
only the tip missing, and two fragments from the shaft
of a jet pin. The latter is likely to be of 3rd- or 4th-
century date. All the bone pins are of Crummy's type 3
(1983, 21–2), which has a more or less spherical head
and the swollen shaft characteristic of later Roman

pins. The commonest type, it appears *c* AD 150–200 and probably survives to the end of the Roman period (ibid), though it is less common in later 4th-century contexts and, where it is present, may in many cases be residual. However, type 3 pins are found with the 4th-century type 5 (ibid, 24) in the bone-working debris in the *palaestra* of the St Margaret's Street baths at Canterbury, Kent (Greep 1995, 1135–41). The debris was secondary in this context, having been dumped, along with other rubbish, in the waterlogged yard in the late 4th century AD in an attempt to raise the ground level (Blockley et al 1995, 207). The date the debris was generated is, therefore, uncertain, but probably belongs in the middle, or first half, of the century.

<S44> Bone hairpin
WFG9 <1>, layer [47]
Tip broken off. Head type B. L 106mm.
<S45> Bone hairpin
WFG9 <2>, layer [47]
Tip broken off. Head type A. L 52mm.
<S46> Bone hairpin
WFG9 <3>, layer [47]
Tip broken off. Head type C. L 57mm.
<S47> Bone hairpin
WFG9 <49>, [-] trench SW, above filling A
Tip broken off. Head type B. L 48mm.
<S48> Bone hairpin
WFG9 <51>, [-] trench SW, filling A
Tip broken off. Head type B. L 63mm.

Gemstone

<S49> Gemstone
WFG9 <24>, layer [9] trench SW
Gemstone. Low quality amethyst. Cupid standing right, probably burning a butterfly. L 7mm; W 5mm. 1st-century type (Henig 1978, 301, no. app 118, pl 28).

Ceramic lamps

<S50> Ceramic lamp (Fig 84)
WFG9 <76>, layer [15]
Verulamium region white ware open lamp of Loeschcke type 11 or 12 (1919).
Date range: second half of 1st century AD to the first half of 2nd century AD (cf Bailey 1988, 171).
<S51> Ceramic lamp (Fig 84)
WFG9 <77>, layer [25]
Nozzle fragment, with traces of burning, of a Verulamium white ware open lamp of Loeschcke 1919, type 11.
Date range: second half of 1st century AD to the first half of 2nd century AD (cf Bailey 1988, 171).

Fig 84 Ceramic lamps <S50> and <S51> of period 4 from 31–32 Noble Street (WFG9) (scale 1:4)

Shale vessel

<S52> Shale platter
WFG9 <82>, layer [10/2]
Rim fragment, laminated at base. Original Diam *c* 120mm.

Gaming pieces

<S53> Bone counter
WFG9 <26>, layer [10a] (2nd), filling A
Diam 22.5mm, with a large (4.5mm Diam) off-centre perforation.
<S54> Pottery counter rough-out
WFG9 <->, [-], trench SW, filling A
Counter made from a wall sherd of a black-burnished ware 1 vessel (BB1). Very abraded on external surface. Diam 36mm.

Miscellaneous objects

<S55> Jet cylinder
WFG9 (south-west) <1>, layer [9] above filling A
Fragment of a cylindrical, slightly tapering length of jet, lathe-turned and decorated with groups of grooves and a low convex moulding. Both ends are broken, and are pierced centrally, but the perforations do not meet. Similar cylinders are often described as handles (Allason-Jones 1996, 48), and Ralph Jackson has suggested that this object may be from an opthalmic handled needle similar to a bone example from Corbridge, Northumberland (Gilson 1981, fig 2, 3).
<S56> Copper-alloy strip
WFG9 (SW), <19>, layer [2]
The centre is slightly raised above the broken terminals. L 40mm; W 3mm.
<S57> Copper-alloy sheet
WFG9 <11>, layer [10]
A length of rolled/folded copper-alloy sheet. L 73mm; W 14.5mm.
<S58> Iron ring
WFG9 (south-west), <4>, layer [10] filling A
Internal Diam 20mm.

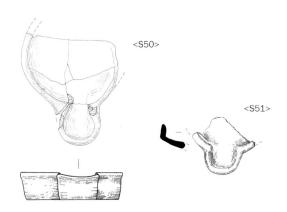

7 Excavations on the south side of Cripplegate

7.1 WFG10, Lillypot Lane (fort wall)

1951 (Grimes 1968, 23; Fig 5; Fig 6; Fig 72). NGR: TQ 32238 81456

Following the identification of the fort in 1949–50, Grimes examined a number of sites along the presumed course of the south wall of the fort (WFG10–WFG14). This site consisted only of a very small trench, scarcely 1 × 2m, which located the site of the wall. It survived as just three courses of ragstone on a rubble foundation (Fig 85). All other details of its construction, internal bank and so forth, were not seen due to modern intrusions and walls. No finds survived from this excavation.

The line of the wall at this point was recently re-examined by MOLA (Lyon 2004, 165–6). These excavations revealed traces of late 1st-century buildings that had been swept away prior to the construction of the fort. The evidence there was not specific about the date of construction, placing it anywhere from *c* AD 120 to *c* AD 160. The fort wall, part of an internal tower and the fort ditch were recorded. Only the foundations, however, were recorded, which were crude in fashion. Sufficient area to the south of the fort was excavated to demonstrate that there was only a single ditch here, unlike at 1–6 Aldersgate where there is a suggestion that there were two ditches on the western side of the fort (Butler 2001, 45).

No new evidence came from these excavations for the date at which the fort may have fallen into disuse, although it was shown that a gravel surface had covered the backfilled ditch at this point during the 3rd century AD.

7.2 WFG11, Staining Lane (fort wall)

1951 (Grimes 1968, 23; Fig 5; Fig 6; Fig 86). NGR: TQ 32286 81437

As for WFG10 (above, 7.1), this site was represented by a very small trench located specifically to identify the line of the south wall of the fort. No details of the wall could be recorded, although part of a robber trench was postulated as the possible line of the wall. No finds survived from this excavation.

7.3 WFG12, Wood Street (fort south gate)

1950–1 (Grimes 1956, 127–8; 1968, 22–4; Fig 5; Fig 6; Fig 86). NGR: fort ditch – TQ 32308 81425

A redevelopment on the west side of Wood Street on the presumed path of the south wall of the fort enabled Grimes to examine the possible location of the south gate of the fort. Four trenches were planned (A–D, Fig 87) but the two westernmost trenches were abandoned owing to the profusion of modern concrete foundations. The course of the fort wall as seen at WFG9, WFG10 and, perhaps, WFG11 (Chapter 6.3; and above, 7.1, 7.2) suggested that it ran under the north wall of the property. As a result, Grimes was aware that the opportunity to examine the gate in detail would not be forthcoming. The basements to the north were much deeper and so all traces of the gate would have been lost. Upon removal of the basement slab, he discovered that the extant archaeology here was very shallow and only deep features survived. None of the pottery surviving for this site could be related to any of the scant surviving records.

Period 1

The natural consisted of brickearth with no traces of any prehistoric activity.

Fig 85 WFG10, view of the wall on the south side of the fort, looking north

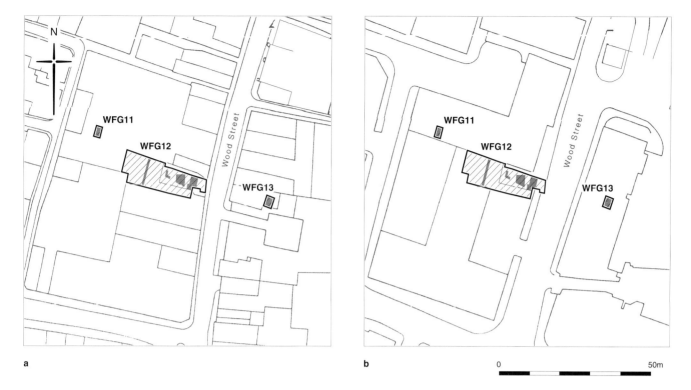

Fig 86 WFG11–WFG13, the sites and trenches: a – located on a contemporary street plan; b – located on a modern street plan (scale 1:1200)

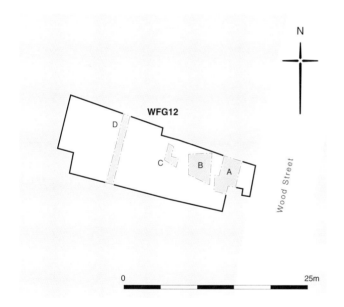

Fig 87 WFG12, location of trenches A–D (scale 1:500)

Period 2

No period 2 activity was recorded. However, on the southern end of the two eastern trenches Grimes recorded a gravel make-up, the top of which had been truncated by the Victorian basement. This appeared to rest directly on natural, but the area available for study was too small to enable the positive identification of any features or layers under this make-up. It is possible that this gravel is part of a road contemporary with the fort gate.

Period 3

Of significance, however, was a V-shaped ditch (Fig 88; Fig 89), which ran east–west across the two trenches on a line parallel with the presumed course of the south wall of the fort. On both sides of the ditch, post- and stakeholes suggested the existence of a timber bridge or platform, which would have carried traffic over the ditch itself. The identification of these features as a small bridge would appear to have been confirmed by the presence of a similar gravel surface on the north side of the ditch and, at the extreme north end of the site, the corner of a masonry wall. The line of this wall did not extend across the north end of the trenches, suggesting that the wall was broken at this point, in the exact position where Grimes postulated the location of the south gate of the fort. This corner, therefore, was identified as one of the door jambs of the south gate. It is possible that the gravel, described above in period 2, may represent a road surface, which led up to the gate from the south and continued into the fort on the north side of the ditch. The bridge connected the two sides. A medieval pit cut into the south side of the ditch.

Coins

<S59> Copper-alloy coin
WFG12 <5>, unstratified
Sestertius.
2nd–early 3rd century AD.
<S60> Copper-alloy coin
WFG12 <6>, unstratified

Fig 88 WFG12, view of the ditch of period 3 in trenches A and B, looking north-west

Diam 24mm.
1st–early 3rd century AD.
<S61> Coin
WFG12 <4>, unstratified
Antoninus Pius, sestertius.
AD 171–2 (*BMC*, iv, 1416–19)

Small finds

BROOCHES
<S62> Copper-alloy brooch (Fig 90)
WFG12 <1>, unstratified
P-shaped brooch with a single bow, coil and pin missing. There are faint traces of rouletting on the hinge cover and on the first of two transverse mouldings on the head. The bow is decorated by vertical ridges framed by a square moulding. There is a large flange at the base of the bow and the foot, which is facetted, is long and zoomorphic. Its debased dragonesque design terminates in a pronounced circular moulding. L 50mm. This is a Continental type, dated to the 2nd and 3rd centuries AD and especially popular with the military (cf Hattatt 1985, 127–9; 1989, 198).

Fig 89 WFG12, view of the ditch and robbed wall foundation of period 3 in trenches A and B, looking west

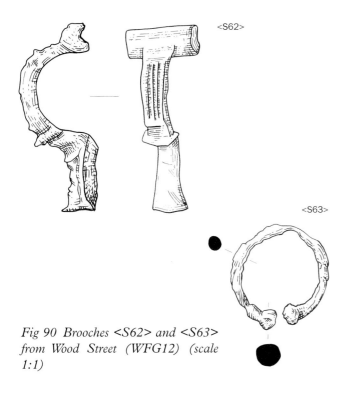

Fig 90 Brooches <S62> and <S63> from Wood Street (WFG12) (scale 1:1)

<S63> Copper-alloy penannular brooch (Fig 90) WFG12 <2>, no context number, but recorded as coming from the fort ditch opposite the south gate Fowler type A2 (1960, 150–2), with rounded bulbous terminals, which consist of simple milled knobs. Pin missing. Internal Diam 20.5mm. These brooches cannot be closely dated.

7.4 WFG13, Wood Street (fort wall)

1951 (Grimes 1968, 24; Fig 5; Fig 6; Fig 86). NGR: TQ 32346 81412

Another small trench located the line of the south wall of the fort on the east side of Wood Street. No details of this excavation survive in the archive. No finds survive for study.

7.5 WFG14, 70a–71 Aldermanbury (fort south-east corner)

1952 (Grimes 1956, 128, 161–2; 1968, 25; Fig 5; Fig 6; Fig 91). NGR: fort wall – TQ 32398 81495

A number of topographical features throughout the Cripplegate area (eg the line of the south wall of the fort, the position of the south gate (as suggested by the scant features at WFG12; above, 7.3) and a kink in the line of the city wall where it met the north wall of the fort in the London Wall area, to the east of St Alphage church) suggested that the site of the south-east corner of the fort would be located on the west side of Aldermanbury, to the south of St Mary Aldermanbury. Three trenches in the basements of a line of adjacent properties were located to straddle the line of the wall and, hopefully, to locate a curve replicating that seen in WFG9 (Chapter 6.3). The results were not as rewarding as had been expected on account of deep

Fig 91 WFG14, the site and trenches: a – located on a contemporary street plan; b – located on a modern street plan (scale 1:1200)

medieval features. The most important observations came from the middle of the three trenches.

Periods 1 and 2

Natural soil was brickearth. There was no evidence for any prehistoric activity and no sign of any pre-fort occupation.

Period 3

The earliest identifiable feature on this site was the fort ditch itself (Fig 92). This had a V-shaped profile, similar to that seen at the south end of Noble Street (WFG9; Chapter 6.3) and at Wood Street (WFG12; above 7.3). It ran from east to west and, on the eastern side of the trench, began to turn slightly to the north-east. This suggested that Grimes's excavations were just to the west of the south-east corner of the fort. This was to be confirmed by the excavation by the Guildhall Museum of a site to the north-east on the site of the Guildhall Library extension (Marsden 1968, 4–10). Grimes did not see the fort wall on this site.

Period 4

At least five sections, A–E (this notation was not used by Grimes but is used here for clarity), were recorded of the ditch profile and its fills. The finds were recovered from the main fills of the sections. The finds list below gives details of these fills and their

corresponding layers above and below. They are as follows:

Section A

Top fill	layer [4]
Middle fill	layer [6]
Lowest fill	layer [7]

Section B

Top fill	layer [56], same as layer [62]
	layer [62], same as layer [56]
Middle fill, upper	layer [57]
Middle fill, lower	layer [64]
Lowest fill	layer [65]

Section C

Top fill	layer [68]
Middle fill	layer [69]
Lowest fill	layer [70]

Section D

Top fill	layer [71]
Middle fill, upper	layer [72]
Middle fill, lower	layer [73]
Lowest fill	layer [74]

Section E

Top fill	layer [75]
Middle fill, upper	layer [76]
Middle fill, lower	layer [77]
Lowest fill	layer [78]

Fig 92 WFG14, view of the fort ditch, looking south-west

A detailed section drawing (Fig 93a), however, shows that the ditch was not backfilled in such an orderly fashion. The section reveals a profusion of individual lenses and thin dumps of material, much of it probably organic in origin. The finds groups came from the larger components of such fills. As was seen in the southern ditch of the fort at Noble Street (WFG9), the ditch appears to have gone out of use after the later part of the 2nd century AD, at least it was no longer kept clean, and rubbish deposits built up in the ditch throughout the 3rd century AD. The date of the earliest fills tends towards the late 2nd or early 3rd century AD, whereas the later fills are 3rd century AD or later. Grimes notes in his records that the upper fills of the ditch were cut by a shallow gully of Roman date. No finds can be identified as coming from this feature – it cannot, therefore, be dated more closely.

Fort ditch section A

LAYER [4] (TOP FILL OF DITCH)

Pottery summary:
Small-sized assemblage.
Earliest date *c* AD 150; latest date *c* AD 250.
Samian ware catalogue:
<SAM236> Probably south Gaul (SAMLG 5DR18)
Flavian–Trajanic.
<SAM237> Central Gaul (SAMCG 6DR27)
Trajanic–Hadrianic.

Other fine and coarse wares:
NKSH; HWC ?3; HWC 3 BDD; HWC; HWC 4F; HWC ?2E BUD; CGBL 3; BB1 2 ?AL; BB2 5J BUD; BB2 4H; BB2 4; SAND 2; SAND; BB2 2; SAND 2A; AHSU, VCWS; OXID; RWS; AHSU 2.
Comments:
This is a fairly abraded assemblage. It is dated post-*c* AD 150 on the presence of a central Gaulish/Lezoux black colour-coated ware beaker (CGBL 3).

LAYER [6] (MIDDLE FILL OF DITCH)

Pottery summary:
Small-sized assemblage.
Earliest date *c* AD 140; latest date *c* AD 250.
Fine and coarse wares:
BAETE 8DR20; OXID; ?BB1 2; HWC 3BDD; BBS 2 ?SL; BB2 4; BB1 2; HWC2; BB2.
Comments:
Several of the sherds are burnt.

LAYER [7] (LOWEST FILL OF DITCH)

Pottery summary:
Small-sized assemblage.
Earliest date *c* AD 120; latest date *c* AD 140.
Fine and coarse wares:
ERSB; ?BB1 2; SAND 9A; FMIC 4.
Comments:
The black-burnished ware 1 jar (?BB1 2) has sherd links to context layer [6] above.

N   S

a
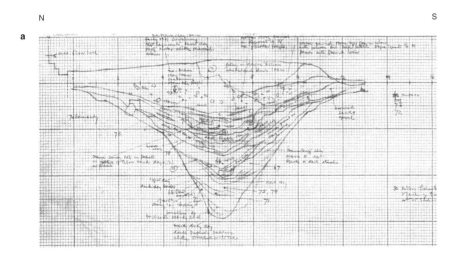

b
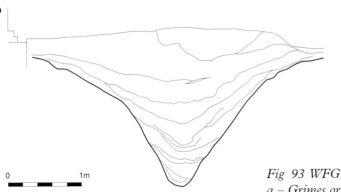

0   1m

Fig 93 WFG14, west-facing section through the ditch (see Fig 92): a – Grimes original; b – interpretive section (scale 1:50)

Fort ditch section B

LAYER [56] (SAME AS [62]; TOP FILL OF DITCH)
Pottery summary:
Small-sized assemblage.
Earliest *c* AD 150; latest date *c* AD 400.
Samian ware catalogue:
<SAM238> ?East Gaulish sherd (SAMEG)
Other fine and coarse wares:
VRW; BB1 4; HWC 2 AL; SAND 2; AHSU 2; CC.

LAYER [62] (SAME AS [56]; TOP FILL OF DITCH)
Pottery summary:
Small-sized assemblage.
Earliest date *c* AD 150; latest date *c* AD 250.
Samian ware catalogue:
<SAM239> Central Gaul (SAMCG 7)
Late Antonine.
Other fine and coarse wares:
VRW; SAND.
Comments:
The central Gaulish samian mortarium is late Antonine in date and shows significant signs of wear on the interior.

LAYER [57] (MIDDLE FILL (UPPER) OF DITCH)
Pottery summary:
Small-sized assemblage.
Earliest date *c* AD 140; latest date *c* AD 200.
Samian ware catalogue:
<SAM240> South Gaulish sherd (SAMLG)
1st century AD.
Other fine and coarse wares:
VCWS 1B7–9; HWC; VRW 2T; SAMLG.

LAYER [64] (MIDDLE FILL (LOWER) OF DITCH)
Pottery summary:
Small-sized assemblage.
Earliest date *c* AD 50; latest date *c* AD 160.
Fine and coarse wares:
AHSU 2.

LAYER [65] (LOWEST FILL OF DITCH)
Pottery summary:
Small-sized assemblage.
Earliest date *c* AD 150; latest date *c* AD 250.
Samian ware catalogue:
<SAM241> Central Gaul (SAMCG 5DR18/31)
Hadrianic to early Antonine.
<SAM242> Central Gaul (SAMCG 5DR31)
Mid to late Antonine.
Other fine and coarse wares:
BB1 2 AL; RWS ?1; CC3 RC.
Comments:
There are two central Gaulish samian Dragendorff type 18/31 dishes (SAMCG 5DR18/31) and one

Dragendorff type 31 dish (SAMCG 5DR31). These vessels have been dated to the Hadrianic–Antonine and mid–later Antonine periods respectively. A few of the sherds in this context are abraded.

Fort ditch section C

LAYER [68] (TOP FILL OF DITCH)
Pottery summary:
Small-sized assemblage.
Earliest date *c* AD 250; latest date *c* AD 400.
Fine and coarse wares:
VRW; AMPH; VCWS; NKSH; HWC; BBS 2F AL; AHFA 4; BB2 4.
Comments:
This context is given the date of *c* AD 250–400 by the presence of an Alice Holt/Farnham ware (AHFA) which is dated post-*c* AD 250. Otherwise the group could be dated *c* AD 120–250.

LAYER [69] (MIDDLE FILL OF DITCH)
Although Grimes noted that finds were retained from this layer, there is no record of any pottery in the archive.

LAYER [70] (LOWEST FILL OF DITCH)
Pottery summary:
Small-sized assemblage.
Earliest date *c* AD 140; latest date *c* AD 200.
Samian ware catalogue:
<SAM243> Les Martres-de-Veyre (SAMMV 5DR15/17R)
Early 2nd century AD.
<SAM244> Central Gaul (SAMCG 4DR37)
Mid–late Antonine.
Other fine and coarse wares:
BAETE 8DR20; BB2 4H; VRW 1; VCWS; BB2 4.
Comments:
The dates of this context had been altered from *c* AD 120–80 due to the identification of the central Gaulish samian Dragendorff type 37 bowls (SAMCG 4DR37) as Antonine. Several of the coarse ware sherds are abraded. The Verulamium region coarse white-slipped ware (VCWS) sherd is probably part of the ring-necked flagon with cupped mouth (1B7–9) in the same fabric that is in contexts [75], [74] and [78].

Fort ditch section D

LAYER [71] (TOP FILL OF DITCH)
Pottery summary:
Small-sized assemblage.
Earliest date *c* AD 250; latest date *c* AD 400.
Samian ware catalogue:
<SAM245> South Gaulish sherd (SAMLG)
1st century AD.
<SAM246> Central Gaulish sherd (SAMCG)
Antonine.
Other fine and coarse wares:
BAETE 8DR20; GAUL1 8G; AHFA 2 WLX; BBS 2

AL; VRW; RWS.
Comments:
Based upon the samian and the majority of the coarse wares, this assemblage could be dated *c* AD 120–250. However, because of the presence of the Alice Holt/Farnham ware (AHFA) jar dates should be amended to *c* AD 250–400. The central Gaulish samian sherd (SAMCG) was dated to the Antonine period.

LAYER [72] (MIDDLE (UPPER) FILL OF DITCH)
Pottery summary:
Small-sized assemblage.
Earliest date *c* AD 140; latest date *c* AD 200.
Samian ware catalogue:
<SAM247> Central Gaul (Fig 94)
The ovolo is not certainly identifiable. The wreath medallion (Rogers 1974, E26) was used by Advocisus and Criciro, while the wavy line border suggests links with such potters as Servus II (Stanfield and Simpson 1958, pl 131 nos 1–7). The satyr is Oswald 1936–7, no. 628 (SAMCG 4DR37).
Antonine.
<SAM248> Central Gaul
The ovolo is Rogers 1974, B32, used by X-5 and X-6 (SAMCG 4DR37).
Hadrianic–early Antonine.
Other fine and coarse wares:
KOLN 3 BFD; VRW 7HOF; VRW; SAND.
Comments:
There are central Gaulish samian Dragendorff type 37 bowls (SAMCG 4DR37) here, one is Antonine and the other is Hadrianic–Antonine in date.

LAYER [73] (MIDDLE (LOWER) FILL OF DITCH)
Pottery summary:
Small-sized assemblage.
Earliest date *c* AD 50; latest date *c* AD 160.
Fine and coarse wares:
The pottery from this context consisted of six sherds of Verulamium region white ware (VRW) which all come from the same vessel.

Fig 94 Samian vessel <SAM247> from period 4 at 70a–71 Aldermanbury (WFG14) (scale 1:1)

LAYER [74] (LOWEST FILL OF DITCH)
Pottery summary:
Small-sized assemblage.
Earliest date *c* AD 150; latest date *c* AD 400.
Fine and coarse wares:
HOO; NVCC 3 BAD; VRW 2T; VCWS 1; RWS; OXID; ?AHSU.
Comments:
There is a mixture of fabrics in this context mostly dating to the 2nd century AD. However, the Alice Holt/Surrey ware (AHSU) is queried as it may be Alice Holt/Farnham ware (AHFA), which is dated post-AD 250. The Verulamium region coarse white-slipped ware (VCWS) sherd is probably part of the ring-necked flagon with cupped mouth (1B7–9) in the same fabric that is in contexts [70], [75] and [78]. There are two unsourced oxidised ware (OXID) sherds, which are possibly from amphorae.

Fort ditch section E

LAYER [75] (TOP FILL OF DITCH)
Pottery summary:
Small-sized assemblage.
Earliest date *c* AD 140; latest date *c* AD 200.
Fine and coarse wares:
VCWS 1B7–9. One vessel.
Comments:
This context has nine sherds, all from the same vessel, which is also found in other contexts ([70], [74], [78]). No other fabrics were found.

LAYER [76] (MIDDLE (UPPER) FILL OF DITCH)
Pottery summary:
Small-sized assemblage.
Earliest date *c* AD 60; latest date *c* AD 150.
Fine and coarse wares:
NKSH 2M STAB.
Comments:
This was a single large sherd from a rolled-rimmed storage jar (2M).

LAYER [77] (MIDDLE (LOWER) FILL OF DITCH)
Pottery summary:
Small-sized assemblage.
Earliest date *c* AD 50; latest date *c* AD 170.
Fine and coarse wares:
BAETE 8DR20.
Comments:
There is only one large sherd of a Baetican early fabric Dressel 20 amphora (BAETE 8DR20) in this context.

LAYER [78] (LOWEST FILL OF DITCH)
Pottery summary:
Small-sized assemblage.
Earliest date *c* AD 120; latest date *c* AD 200.
Fine and coarse wares:
VCWS 1 ROD; VCWS 1; HWC 3 BDD; BB2 2.

Comments:
This assemblage contained one vessel of exceptional interest, a Verulamium region coarse white-slipped ware flagon with rouletted decoration (VCWS 1 ROD). There are 11 sherds of this vessel in context layer [78] and there is more of what is probably the same vessel in context layer [60a]. The context also has likely sherd links with context layers [70], [74] and [75] as the Verulamium region coarse white-slipped ware (VCWS) sherd is probably part of the ring-necked flagon with cupped mouth (1B7–9) from these contexts.

Building material

Only one tile was recorded, the rest of the material had apparently not been retained for study. The tile recorded is a late 2nd- or 3rd-century imbrex. This is an import into Roman London, although the kiln source is currently unknown.

Small finds

<S64> Copper-alloy brooch
WFG14 <24>, layer [73] bag 10, area 2 cut 1
Fragment of a circular disc brooch with the fitting for a hinged pin. Diam *c* 28mm.
<S65> Copper-alloy fitting
WFG14 <14>, layer [71] bag 4
Convex semicircular fitting, possibly a lid. The upper surface is incised with lines radiating from a flat hook rolled over to take a hinge bar. L excluding hinge 20mm; max W 26mm.

8 Excavations in the north-east area of Cripplegate

8.1 WFG15, Brewers' Hall

1958 (Grimes 1968, 170–2; Fig 5; Fig 6; Fig 95).
NGR: TQ 32429 81542

The Brewers' Hall was a site on which Grimes believed that the survival of both Roman and medieval deposits would be very substantial. The excavations, however, revealed that the remodelling of the medieval hall following its destruction in the Great Fire had severely damaged much of the underlying deposits. The narrow trenches which Grimes was obliged to excavate among the small rooms of the post-medieval hall made it difficult to examine in detail the earlier phases of activity.

Natural brickearth was seen only in the bottom of some deep medieval pits. Apart from a small fragment of ragstone wall, which he believed to be Roman in date and belonging to the fort, no other features pre-dating the medieval period were seen.

Only 22 small-sized ceramic assemblages were recorded. None of these can now be accurately located on the site, but none contain pottery earlier than the early 2nd century AD, with just a couple dating from the 3rd and 4th century AD. The samian assemblage from these layers contains just 21 sherds, including four small south Gaulish fragments dated to the 1st century AD. The remainder are all south or central

Gaulish sherds of Hadrianic–Antonine date and one late 2nd- to mid 3rd-century east Gaulish bowl fragment.

8.2 WFG15a, Aldermanbury (fort wall)

1951 (Grimes 1968, 25; Fig 5; Fig 6; Fig 95). NGR: TQ 32473 81567

A small trench was located across a basement in the hope of locating the line of the fort wall and ditch. However, later features had totally destroyed all evidence of earlier occupation.

8.3 WFG16, Aldermanbury Postern

1958 (Grimes 1968, 25–6; Fig 5; Fig 6; Fig 96). NGR: TQ 32489 81605

An area *c* 8m west of Aldermanbury postern was examined with the aim of locating the north-east corner of the fort. The basement in question lay just outside the line of the city wall. However, no part of the city wall or the fort wall was recorded. Only slight

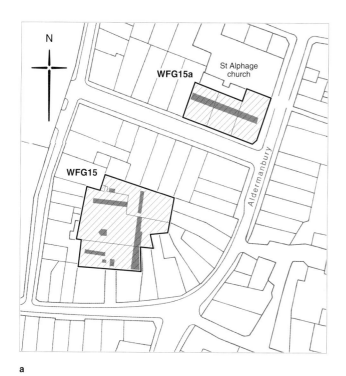

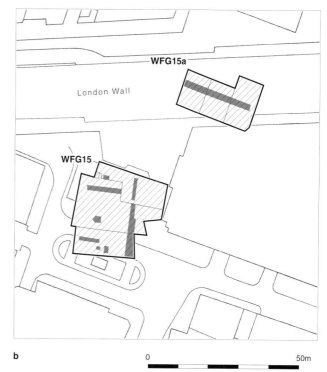

Fig 95 WFG15 and WFG15a, the sites and trenches: a – located on a contemporary street plan; b – located on a modern street plan (scale 1:1200)

113

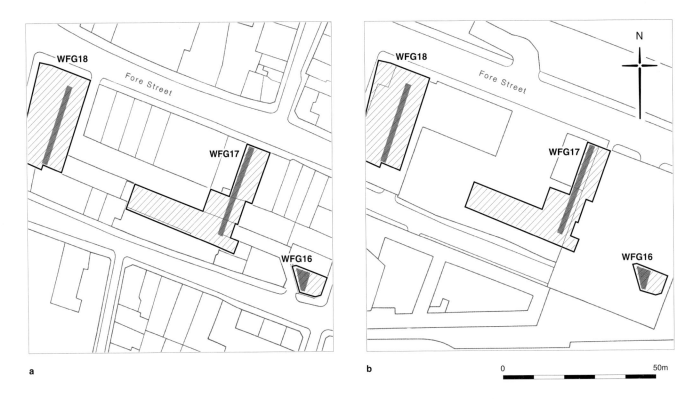

Fig 96 WFG16–WFG18, the sites and trenches: a – located on a contemporary street plan; b – located on a modern street plan (scale 1:1200)

remains of the fort ditch were recorded. It was seen to curve slightly to the north-west and appeared to merge with a U-shaped feature, which, Grimes believed, was the ditch associated with the city wall (seen also at WFG4, Chapter 5.5; WFG17 and WFG18, below, 8.4, 8.5). No finds survive from this site for further study.

8.4 WFG17, St Alphage churchyard, Fore Street

1946–7 (Grimes 1968, 27–8, 64, 78–81, 83–4, 86–9; Fig 5; Fig 6; Fig 96). NGR: city wall – TQ 32505 81596

Two of the earliest excavations undertaken by the RMLEC in the Cripplegate area were across the city defences on the northern side of the site (WFG17 and WFG18; below, 8.5). The removal of destroyed Victorian buildings there enabled, for the first time, a detailed examination of the sequence of city ditches. This was the first time that such a detailed record had been made of the ditches for the city as a whole (Fig 23; see also Fig 25 and Fig 26 showing the clearance of this site by the Corporation of London in 1951 after Grimes had completed his work here).

In brief, the surviving wall is of many phases with, at the lowest part on the exterior, traces of the Roman fort wall. On the east side of the surviving stretch, the city wall thickening can be seen abutting this wall (Fig 97). Above this is a sequence of medieval rebuilds and repairs in a variety of construction methods.

Fig 97 WFG17, detail of the fort wall (right) and city wall thickening (left) abutting it

8.5 WFG18, Cripplegate Buildings, Wood Street

1946–7 (Grimes 1968, 85; Fig 5; Fig 6; Fig 96). NGR: TQ 32407 81656

Along with WFG17 (above, 8.4), this site was one of the first to be examined by the RMLEC in the Cripplegate area. It too was one of the first examinations of the city defences beyond the wall itself.

Natural soil consisted of brickearth throughout the site, even though the ditch profiles were very deep in parts. The earliest feature recorded was a Roman ditch, U-shaped in profile, close to the line of the city wall itself. The face of this wall, which presumably should have been the north wall of the fort, was not seen. The Roman ditch had been cut on its north side by a succession of broad, deep ditch cuts and recuts which date from the medieval period up to the 17th century. These are examined in greater detail by Milne (2001, 9–18).

Miscellaneous object

<S66> Bone ?handle
WFG18 <45>, layer [5]
Fragment of a tapering bone tube with seven grooves at the wider end. Probably a handle, perhaps, like the jet object <S55> (Chapter 6.3), for a handled needle, or possibly the grip from a sword or dagger handle (cf Oldenstein 1976, table 10, 17–22). Max Diam 11.5mm; surviving L 80mm.

9 Excavations in the interior of the fort circuit

9.1 WFG19, Silver Street (headquarters building)

1957 (Grimes 1968, 34–5; Fig 5; Fig 6; Fig 98). NGR: TQ 32337 81541

The route of the new London Wall ran across the centre of the area of the fort at the junction of Silver Street with Wood Street. There arose, therefore, an opportunity to examine a site on the north-west corner of this junction with the hope of discovering evidence of the main headquarters building of the fort. From the start, the depth of the basements did not lead Grimes to be optimistic. Excavations revealed only the lower parts of a few Roman and medieval rubbish pits, and a few undatable postholes, probably Roman on account of their depth. The archive contains very little data about these features and no finds survive from the site.

9.2 WFG20, 15–17 Silver Street

1956–7 (Grimes 1968, 35, 37; Fig 5; Fig 6; Fig 99). NGR: TQ 32273 81500

MOLA in 1992–2000

This site was re-excavated by MOLA between 1992 and 2000, and published by Howe and Lakin (2004).

In summary, their work discovered some evidence of Bronze Age occupation in the form of field ditches. This had been truncated and then overlain by redeposited brickearth during the late 1st century AD. The area appears to have been marginal during the earliest period of Roman occupation in London, but there was some evidence of enclosures and slightly founded buildings here after c AD 70. There was no evidence to support the theory that there was a timber fort on this site prior to the construction of the masonry Cripplegate fort.

The recent excavations confirmed an early 2nd-century, *de novo*, construction date for the fort – perhaps in the AD 120s – and also expanded our knowledge of the interior layout of the fort, elaborating upon Grimes's discoveries of 1956. They also showed that the internal buildings did not appear to remain much in use beyond the end of the 2nd century AD. Modern building had severely truncated the later levels, but it appears that, while the buildings were not used, some of the interior roads continued to be maintained. Unfortunately, again mirroring the results of Grimes's work, finds assemblages, other than building materials, were not prolific. No useful pottery groups were found to assist in interpreting function or use of particular parts of the buildings.

a

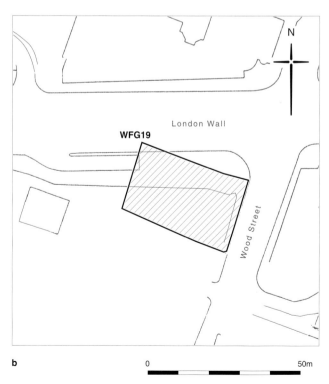

b

Fig 98 WFG19, the site: a – located on a contemporary street plan; b – located on a modern street plan (scale 1:1200)

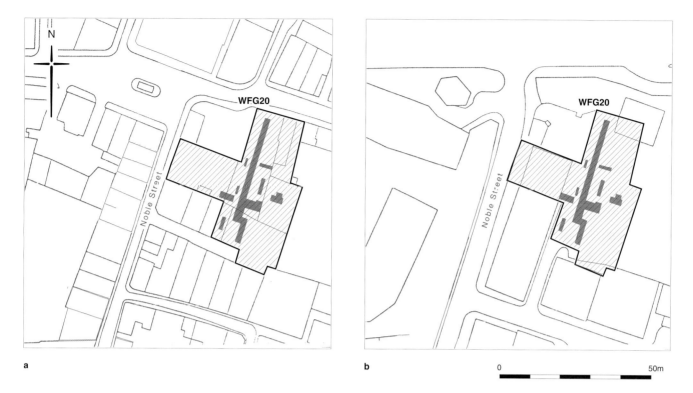

Fig 99 WFG20, the site and trenches: a – located on a contemporary street plan; b – located on a modern street plan (scale 1:1200)

Grimes in 1956

For the record (and with thanks to Trevor Brigham), the following were the results of excavations carried out on this site in 1956 in the cleared basements of buildings destroyed by the bombing in December 1940. The records indicate that Grimes established a fixed, horizontal datum but unfortunately, due to the varying basement levels, the recorded depth of the datum below the contemporary street level can no longer be accurately calculated. As a result the archive records, where depths below datum are mentioned, are confusing and misleading. Locating many of the pottery assemblages, therefore, has proved to be very unproductive. However, as was the case with the more recent excavations, all the assemblages were small and none could be used objectively to recreate activities on this site.

Eleven trenches were excavated to natural, and deep intrusions emptied as far as possible (Fig 99). All Roman walls, tessellated floors and a hearth were left intact. No attempt was made to examine earlier deposits in these areas. The presence of any pre-Roman material, therefore, was not explored.

Period 1

Natural soil consisted of brickearth. No changes in slope were recorded and indeed, deturfing and small-scale terracing may have erased any natural contours. Evidence from recent observations nearby (29 Noble Street (NOB73); Chapter 11.1), with reference to

Grimes's records, suggests that the height of natural lay at 12.7–12.9m OD.

Period 2

The earliest occupation, during the late 1st and early 2nd century AD, can be interpreted as:

1 – deturfing;
2 – isolated pits and ditches, aligned broadly east–west, and clusters of postholes, which may be predecessors of the later stone-founded barracks;
3 – redeposited brickearth.

Period 3

Cutting through the redeposited brickearth layers were the foundations for masonry walls, which can be interpreted as barracks in the south-west corner of the Cripplegate fort (Fig 100; cf Grimes's results with MOLA's in Fig 101). Two gauges of wall can be identified: east–west aligned walls were 0.48m wide; north–south aligned walls were 0.64m wide. The best-preserved sections had level tops suggesting that superstructures may have been of clay and timber, a constructional technique well recorded in Roman London (Fig 102).

The walls formed a north–south oriented building at least 25m long, identified as the central section of a barracks. The barracks was 7.5–8.0m wide for most of its length, with a 2m veranda along the east side. This veranda did not continue beyond the northernmost

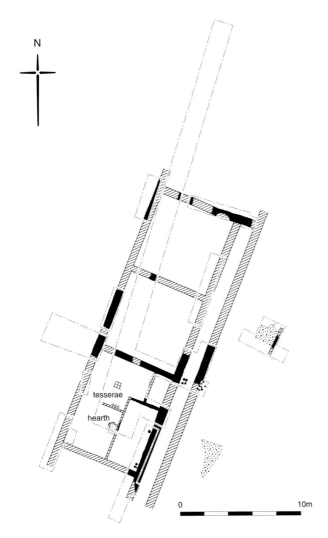

N

Fig 100 WFG20, the location of trenches and interpretation plan of the barracks (scale 1:300)

east–west wall, suggesting that the ground plan of the barracks conformed to standard barracks design.

The interior details of the barracks suggest a higher level of decoration and comfort than normally anticipated. For the most part the floors were initially of trodden brickearth but one room was subsequently floored with tesserae set in *opus signinum* (Fig 103; Fig 104). The presence of parallel *opus signinum* and mortar ridges in the floors of other rooms suggests timber partitioning. A hearth consisting of a single bipedalis tile surrounded with small rectangular tiles, normally used for herringbone floors, set on their flat sides was discovered in one room.

The walls and veranda were plastered and painted, mainly in plain red, but occasional red and black lines on unpainted or white backgrounds suggest that simple panelled designs were used. These details indicate a considerable investment in the standard of this

particular barracks: such refinements would not be expected in the standard men's quarters.

Period 4

The walls and floors were sealed by brickearth deposits, which were probably the slumped walls of the barracks. These contained the plaster described above, mortar deposits and late 2nd- or early 3rd-century pottery which implies that the demolition of the structures occurred in the mid Roman period, possibly around the time that the fort was incorporated in the new town defences (*c* AD 200). Overlying deposits contained coins and pottery of the mid 3rd and 4th century AD. The nature of the occupation in this area during this period is not known.

Material from later periods is very sparse. There was no direct evidence for Saxon or early medieval activity, although several sections of the barracks appear to have been robbed during the medieval period, probably before the 13th century.

Pottery

As mentioned above, all of the ceramic assemblages from this site were small and none can be located to the records.

Coins

<S67> Copper-alloy coin
WFG20 <11>, layer [108]
?Claudius; ?copy as.
?Mid 1st century AD.
<S68> Copper-alloy coin
WFG20 <6>, layer [B27]
Claudius; plated denarius.
AD 41–50.
<S69> Copper-alloy coin
WFG20 <7>, layer [B2]
Radiate copy.
c AD 270–80.
<S70> Copper-alloy coin
WFG20 <10>, layer [B10]
Maximian I; antoninianus.
AD 286–93 (*RIC*, Carausius 34–6).
<S71> Copper-alloy coin
WFG20 <8>, layer [cut P]
Constantine II; follis.
AD 321 (*RIC*, 148, 149).
<S72> Copper-alloy coin
WFG20 <9>, layer [B10]
Valentinian I; Diam 18mm.
AD 367–75 (*LRBCII*, no. 527).

Fig 101 (facing) WFG20, the results of the MOLA excavations in the 1990s; Grimes located the north end of Building 12 and the west side of Building 13, lack of survival in the 1990s led to a different interpretation (scale 1:500)

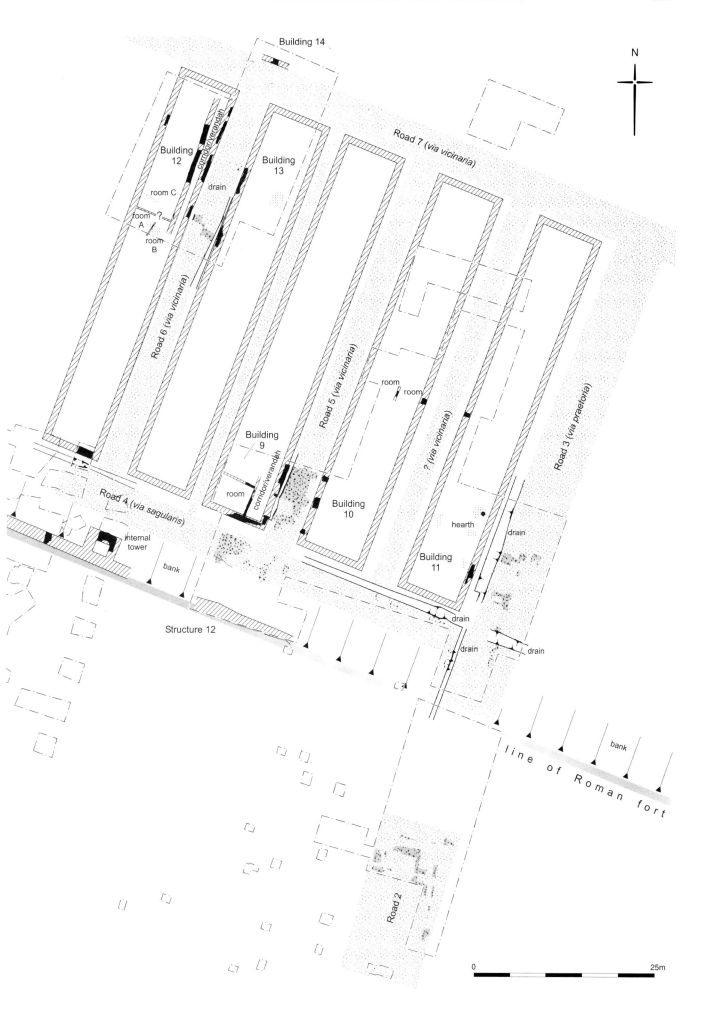

Fig 102 WFG20, detail of walls showing two modules; note also the stakehole clusters in the foreground, view looking north (3ft (0.91m) scales)

Fig 103 WFG20, plain mosaic with hearth in the foreground, view looking south (1ft (0.30m) scale)

Fig 104 WFG20, detail of plain mosaic; note quarter-moulding alongside the scale, view looking north (1ft (0.30m) scale)

Other small finds

Hairpins

<S73> Bone hairpin
WFG20 <18>, layer [K.51]
Complete; head type B. L 67mm.

Toilet, surgical or pharmaceutical instrument

<S74> Copper-alloy probe
WFG20 <2>, unstratified
Probe with decorated zoomorphic terminal and shaft either twisted or with grooves where wire in a contrasting metal was originally inlaid. Similar zoomorphic decoration has been noted on a toilet spoon with twisted shaft from Colchester (Crummy 1983, fig 64, 1917), which has also produced a copper-alloy spoon-probe with a shaft inlaid with both white metal wire and possibly niello (ibid, fig 65, 1927).

Ceramic lamps

<S75> Ceramic lamp (Fig 105)
WFG20 <22>, layer [C.81]
Fragment of a picture lamp with the upper half of the discus surviving. The design shows an eagle with outspread wings and raised left foot (Loeschcke 1919, pl 13, 281; Bailey 1988, 78–9, fig 99). Shoulder type 2a; lamp possibly type 4 (Loeschcke 1919). Central Gaulish colour-coated ware (other fabric) (CGOF).

<S75>

Fig 105 Ceramic lamp <S75> from 15–17 Silver Street (WFG20) (scale 1:2)

<S76> Ceramic lamp
WFG20 <21>, layer [M.54]
Fragment of a small type 9 factory lamp (Loeschcke 1919) with closed channel. Local product. Cologne colour-coated ware (KOLN).
2nd century AD.

Shale vessels

<S77> Shale platter
WFG20 <20>, layer [D.29]
Fragment only, with parts of the simple raised rim and the foot ring surviving (Aitken and Aitken 1982, fig 14, 98). Original Diam *c* 200mm.

Fastenings and fittings

<S78> Copper-alloy loop
WFG20 <4>, layer [31]
Split-spike loop, broken. L 36.5mm.

9.3 WFG21, Addle Street

1956 (Grimes 1968, 159; Fig 5; Fig 6; Fig 106). NGR: TQ 32355 81502

The route of the new London Wall, running diagonally across the area of the fort, encouraged Grimes to examine the site on the south-east corner of the junction of Wood Street and Addle Street. It was hoped that this site, with seemingly shallow basements, would disclose further evidence for the interior detail of the Roman fort. Unfortunately, later features had all but obliterated any Roman occupation.

Periods 1 and 2

Natural soil consisted of brickearth with no evidence for prehistoric activity. However, very little of the surface of the brickearth was seen, the greater part of the site being taken up with cut features of medieval date.

Period 3

Only a small fragment of ragstone wall, probably Roman in date, was found in the north-west corner of the site. The entire site was covered with a profusion of medieval pits but it was possible to determine that these had cut through an earlier medieval phase of activity. This was represented by at least two sunken buildings, with wattle walls. These are probably of the 11th or 12th century.

9.4 WFG22, St Alban's church, Wood Street

1962–4 (Grimes 1968, 37, 203–9; Fig 5; Fig 6; Fig 106). NGR: TQ 32350 81465

The site of St Alban's church, Wood Street, was one which Grimes had identified as an important area of study early in the activities of the RMLEC. It was not until 1961–2 that he was given the opportunity to examine the interior of the church, when this building was being demolished to make way for a road rewidening scheme and the building of a new police station. Before he was able to work there, however, he had to await the removal of the burials in the interior and the churchyard by a contracted firm. This phase was carried out over a long period of time thus

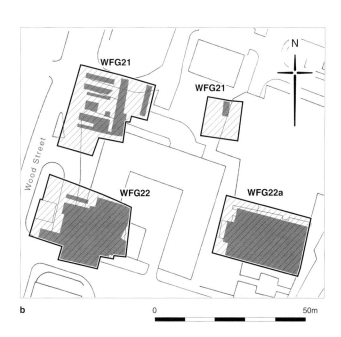

Fig 106 WFG21, WFG22 and WFG22a, the sites and trenches: a – located on a contemporary street plan; b – located on a modern street plan (scale 1:1200)

severely encroaching upon the time Grimes had to examine the site. Although the staff of the firm cooperated as best as possible, no records of the burials for the church could be made, a matter that caused Grimes much concern. The removal of the burials also damaged the upper levels of stratigraphy, especially of the medieval period associated with the church, which meant that, although wall lines could be identified, the floors associated with them could not be recorded (Fig 107).

Period 1

The natural soil on the site was brickearth. No prehistoric activity was recorded.

Period 2

The earliest evidence for human activity dated to the second half of the 1st century AD and was represented by gullies, pits and postholes (Fig 108). It may be of importance that the period 3 Roman building phase on this site retained the alignments of the gullies; this suggested to Grimes the possibility that the structures represented by the 1st-century features had the same function as the later structures. It is, however, equally possible that those features

Fig 107 WFG22, view of the north churchyard of St Alban, looking east (3ft (0.91m) scales)

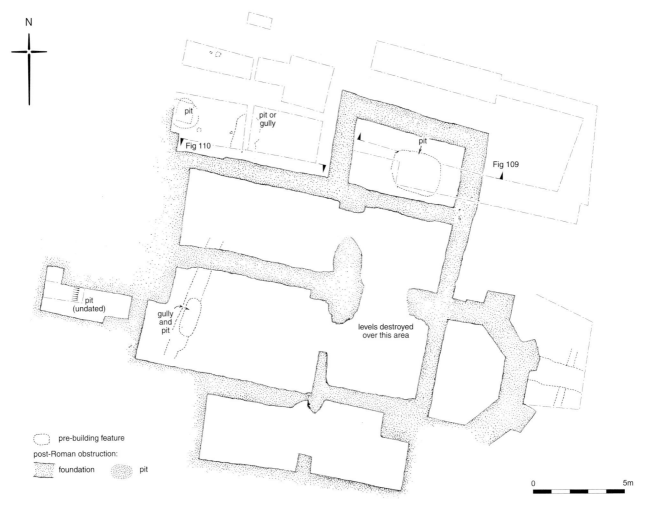

Fig 108 WFG22, plan of the period 2 features (scale 1:200)

which Grimes believed to be earlier than the fort may be the initial early 2nd-century phase of construction and the stone buildings date from later in the 2nd century AD – both phases, however, being contemporary with the masonry fort itself. This is suggested by the dating evidence in the other pits (especially layers [34] and [35] (below, 'Period 3') dated to the early 2nd century AD), which are under the gully associated with the masonry building.

The sections recorded by Grimes through the northern part of the churchyard and the north transept of St Alban's church (Fig 109; Fig 110) demonstrate well the degree of activity on this particular site before the construction of the masonry walls of the fort. A large pit (Grimes's 'Big early pit' see layer [12], below; Fig 109) had been dug, almost 4m wide at the top with what appears to be a step down on the east side. The base of

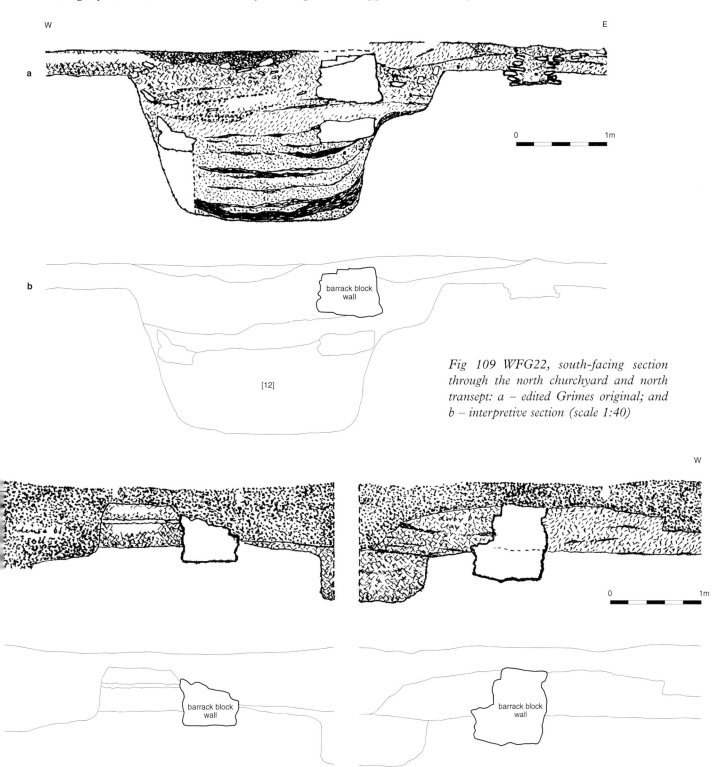

Fig 109 WFG22, south-facing section through the north churchyard and north transept: a – edited Grimes original; and b – interpretive section (scale 1:40)

Fig 110 WFG22, north-facing section through north churchyard and pit or gully: a – edited Grimes original; and b – interpretive section (scale 1:40)

the pit was *c* 2.4m wide. The precise function of this feature is not clear – it was not a well so perhaps it may have been a simple gravel extraction pit. The first 1m-fill consisted of interleaved layers of silt and organic material, suggesting that it had built up over a period of time (eg months) rather than backfilled in a single episode. The upper part of the fill of the pit, dumped layers of gravel and brickearth, is more consistent with a single backfilling and levelling exercise. Into this soft material, and evidently affected by subsidence and shrinking of the lower fills, the foundation of the barrack block had been built. In fact, the section shows a large section of wall foundation with, immediately below it and separated by more gravel and clay fill, another section of masonry. Could this be evidence of major subsidence of the foundation and a replacement being built above it? It is likely that this would have required a substantial rebuild of this part of the barracks.

Pre-barracks layers

LAYER [12] ('LAYER IN MIDDLE OF BIG, EARLY PIT')

Pottery summary:
Small-sized assemblage.
Earliest date *c* AD 70; latest date *c* AD 100.

Samian ware catalogue:
<SAM249> South Gaul (SAMLG 4DR29) (Fig 111)
Sherd link with layer [39].
There are links with a bowl from Vechten stamped OFCEN, which has an upper frieze scroll with what may be the same bud; the lower frieze on the Vechten bowl includes all the elements here, with the exception of the small dog, in a similar arrangement.
c AD 70–85.

Fig 111 Selected samian vessels <SAM249> and <SAM251> of period 2 from St Alban's church, Wood Street (WFG22) (scale 1:1)

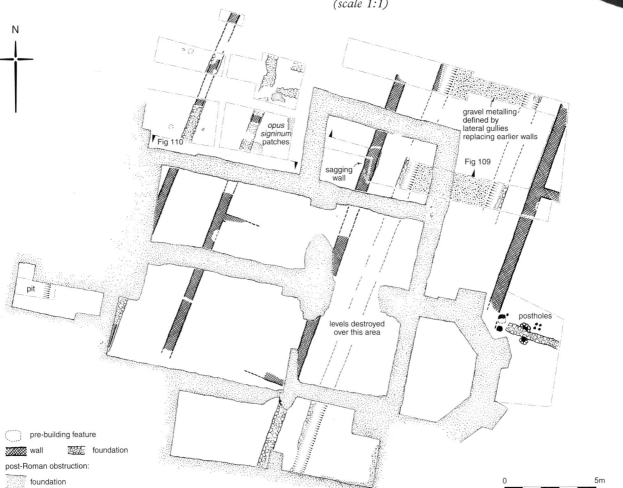

Fig 112 WFG22, plan of the period 3 features (scale 1:200)

<SAM250> DR29, south Gaul, (SAMLG 4DR29)
Fragment of scroll in upper frieze.
c AD 70–85.
<SAM251> DR37, south Gaul (SAMLG 4DR37)
(Fig 111)
The general style is characteristically early to mid Flavian (see for example Atkinson 1914, pl 12 no. 60; Hermet 1934, pl 82 no. 7); a trident ovolo, chevron band, panels with triple medallions, and s-gadroons at base. The animal may be the stag, Oswald 1936–7, no. 1738.
c AD 75–90.
<SAM252> Three DR 27 sherds, south Gaul (SAMLG 6DR27)
Flavian.
<SAM253> South Gaul (SAMLG 4DR30)
Pre-Flavian.
<SAM254> Three sherds, south Gaul (SAMLG 5DR18)
Flavian.

<SAM255> DR18R, south Gaul (SAMLG 5DR18R)
Flavian.
Other fine and coarse wares:
SAND II.

Period 3

The period of activity was represented by the construction of three buildings with a narrow, c 3.5m, gravel road between the eastern and the central building (Fig 112; Fig 113). The middle of these buildings, and the best recorded, had three parallel walls aligned north–south with east–west aligned partition walls. Their arrangement was reminiscent of Roman barracks, with a narrow veranda on the east side overlooking the road and the barracks rooms in the range on the west. The building on the east side of the road also had partition walls in the eastern range and a veranda on the west. A small alleyway, with no traces of any gravel metalling,

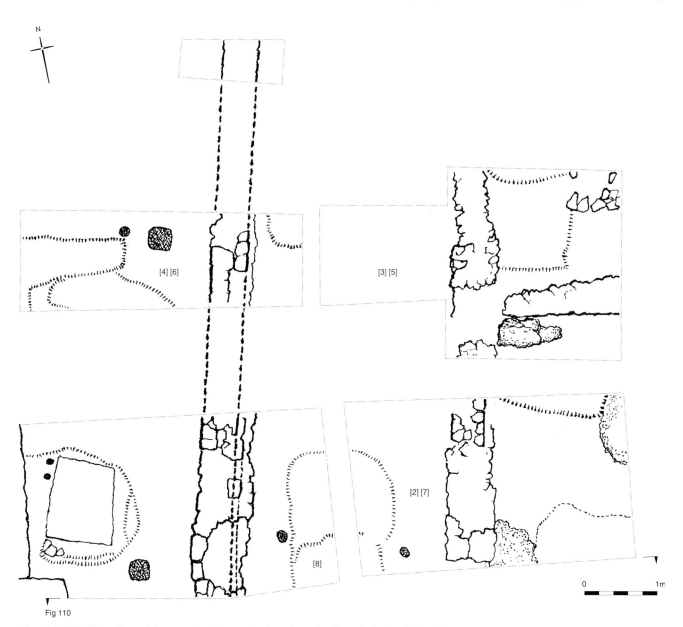

Fig 110

Fig 113 WFG22, plan of features in the north churchyard, all periods (scale 1:50)

separated the western block from the rear wall of another block to its west. Traces of *opus signinum* in one of the rooms in the central building gave an indication of the internal decoration, but there was little other evidence to show the function or decoration of these buildings. A partition wall in the central building had slumped into the fill of one of the underlying pits. Its repair included much reused material including a fragmentary tile with a PR BR LON stamp. The large pit containing layers [8] and [9] (Fig 110; Fig 113), dated to the mid 2nd century AD, represents a feature contemporary with the life of the fort that was used for rubbish disposal by its occupants. Significant finds from this period are illustrated on Fig 114 and Fig 115.

Layers contemporary with barracks

LAYER [5]
Pottery summary:
Small-sized assemblage.
Earliest date *c* AD 180; latest date *c* AD 400.

Fine and coarse wares:
HWC 2T; HWC 3 BDD; OXWW 7M11; BBS 5J.

LAYER [7]
Pottery summary:
Small-sized assemblage.
Earliest date *c* AD 120; latest date *c* AD 160.
Samian ware catalogue:
<SAM256> Central Gaul, with Cinnamus ovolo 1 (SAMCG 4DR37)
c AD 155–75.
<SAM257> South Gaul (SAMLG 5DR18)
Flavian–Trajanic.
Other fine and coarse wares:
BB2 2F; VRW 2; HWB 2.

LAYER [8] (LAYER FROM THE BOTTOM OF PIT 1 CONTEMPORARY WITH BARRACKS)
Pottery summary:
Medium-sized assemblage.
Earliest date *c* AD 140; latest date *c* AD 160.
Samian ware catalogue:
<SAM258> South Gaul (Fig 114)

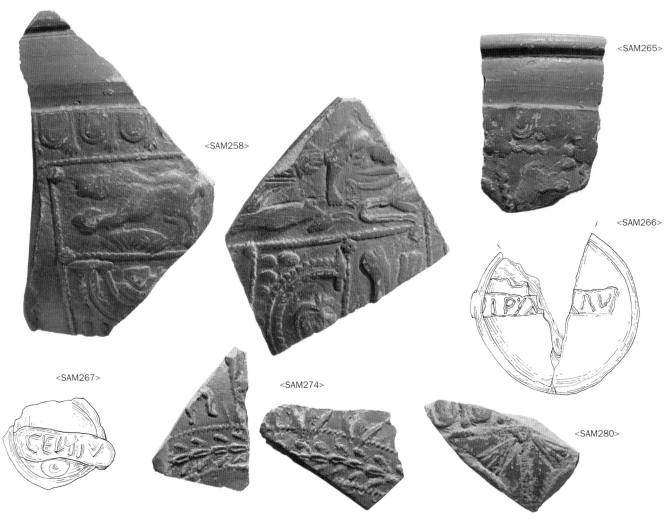

Fig 114 (above and facing) Selected samian vessels of period 3 from St Alban's church, Wood Street (WFG22): <SAM258>, <SAM265>–<SAM267>, <SAM274>, <SAM280>, <SAM284>, <SAM285>, <SAM287>, <SAM290>, <SAM295>, <SAM301>–<SAM305>, <SAM312> and <SAM314> (scale 1:1, stamp details 2:1)

<SAM284>

<SAM290>

<SAM285>

<SAM295>

<SAM301>

<SAM302>

<SAM303>

<SAM304>

<SAM287>

<SAM305>

<SAM312>

<SAM314>

Sherd link with layer [34], <SAM300>.

The style is characteristically late Flavian (cf eg the Holt material, Grimes 1930, especially no. 28). The Diana and hind is Oswald 1936–7, no. 103A, the boar, ibid, no. 1672 (SAMLG 4DR37).

c AD 85–105.

<SAM259> South Gaul (SAMLG 6DR27)

Flavian–Trajanic.

<SAM260> Central Gaul (SAMCG 5DR18/31)

Hadrianic–Antonine.

<SAM261> South Gaul (SAMLG 6DR27)

Late Flavian–Trajanic.

<SAM262> Two sherds, central Gaul (SAMCG 5DR18/31)

Hadrianic.

<SAM263> South Gaul (SAMLG 5DR18)

Flavian.

<SAM264> Central Gaul (SAMCG 6DR33)

Hadrianic.

Other fine and coarse wares:

LONW 4; AHSU 2D; AHSU 2C; AHSU 2T; LOXI 9A; HWC 2E; HWC 4; HWC+ 2F; HWC 3 BDD; BB1 2F6; BB1 2 AL; BB1 2F; HWC+ 2F AL; BB2 2F; BB2 4H1; ?BB1 4; BBS 4G AL; AHSU 2A; MLEZ ?5DR18; VRW 5J; VRW 4A; VRW 1E NFSE 1B7–9; AHSU 2T; HWC 3.

LAYER [9] (INCLUDING A–D INCLUSIVE) (FROM THE BOTTOM OF PIT 2 CONTEMPORARY WITH BARRACKS, BENEATH NORTH CHURCHYARD)

Pottery summary:

Large-sized assemblage.

Earliest date *c* AD 140; latest date *c* AD 160.

Samian ware catalogue:

<SAM265> In the style of Igocatus of les Martres-de-Veyre (SAMMV 4DR37) (Fig 114)

The ovolo and rosette are probably those on Stanfield and Simpson 1958, pl 17 nos 208, 209; the figure is not identifiable.

c AD 100–25.

<SAM266> Stamped by Epapra (die 1b) of les Martres-de-Veyre (SAMMV 6DR27) (Fig 114)

c AD 100–25.

<SAM267> Stamped by Genialis iii (die 3a) (SAMMV 6DR27) (Fig 114)

Genialis iii dies are found at les Martres-de-Veyre and at Lezoux. This example comes from les Martres-de-Veyre, by fabric.

c AD 110–25.

<SAM268> Central Gaul (SAMCG 6DR33)

Hadrianic–early Antonine.

<SAM269> South Gaul (SAMLG 5DR18/31)

Flavian–Trajanic.

<SAM270> Central Gaul (SAMCG 5DR18/31)

Trajanic–Hadrianic.

<SAM271> South Gaul (SAMLG 4CU11)

Flavian.

<SAM272> Central Gaul (SAMCG 6DR27)

Hadrianic–early Antonine.

<SAM273> South Gaul (SAMLG 5DR18R)

Flavian–Trajanic.

<SAM274> In the style of the Ioenalis-Donnaucus group at les Martres-de-Veyre (SAMMV 4DR37) (Fig 114)

Sherd link with layer [4].

The Hercules (Oswald 1936–7, no. 785) is on Stanfield and Simpson 1958, pl 40 no. 468, the small warrior (Oswald 1936–7, no. 202) on Stanfield and Simpson 1958, pl 36 no. 419, the basal wreath on pl 40 no. 462 and pl 47 no. 555. The foliage motif is also on pl 47 no. 555. The small warrior is not certainly identifiable.

c AD 100–25.

<SAM275> Early east Gaulish and probably la Madeleine (SAMEG 5DR18/31)

Hadrianic–early Antonine.

<SAM276> South Gaul (SAMLG 6DR27)

Flavian–Trajanic.

<SAM277> South Gaul (SAMLG 5DR18)

Flavian–Trajanic.

<SAM278> South Gaul (SAMLG 5DR18R)

Flavian–Trajanic.

Other fine and coarse wares:

LONW NCD; AHSU 2; ?AHSU 2T; SAND; HWC 3F; HWC 3 BDD; HWC 2F; HWC 4A; ?HWC 2T; HWC+ 4F; HWC 4F; HWC ?2E; HWC 3E; HWC 3 BDD; BB2 2 AL; BB2 2F AL; BB2 4H1; BB2 4; BB1 2A/6; BB1 2F AL; BB1 4G/H; BB1 4G AL; BB1 IV BUD; BB1 2F; VRW 4A; VCWS 1B7–9; VRW 1B; VRW 4; VRW 4A; VRW; VRW 7 HOF; BB1 4 AL.

LAYER [11] (CONTEMPORARY WITH BARRACKS)

Pottery summary:

Small-sized assemblage.

Earliest date *c* AD 120; latest date *c* AD 160.

Samian ware catalogue:

<SAM279> South Gaul (SAMLG 5DR18R)

Flavian–Trajanic.

Other fine and coarse wares:

VRG 4A; ERMS 2B; BB2 5J BUD; HWC 4F; BB2 4; VRW 7HOF; VRMI 3B EMB.

Pottery catalogue:

<P129> Early Roman micaceous sandy ware round-bodied jar with thickened or out-turned rim (ERMS 2B); (WFG22 P1) (Fig 115)

<P130> Verulamium region mica-dusted ware ovoid beaker with impressed decoration (VRMI 3B MPD); (WFG22 P2) (Fig 115)

<P131> Verulamium region grey ware reed-rimmed bowl (VRG 4A); (WFG22 P3) (Fig 115)

<P132> Highgate Wood ware C bowl with curved walls and flat, hooked or folded rim (HWC 4F); (WFG22 P4) (Fig 115)

<P133> Black-burnished ware 2 shallow simple dish with wavy line decoration (BB2 5J WL); (WFG22 P5) (Fig 115)

<P134> Verulamium region white ware hook-flanged mortarium (VRW 7HOF); (WFG22 P6) (Fig 115)

LAYER [19] (CONTEMPORARY WITH BARRACKS)

Pottery summary:
Small-sized assemblage.
Earliest date *c* AD 140; latest date *c* AD 200.
Samian ware catalogue:
<SAM280> In the style of DIVIXTUS of Lezoux (SAMCG 4DR37) (Fig 114)
The ovolo is on Stanfield and Simpson 1958, pl 116 no. 8, the fan motif on pl 116 no. 18.
c AD 145–75.
<SAM281> Central Gaul (SAMCG 5DR31R)
Late Antonine.
<SAM282> East Gaul (Trier) (SAMEG 5DR18R/ LUD Sb)
Late 2nd–mid 3rd century AD.
<SAM283> South Gaulish sherd (SAMLG)
Flavian.
Other fine and coarse wares:
VRW 7 BEF.
Pottery catalogue:
<P135> Verulamium region white ware bead and flange mortarium (VRW 7BEF) (Fig 115)

LAYER [23] (FROM FILL OF ROADSIDE GULLY)

Pottery summary:
Small-sized assemblage.
Earliest date *c* AD 160; latest date *c* AD 250.
Samian ware catalogue:
<SAM284> South Gaul (SAMLG 4DR37) (Fig 114)
Coarse cable borders, heavy arcading; the figure is probably Victory (Hermet 1934, pl 20 no. 103).
c AD 90–110.
<SAM285> (SAMMV 4DR37) (Fig 114)
With the ovolo and wavy lines used by Igocatus of les Martres-de-Veyre (Stanfield and Simpson 1958, pl 18 no. 228).
c AD 100–25.
<SAM286> Central Gaul (SAMCG 5DR18/31)
Early 2nd century AD.
Other fine and coarse wares:
HWC 3F; LOEG 4; BB2 2F9; BB1 2F; BB1 ?6.
Pottery catalogue:
<P136> Black-burnished ware 1 everted-rimmed jar with continuous curve (BB1 2F3); (WFG22 P8) (Fig 115)
<P137> Black-burnished ware 2 everted-rimmed jar with cavetto rim and vertical lines (BB2 2F9 VL); (WFG22 P9) (Fig 115)
<P138> Highgate Wood ware C everted-rimmed jar (HWC 2F); (WFG22 P10) (Fig 115)
<P139> Black-burnished ware 1 beaker (BB1 3); (WFG22 P11) (Fig 115)
<P140> Highgate Wood ware C poppy-head beaker (HWC 3F); (WFG22 P12) (Fig 115)
<P141> London eggshell ware bowl (LOEG 4); (WFG22 P13) (Fig 115)

LAYER [26] (PIT CONTEMPORARY WITH BARRACKS, IMMEDIATELY SOUTH OF CHURCH TOWER, UPPER LAYER)

Pottery summary:
Small-sized assemblage.
Earliest date *c* AD 120; latest date *c* AD 180.
Fine and coarse wares:
HWC 2T; BB2 4H.

LAYER [27] (PIT CONTEMPORARY WITH BARRACKS, IMMEDIATELY SOUTH OF CHURCH TOWER, LOWER LAYER)

Pottery summary:
Small-sized assemblage.
Earliest date *c* AD 70; latest date *c* AD 160.
Samian ware catalogue:
<SAM287> In the style of Ioenalis of les Martres-de-Veyre (SAMMV 4DR37) (Fig 114)
The warrior (Oswald 1936–7, no. 220) is on Stanfield and Simpson 1958, pl 36 no. 417, the crane (Oswald 1936–7, no. 2196) and beaded circles on Stanfield and Simpson 1958, pl 40 no. 470, and the basal wreath on pl 40 no. 472.
c AD 100–25.
<SAM288> South Gaul (SAMLG 5DR18)
Flavian.
<SAM289> Central Gaul (SAMCG 6DR27)
Early 2nd century AD.
Other fine and coarse wares:
HWC; HWC 2T; AHSU 2C; AHSU ?2D BUD; SAND 2T; CCGW; OXID 2.
Pottery catalogue:
<P142> Copthall Close grey ware necked jar (CCGW 2T); (WFG22 P14) (Fig 115)
<P143> Unsourced oxidised ware jar (OXID 2); (WFG22 P15) (Fig 115)

LAYER [28] (FILLING OF WEST GULLY, UNDER SOUTH TRANSEPT OF CHURCH)

Pottery summary:
Small-sized assemblage.
Earliest date *c* AD 70; latest date *c* AD 250.
Samian ware catalogue:
<SAM290> In the style of Donnaucus of les Martres-de-Veyre (Fig 114)
The horse and rider (Oswald 1936–7, no. 251) is on Stanfield and Simpson 1958, pl 44 no. 512, the lion (Oswald 1936–7, no. 1450) on pl 47 no. 558, the boar (ibid, no. 1664 or 1666), snake and rocks (ibid, no. 2155), ovolo and beads on Stanfield and Simpson 1958, pl 47 no. 555. The incomplete male figure is not certainly identifiable.
c AD 100–25.
Other fine and coarse wares:
Now missing.

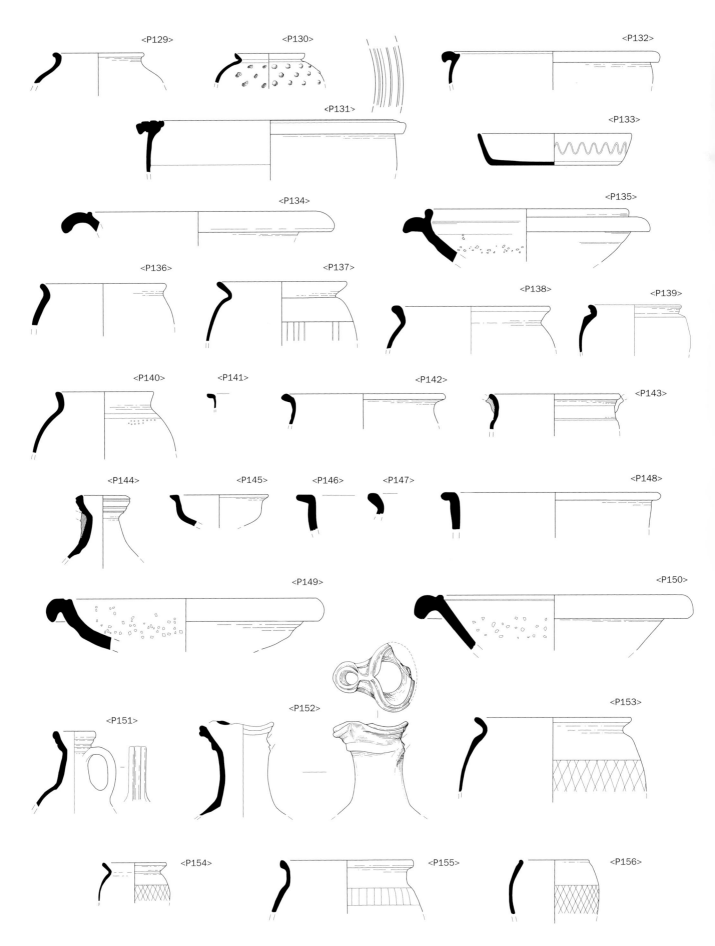

Fig 115 (above and facing) Selected pottery of period 3 from St Alban's church, Wood Street (WFG22): <P129>–<P172> (scale 1:4)

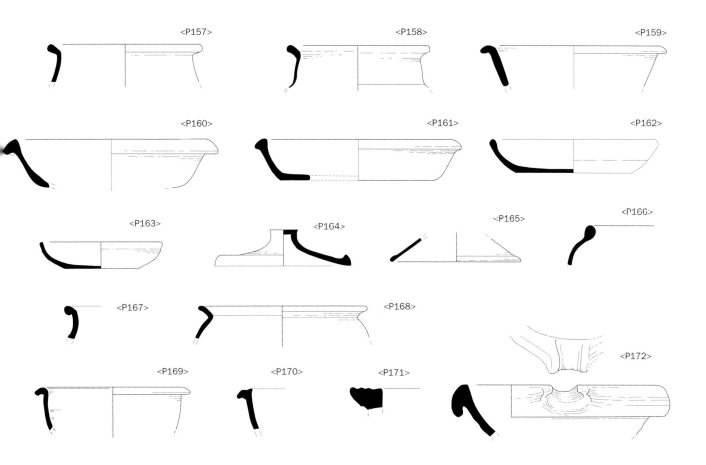

LAYER [32] (FROM TOP OF GULLY ON WEST SIDE OF BARRACKS)

Pottery summary:

Small-sized assemblage.

Earliest date *c* AD 140; latest date *c* AD 200.

Samian ware catalogue:

<SAM291> Central Gaul (SAMCG 5DR18/31)
Early 2nd century AD.

<SAM292> South Gaul, riveted (SAMLG 5DR31R)
Later Antonine.

<SAM293> Two central Gaulish sherds (SAMCG)

Other fine and coarse wares:

VCWS 1 B7–9; LOMI 4 MT35; VRW 7HOF; BB2 4H1; BB1 2F; BB2 2F.

Pottery catalogue:

<P144> Verulamium region coarse white-slipped ware ring-necked flagon with cupped mouth (VCWS 1B7–9); (WFG22 P16) (Fig 115)

<P145> London mica-dusted ware Marsh form 35 bowl (LOMI 4M35); (WFG22 P17) (Fig 115)

<P146> Black-burnished ware 1 everted-rimmed jar (BB1 2F); (WFG22 P18) (Fig 115)

<P147> Black-burnished ware 1 everted-rimmed jar (BB1 2F); (WFG22 P19) (Fig 115)

<P148> Black-burnished ware 2 round-rimmed bowl with acute lattice decoration (BB2 4H AL); (WFG22 P20) (Fig 115)

<P149> Verulamium region white ware hook-flanged mortarium (VRW 7HOF); (WFG22 P21) (Fig 115)

<P150> Verulamium region white ware hook-flanged mortarium (VRW 7HOF); (WFG22 P22) (Fig 115)

LAYER [33] (FROM BASE OF GULLY ON WEST SIDE OF BARRACKS)

Pottery summary:

Medium-sized assemblage.

Earliest date *c* AD 150; latest date *c* AD 250.

Samian ware catalogue:

<SAM294> Probably from Rheinzabern, with vertical incised palm leaves round the body (SAMEG 2DE72)
Antonine–early 3rd century AD.

<SAM295> Stamped by Viducos ii (die 5b) of les Martres-de-Veyre (SAMMV 6DR33) (Fig 114)
c AD 100–25.

<SAM296> Central Gaul, with unidentifiable stamp (SAMCG 5DR18/31)
Hadrianic–early Antonine.

<SAM297> South Gaul (SAMLG 5DR18/31)
Trajanic.

<SAM298> Central Gaul (SAMCG 5DR18/31)
Hadrianic.

<SAM299> South Gaul (SAMLG 6DR33)
Flavian–Trajanic.

Other fine and coarse wares:

NKSH; HWC 2E; HWC 9A; BB1 ?2F; BB1 4G; BB1 2F; BB2 4H1; BB2 2 AL; BB2 2F; BB2 2A F6; SAND 4/5; VCWS 1C; VCWS 1B7–9; OXID LOXI 9A; VRW; VRW 2H; NVCC 3; VRW ?2K; OXID 5.

Pottery catalogue:

<P151> Verulamium region coarse white-slipped ware ring-necked flagon with cupped mouth (VCWS 1B7–9); (WFG22 P23) (Fig 115)

<P152> Verulamium region coarse white-slipped ware pinch-mouthed flagon (VCWS 1C); (WFG22 P24) (Fig 115)

<P153> Black-burnished ware 1 everted-rimmed jar with acute lattice decoration (BB1 2F AL); (WFG22 P25) (Fig 115)

<P154> Black-burnished ware 2 everted-rimmed jar with acute lattice decoration (BB2 2F AL); (WFG22 P26) (Fig 115)

<P155> Highgate Wood ware C round-bodied necked jar with decorated shoulder (HWC 2E); (WFG22 P27) (Fig 115)

<P156> Black-burnished ware 2 bead-rimmed jar (BB2 2A17); (WFG22 P28) (Fig 115)

<P157> Verulamium region white ware large neckless jar with near-horizontal rim (VRW 2H); (WFG22 P29) (Fig 115)

<P158> Verulamium region white ware jar (VRW 2); (WFG22 P30) (Fig 115)

<P159> Black-burnished ware 1 flat-rimmed bowl with vertical wall and acute lattice decoration (BB1 4G AL); (WFG22 P31) (Fig 115)

<P160> Black-burnished ware 2 round-rimmed bowl with acute lattice decoration (BB2 4H AL); (WFG22 P32) (Fig 115)

<P161> Black-burnished ware 2 round-rimmed bowl with acute lattice decoration (BB2 4H AL); (WFG22 P33) (Fig 115)

<P162> Unsourced sand-tempered ware shallow simple dish (SAND 5J); (WFG22 P34) (Fig 115)

<P163> Unsourced oxidised ware dish (OXID 5); (WFG22 P35) (Fig 115)

<P164> London oxidised ware lid (LOXI 9A); (WFG22 P36) (Fig 115)

<P165> Highgate Wood ware C lid (HWC 9A); (WFG22 P37) (Fig 115)

LAYER [34] (FROM LAYER BENEATH GULLY TO EAST OF ROMAN FOUNDATION)

Pottery summary:
Small-sized assemblage.
Earliest date *c* AD 100; latest date *c* AD 160.
Samian ware catalogue:
<SAM300> South Gaul (SAMLG 4DR37)
Sherd link with layer [8].
The style is characteristically late Flavian (cf eg the Holt material, Grimes 1930, especially no. 28). The Diana and hind is Oswald 1936–7, no. 103A, the boar no. 1672.
c AD 85–105.
Other fine and coarse wares:
NKSH; LONW 4 NCD; AHSU 4K; OXID LOXI 9A.

LAYER [35] (FROM LAYER BENEATH GULLY TO EAST OF ROMAN FOUNDATION, INCLUDING 35C, E AND F)

Pottery summary:
Small-sized assemblage with some large sherds.
Earliest date *c* AD 120; latest date *c* AD 160.

Samian ware catalogue:
<SAM301> In the style of Ioenalis of les Martres-de-Veyre (SAMMV 4DR37) (Fig 114)
Stanfield and Simpson 1958, pl 40 no. 470 has the central chevron wreath, the plants and rosettes of the lower frieze and the basal band of circles; it may be from the same mould. Ibid, pl 40 no. 462 has the festoons with large rosettes, no. 461 the beaded circles used as an ovolo.
c AD 100–25.
<SAM302> In the style of Donnaucus of les Martres-de-Veyre (SAMMV 4DR37) (Fig 114)
The triton (Oswald 1936–7, no. 18) and foliage motif are on Stanfield and Simpson 1958, pl 45 no. 52, the dolphin (Oswald 1936–7, no. 2384) on Stanfield and Simpson 1958, pl 43 no. 491, and the snake and rocks (Oswald 1936–7, no. 2155) on Stanfield and Simpson 1958, pl 49 no. 584.
c AD 100–25.
<SAM303> Les Martres-de-Veyre (SAMMV 4DR37) (Fig 114)
The gladiator (Oswald 1936–7, no. 1004, usually paired with no. 1003), shield and crown motif are on Stanfield and Simpson 1958, pl 10 no. 127, the anchor motif on pl 11 no. 129, all by Drusus I.
c AD 100–25.
<SAM304> Les Martres-de-Veyre (SAMMV 4DR37) (Fig 114)
Sherd link with layer [29].
The small ovolo is probably one used by Ioenalis-Donnaucus (Stanfield and Simpson 1958, fig 10 no. 1).
c AD 100–25.
<SAM305> Dish stamped by Avitus iii (die 2a) of Lezoux (SAMCG 5DR42) (Fig 114)
c AD 125–50.
<SAM306> Central Gaul (SAMCG 5DR18/31)
Hadrianic.
<SAM307> East Gaul, probably la Madeleine (SAMEG 5DR18/31)
Mid 2nd century AD.
<SAM308> South Gaul (SAMLG INKWELL RI13)
Late 1st century AD.
<SAM309> Central Gaul (SAMCG 5DR36)
Hadrianic.
<SAM310> South Gaul (SAMLG 5DR18R)
Trajanic.
<SAM311> South Gaul (SAMLG 6DR27)
Flavian–Trajanic.
Other fine and coarse wares:
VRW 7 HOF, stamp LALLANS AD 90–130; VRW 1J; OXID LOXI 9A; VRW 7 stamp GISSUS AD 100–35; HOO/NKWS CAM 56; VRW ?1B5; OXID TRI; BB1 2F BUD; BBS 4H1; BB2 2F; BB1 2F; HWC 2F HWC ?2F AL; AHSU 2C.

LAYER [39] (LAYER AT TOP OF LARGE EARLY PIT UNDER WALL OF BARRACKS)

Pottery summary:
Small-sized assemblage.

Earliest date *c* AD 120; latest date *c* AD 160.
Samian ware catalogue:
<SAM312> South Gaul (SAMLG 4DR29) (Fig 114)
Sherd link with layer [12].
There are links with a bowl from Vechten stamped OFCEN, which has an upper frieze scroll with what may be the same bud; the lower frieze on the Vechten bowl includes all the elements here, with the exception of the small dog, in a similar arrangement.
c AD 70–85.
<SAM313> Bowl sherd, south Gaul (SAMLG 4)
Flavian.
Other fine and coarse wares:
ANSU 2A; AHSU 2T; AHSU 2; BB2 2F; ?AHSU 4F; VRMI 3 EMB; VRW 4A; OXID; NFSE 7.
Pottery catalogue:
<P166> Alice Holt/Surrey ware bead-rimmed jar (AHSU 2A); (WFG22 P38) (Fig 115)
<P167> Alice Holt/Surrey ware necked jar (AHSU 2T); (WFG22 P39) (Fig 115)
<P168> Black-burnished ware 2 everted-rimmed jar (BB2 2F); (WFG22 P40) (Fig 115)
<P169> ?Alice Holt/Surrey ware bowl with curved walls and flat, hooked or folded rim (?AHSU 4F); (WFG22 P41) (Fig 115)
<P170> Verulamium region white ware reed-rimmed bowl (VRW 4A); (WFG22 P42) (Fig 115)
<P171> Verulamium region white ware reed-rimmed bowl (VRW 4A); (WFG22 P43) (Fig 115)
<P172> North French/south-east English oxidised ware mortarium (NFSE 7); (WFG22 P44) (Fig 115)

LAYER [41] (FROM BUFF LOAM AROUND BARRACKS WALL AT EAST END OF SITE)
Pottery summary:
Small-sized assemblage.
Earliest date *c* AD 120; latest date *c* AD 160.
Samian ware catalogue:
<SAM314> Stamped by Felicio iii of Montans (SAMMT 5DR18/31) (Fig 114)
c AD 110–45.
<SAM315> Two sherds, central Gaul (SAMCG 5DR18/31)
First half of 2nd century AD.
Other fine and coarse wares:
Now missing.

Period 4

Evidence for the end of Roman activity on this site is sparse. Truncation and disturbance by medieval grave digging, including the clearance of these graves by contractors in the 1950s (W F Grimes, pers comm), considerably disturbed the upper levels of this site. Part of one of the barracks walls had been cut by a shallow pit (layers [2], [3], [3a]), which might be an early medieval feature. Material found in it, however, is consistent with a 3rd- or 4th-century date. Some of the

material immediately over the barracks was described as 'dark earth'.

Layers post-dating the barracks

LAYER [1] (IN 'DARK EARTH' ABOVE BARRACKS)
Pottery summary:
Small-sized assemblage.
Earliest date *c* AD 270; latest date *c* AD 400.
Samian ware catalogue:
<SAM316> Central Gaul in the style of Divixtus (SAMCG 4DR37) (Fig 116)
The Minerva (Oswald 1936–7, no. 126) is on Stanfield and Simpson 1958, pl 115 no. 6, the beads and hollow circle on pl 116 no. 17; the Venus is Oswald 1936–7, no. 293A.
c AD 145–75.
<SAM317> In the style of Cinnamus of Lezoux (SAMCG 4DR37) (Fig 116)
His ovolo with a mask in a wreath festoon is as Stanfield and Simpson 1958, pl 159 no. 23.
c AD 155–75.
<SAM318> Central Gaul (SAMCG 4DR37)
Hadrianic–Antonine.
<SAM319> Central Gaulish bowl sherds (SAMCG 4)
Other fine and coarse wares:
HWC 2E; HWC 3F; OXRC 4DR38; NVCC; CC; RWS 7 BEF; GROG 4M; BB1 2FX; BB2 4H1.
Pottery catalogue:
<P173> Black-burnished ware 1 everted-rimmed jar (BB1 2F); (WFG22 P45) (Fig 117)
<P174> Highgate Wood ware C round-bodied necked jar with decorated shoulder (HWC 2E); (WFG22 P46) (Fig 117, decoration not shown)
<P175> Highgate Wood ware C poppy-head beaker (HWC 3F); (WFG22 P47) (Fig 117)
<P176> Black-burnished ware 2 round-rimmed bowl (BB2 4H); (WFG22 P48) (Fig 117)
<P177> Unsourced grog-tempered ware flanged bowl (GROG 4M); (WFG22 P49) (Fig 117)
<P178> Unsourced white-slipped ware bead and flange mortarium (RWS 7BEF); (WFG22 P50) (Fig 117)

LAYER [4] (IN 'DARK EARTH' ABOVE BARRACKS)
Pottery summary:
Small-sized assemblage.
Earliest date *c* AD 250; latest date *c* AD 400.
Samian ware catalogue:
<SAM320> Central Gaul, with Cinnamus ovolo 1 (SAMCG 4DR37) (Fig 116)
The figure is probably Oswald 1936–7, no. 394; beaded rosettes are not common in Cinnamus's work, but cf Stanfield and Simpson 1958, pl 157 no. 8, which is unstamped.
c AD 155–75.
<SAM321> In the style of the Ioenalis-Donnaucus

Fig 116 Selected samian vessels of period 4 from St Alban's church, Wood Street (WFG22): <SAM316>, <SAM317>, <SAM320>– <SAM322>, <SAM340> and <SAM341> (scale 1:1)

group at les Martres-de-Veyre (SAMMV 4DR37) (Fig 116)
Sherd link with layer [9].
The Hercules (Oswald 1936–7, no. 785) is on Stanfield and Simpson 1958, pl 40 no. 468, the small warrior (Oswald no. 202) on pl 36 no. 419, the basal wreath on pl 40 no. 462 and pl 47 no. 555 and the foliage motif is also on pl 47 no. 555. The small warrior is not certainly identifiable.
c AD 100–25.
<SAM322> (SAMCG 4DR37) (Fig 116)
With the small ovolo used by Ioenalis-Donnaucus (Stanfield and Simpson 1958, fig 10 no. 1). The cupid is probably Oswald 1936–7, no. 422.
c AD 100–25.
<SAM323> South Gaul (SAMLG 5DR35)
Flavian.
<SAM324> South Gaul (SAMLG 5DR18)
Flavian.
<SAM325> South Gaul, unstamped (SAMLG 6DR27)
Trajanic.
<SAM326> South Gaul (SAMLG 5DR18)
Flavian–Trajanic.
<SAM327> South Gaul (SAMLG 6DR27)
Flavian–Trajanic.
Other fine and coarse wares:
VRW 9C; DR20 stamp; VRW 5J; LOEG 4 M34;

HWC 2E; BB2 2F; BBS 4M; CC 4A CC; NKSH; BB2 4H5; LOMA 4; VRW 2T; VRW 1; VRW 7; HWC 3F.

LAYER [6] (IN 'DARK EARTH' ABOVE BARRACKS)
Pottery summary:
Small-sized assemblage.
Earliest date *c* AD 350; latest date *c* AD 400.
Samian ware catalogue:
<SAM328> South Gaul (SAMLG 5DR18)
Early–mid Flavian.
<SAM329> South Gaul (SAMLG 5DR18R)
Early–mid Flavian.
Other fine and coarse wares:
PORD 2; OXID LOXI 4A; HWC 3 BDD; BB1 2F; BB1 4M BUD; OXID 1/AMPH HANDLE.

LAYER [31] (IN 'DARK EARTH' ABOVE BARRACKS)
Pottery summary:
Small-sized assemblage.
Earliest date *c* AD 270; latest date *c* AD 400.
Samian ware catalogue:
<SAM330> East Gaul (Trier) (SAMEG 4DR45)
Late 2nd–mid 3rd century AD.
<SAM331> South Gaul (SAMLG 6DR27)
Flavian.

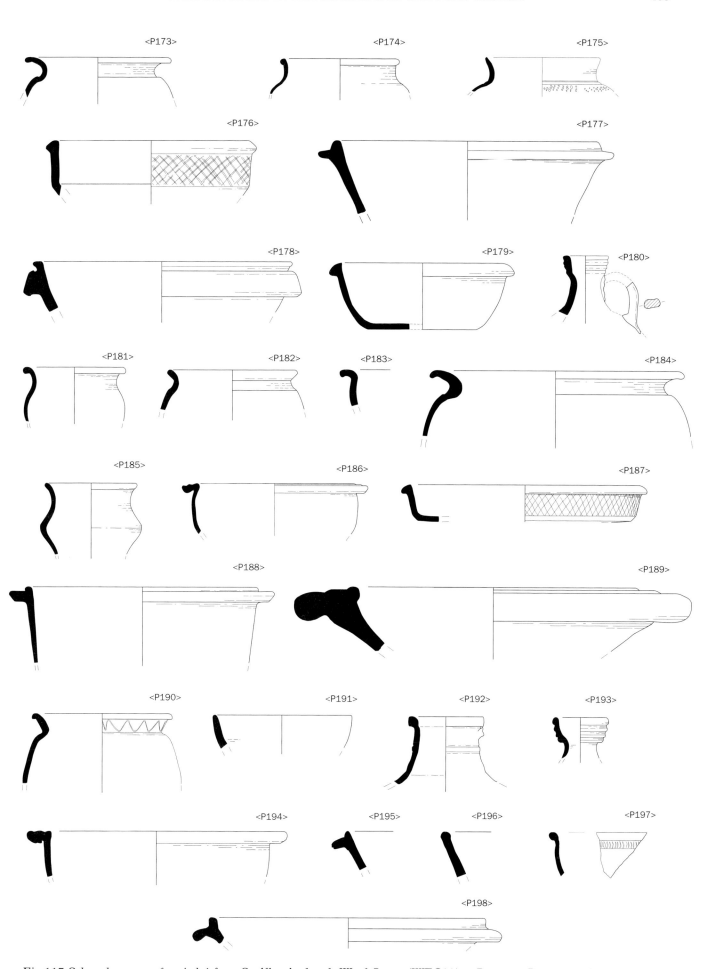

Fig 117 Selected pottery of period 4 from St Alban's church, Wood Street (WFG22): <P173>–<P198> (scale 1:4)

Other fine and coarse wares:
BB2 4H1 AL; OXRC ROD.
Pottery catalogue:
<P179> Black-burnished ware 2 round-rimmed bowl with acute lattice decoration (BB2 4H AL); (WFG22 P51) (Fig 117, decoration not shown)

LAYER [2] (IN SHALLOW HOLLOW CUTTING TOP OF BARRACKS WALL)

Pottery summary:
Small-sized assemblage.
Earliest date *c* AD 270; latest date *c* AD 400.
Samian ware catalogue:
<SAM332> Central Gaul with Cinnamus ovolo (SAMCG 4DR37)
c AD 155–75.
<SAM333> South Gaul (SAMLG 5DR18)
Flavian.
<SAM334> Central Gaul, top of ovolo (SAMCG 4DR37)
Antonine.
<SAM335> Central Gaul (SAMCG 5DR31)
Antonine.
<SAM336> Central Gaul, over fired (SAMCG 5DR31)
Antonine.
<SAM337> East Gaul (Trier) (SAMEG 5DR18/LUD Sa)
Late 2nd–mid 3rd century AD.
<SAM338> Bowl, east Gaul, worn inside (SAMEG 4)
Late 2nd–mid 3rd century AD.
Other fine and coarse wares:
RHWW VERECUNDUS TYPE; VRW 1; VRW 4A; CC ?1; NVCC 3; OXRC 4 WPD; MHAD RLD; BB2 2F; OXWW; HWC 3 BDD; BB1 2F BUD; SAND ?4 4G.
Pottery catalogue:
<P180> Verulamium region white ware ring-necked flagon (VRW 1B); (WFG22 P52) (Fig 117)
<P181> Unsourced sand-tempered ware necked jar (SAND 2T); (WFG22 P53) (Fig 117)
<P182> Black-burnished ware 1 everted-rimmed jar (BB1 2F); (WFG22 P54) (Fig 117)
<P183> Black-burnished ware 2 everted-rimmed jar (BB2 2F); (WFG22 P55) (Fig 117)
<P184> Black-burnished ware 1 later everted-rimmed jar (BB1 2FX); (WFG22 P56) (Fig 117)
<P185> Unsourced sand-tempered ware carinated beaker with tall upright plain rim (SAND 3G); (WFG22 P57) (Fig 117)
<P186> Verulamium region white ware reed-rimmed bowl (VRW 4A); (WFG22 P58) (Fig 117)
<P187> Black-burnished ware 2 round-rimmed bowl with acute lattice decoration (BB2 4H AL); (WFG22 P59) (Fig 117)
<P188> Black-burnished-style ware flanged bowl with intersecting arcs decoration (BBS 4M ARCS); (WFG22 P60) (Fig 117, decoration not shown)
<P189> Rhineland white ware mortarium (RHWW

7); (WFG22 P61) (Fig 117)

LAYER [3] AND [3A] (IN SHALLOW HOLLOW CUTTING TOP OF BARRACKS WALL)

Pottery summary:
Small-sized assemblage.
Earliest date *c* AD 250; latest date *c* AD 400.
Samian ware catalogue:
<SAM339> South Gaul, broken ovolo (SAMLG 4DR37)
Flavian.
<SAM340> In the style of Advocisus of Lezoux (SAMCG 4DR37) (Fig 116)
The ovolo with similar beads, arrowhead motif and double festoon are on Stanfield and Simpson 1958, pl 114 no. 28; the boar is Oswald 1936–7, no. 1668.
c AD 150–80.
Other fine and coarse wares:
VRW 4; VRW 1; VRW IMP; VRW 4A; OXWS M17; RWS 1B7–9; NVCC 3; BB1 4M BUD; AHFA 2T; OXRC 4DR38; OXRC NE ROD; MHAD; VRW 1B; BB1 2FX; BBS 4M; BB2 4H1; ?HWC 2T; FINE 2/3; BB1 2F BUD; AHFA 5J.
Pottery catalogue:
<P190> Black-burnished ware 1 everted-rimmed jar with slightly upright decorated rim (BB1 2F2 AL BUD); (WFG22 P62) (Fig 117)
<P191> Alice Holt/Farnham ware shallow simple dish (AHFA 5J); (WFG22 P63) (Fig 117)
<P192> Verulamium region white ware two-handled flagon with squat bulbous body (VRW 1E); (WFG22 P64) (Fig 117)
<P193> Brockley Hill white-slipped ware ring-necked flagon with cupped mouth (BHWS 1B7–9); (WFG22 P65) (Fig 117)
<P194> Verulamium region white ware reed-rimmed bowl (VRW 4A); (WFG22 P66) (Fig 117)
<P195> Black-burnished ware 1 flanged bowl with intersecting arcs decoration (BB1 4M ARCS); (WFG22 P67) (Fig 117, decoration not shown)
<P196> Verulamium region white ware bowl (VRW 4); (WFG22 P68) (Fig 117)
<P197> Oxfordshire red/brown colour-coated ware necked bowl with rouletted decoration (OXRC 4N ROD); (WFG22 P69) (Fig 117)
<P198> Oxfordshire white-slipped ware necked Young form 17 mortarium (OXWS 7M17); (WFG22 P70) (Fig 117)

LAYER [20] (AS LAYER [37] TOP)

Pottery summary:
Small-sized assemblage.
Earliest date *c* AD 270; latest date *c* AD 400.
Other fine and coarse wares:
OXRC 4DR38; HWC 3B BDD; BB2 4H1.

LAYER [37] (AS LAYER [20] TOP)

Pottery summary:
Small-sized assemblage.

Earliest date *c* AD 270; latest date *c* AD 400.

Samian ware catalogue:

<SAM341> In the style of Doeccus of Lezoux (SAMCG 4DR37) (Fig 116)

The leaf in a double medallion is on Stanfield and Simpson 1958, pl 151 no. 55 and the figure may be the boar shown there; the two small leaves are on pl 150 no. 42.

c AD 165–200.

<SAM342> Central Gaul (SAMCG 4DR37)

Several potters used the ornamental leaf; the details are too abraded to suggest attribution.

c AD 130–60.

<SAM343> East Gaul (Rheinzabern) (SAMEG 5DR31R/LUD Sb)

Late 2nd or 3rd century AD.

Other fine and coarse wares:

OXRC 4; OXRC 4DR38; BB1 4M; OXRC 4DR38.

9.5 WFG22a, St Mary the Virgin, Aldermanbury

1967–8 (unpublished by W F Grimes; Fig 5; Fig 6; Fig 106). NGR: TQ 32414 81455

The church of St Mary Aldermanbury was the last major excavation conducted by the RMLEC (Fig 118). The fabric of the church had been dismantled between 1961 and 1963 and transported to Fulton, Missouri, USA, where its rebuilding was completed in May 1969.

The excavations on the site of the church were conducted in 1967–8, too late for a summary to appear in Grimes's 1968 summary of work. Only material from a gully pre-dating the fort could be associated with the records for this site. The remaining finds assemblages of Roman date are all small, with samian ware coming from the late 1st to mid 2nd century AD. A few east Gaulish sherds were noted as well as a single Argonne ware (ARGO) fragment (of a Chenet 320 from layer [17]; Chenet 1941).

Period 1

Natural soil consisted of brickearth. It was not possible to examine it in any detail and so no evidence for pre-Roman activity could be identified.

Period 2

The earliest features on the site were sealed by the gravel alleyway, which ran between the two later buildings identified here (Fig 119). These consisted of some shallow pits and an approximately north–south aligned gully. Finds from this feature (layers [12b]–[12d] inclusive) are all Flavian. Unfortunately, this was the only Roman feature that could be associated with its finds.

In one deep excavation trench under the church a black loam layer seen at the base of the trench was identified as a redeposited natural soil. It lay directly on dirty brickearth, which in its turn lay over and

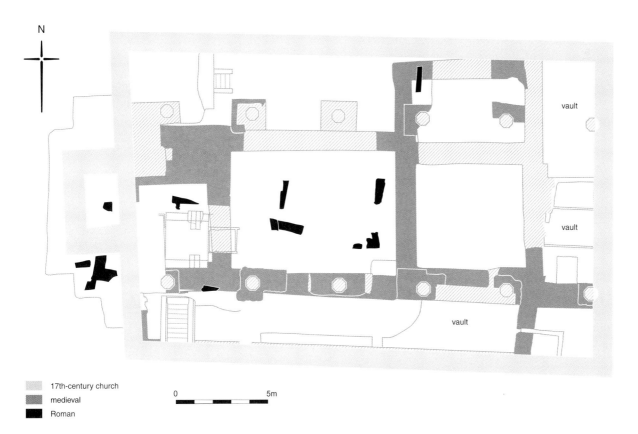

N

17th-century church
medieval
Roman

0   5m

Fig 118 WFG22a, general plan of excavations at the site of St Mary Aldermanbury (scale 1:200)

N

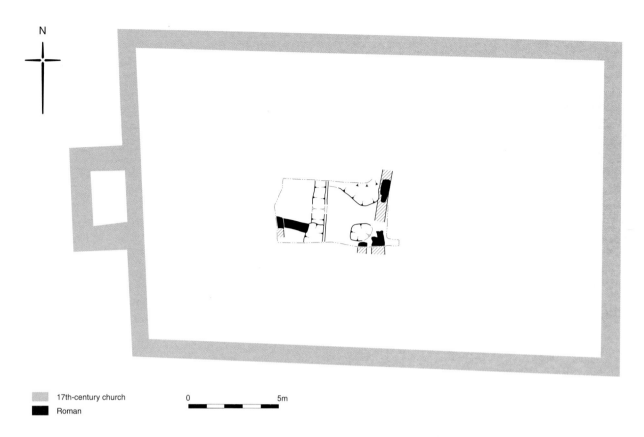

☐ 17th-century church

■ Roman

0   5m

Fig 119 WFG22a, plan of the period 2 features (after G Brown) (scale 1:200)

continued beneath the mortared wall foundation of one of the walls of the buildings associated with the fort. This brickearth was clearly redeposited; it produced some pottery throughout its depth, and where it rested on natural soil (readily distinguished by its redder colour) the interface between the two was demarcated by a charcoal-stained silty deposit. Significant finds are illustrated in Fig 120.

Fill of gully pre-dating gravel alleyway between the Roman buildings

LAYER [12B]
Pottery summary:
Small-sized assemblage.
Earliest date *c* AD 70; latest date *c* AD 100.
Samian ware catalogue:
<SAM344> South Gaul, stamped by Rufinus (SAMLG 4DR29) (Fig 120)
Sherd links with layers [12C] and [12D].
The upper frieze consists of panels of arrowheads separating alternate panels of two birds and an eagle (Oswald 1936–7, no. 2175, no. 2231 and no. 2271) and of paired festoons with birds (no. 2289 and incomplete). The lower frieze scroll includes elements found on other Rufinus bowls; the small goose (Knorr 1919, table 68 no. 5), the triple poppy heads (ibid, table 68 no. 18) and the leaves at the base (as on a bowl from Torre Annunziata; B R Hartley, pers comm). A bowl from the same mould as Neuss is stamped

PRIMIM (Mary 1967, table 10 no. 1). The stamp reads OF.RVFIN, die 2b, Rufinus ii of la Graufesenque.
c AD 80–95, but probably before AD 85 on this form.
<SAM345> DR27, stamped OFRVFU[N]: die 4c, Rufinus ii of la Graufesenque (SAMLG 6DR27) (Fig 120)
c AD 70–90.
<SAM346> Stamped SILVINIF: die 8a, Silvinus of la Graufesenque (SAMLG 5DR18) (Fig 120)
c AD 70–85.
<SAM347> South Gaul (SAMLG 5DR18)
Neronian–Flavian.
<SAM348> Two sherds, south Gaul (SAMLG 6DR27)
Neronian–Flavian.
Other fine and coarse wares:
HWB/C 4F; ERMS 2B; ?AHSU 2T; SAND RUST; VRW 1B2; LOMI 4 MT14; VRW 7 HOF stamp ...]LVD.
Pottery catalogue:
<P199> Verulamium region white ware ring-necked flagon with flared mouth (VRW 1B2)
<P200> Early Roman micaceous sandy ware round-bodied jar with thickened or out-turned rim (ERMS 2B)
<P201> Alice Holt/Surrey ware necked jar (AHSU 2T)
<P202> Alice Holt/Surrey ware necked jar (AHSU 2T)
<P203> Unsourced sand-tempered ware jar with rusticated decoration (SAND 2 RUST)
<P204> Copthall Close ?grey ware bowl with curved walls and flat, hooked or folded rim (CCGW 4F)
<P205> London mica-dusted ware bowl (LOMI 4)

<SAM344>

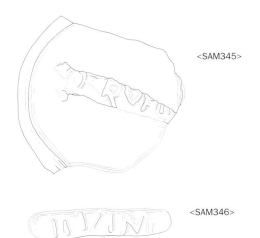

<SAM345>

<SAM346>

*Fig 120 Selected samian vessels <SAM344>–<SAM346>
of period 2 from St Mary Aldermanbury (WFG22a) (scale
1:1, stamp details 2:1)*

LAYER [12C]
Pottery summary:
Small-sized assemblage.
Earliest date *c* AD 70; latest date *c* AD 100.
Samian ware catalogue:
<SAM349> (SAMLG 4DR29)
Sherd link with <SAM344> from [12B] and
<SAM353> from [12D].
<SAM350> Two sherds, south Gaul (SAMLG 5DR18)
Flavian.
<SAM351> South Gaul (SAMLG 5DR35)
Flavian.
<SAM352> South Gaul (SAMLG 5DR18R)
Flavian.

LAYER [12D]
Pottery summary:
Small-sized assemblage.

Earliest date *c* AD 70; latest date *c* AD 100.

Samian ware catalogue:

<SAM353> (SAMLG 4DR29)

Sherd link with <SAM344> from [12B] and <SAM349> from [12C].

<SAM354> South Gaul (SAMLG 4DR29)

Panels in lower frieze with ?hare and tendrils. Heavily burnt.

c AD 70–85.

<SAM355> South Gaul (SAMLG 6DR27)

Stamped with illiterate die.

Flavian.

<SAM356> South Gaul (SAMLG 6DR27)

Flavian.

<SAM357> Two sherds, south Gaul (SAMLG 5DR18)

Neronian–Flavian.

Other fine and coarse wares:

Now missing.

Period 3

The wall referred to in period 2 above seemed, therefore, to have been set in made-up ground, perhaps the filling of a large pit or hollow. This could not be explored further. The wall seemed to be entirely foundation; an irregular offset, which might have indicated its dimensions and limit, was not continuous.

An adjacent wall was only partially seen; *c* 1.25m in length and a maximum width of just 0.25m at the south end. It passed obliquely out of the cutting under the medieval chapel foundation on the north side and under one of Wren's pier base foundations to the south. The justification for regarding it as Roman was that it was entirely made of ragstone fragments set in a green-yellow clay. The foundation was set in dirty looking buff clay which may not be natural but, the excavator believed, could not be far off it. The surface of the buff clay was burnt (truly burnt) in the area below the north-west angle of the chapel, the burning passing into the trench sides. This surface was *c* 3.3m below the church floor. The whole deposit between the buff clay and the bottom of the church floor was disturbed burial soil.

As can be seen, the Roman features related to the fort were very fragmentary but can be reconstructed as two north–south aligned barracks rooms with a narrow gravelled alleyway between (Fig 121).

Period 4

No post-fort activity could be identified with precision. All of the coins from the later levels, however, are late Roman in date.

Coins

Four coins of late 3rd- and 4th-century date were recovered. These can no longer be associated with the site sequence.

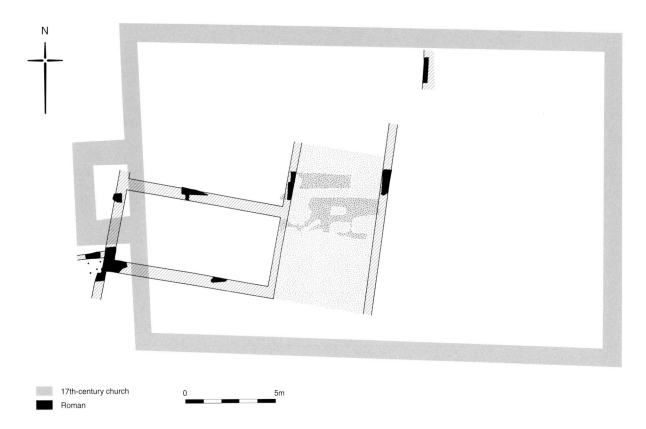

N

| | 17th-century church |
| | Roman |

0   5m

Fig 121 WFG22a, plan of the period 3 features (after G Brown) (scale 1:200)

<S79> Copper-alloy coin
WFG22a <6>, unstratified
Radiate copy.
?Late 3rd century AD.
<S80> Copper-alloy coin
WFG22a <2>, layer [6]
Associated with late 3rd- and 4th-century pottery.
Diam 18mm.
?Late 3rd or 4th century AD.
<S81> Copper-alloy coin
WFG22a <5>, layer [16e]
House of Constantine; Diam 17mm.
Associated with 3rd- and 4th-century pottery;
early–mid 4th century AD.
<S82> Copper-alloy coin
WFG22a <20>, layer [19a]
Diam 18mm.
Associated with a small assemblage of 4th-century
pottery. ?Late 3rd or 4th century AD.

Tools

<S83> Greensand hone
WFG22a <22>, layer [8]
One end straight, the other angled. Max dimensions:
L 102mm; W 61mm; Th 24.5mm.
Associated with late 3rd- and 4th-century pottery.
<S84> Hone fragment
WFG22a <24>, layer [16B]
One end, though rough, is probably original. Surviving
L 42mm; section 23 × 26mm.
Associated with late 3rd- and 4th-century pottery.

Miscellaneous object

<S85> Copper-alloy ring
WFG22a <31>, layer [16C]
Penannular ring. Internal Diam 13.5mm.
Associated with 2nd- to 4th-century pottery.

10 The Cripplegate fort and Londinium

John Shepherd and Stephanie Chettle

10.1 Introduction

We have known of a Roman fort in the Cripplegate area of the City of London for over 60 years now. Along with structures such as the forum and basilica buildings on the opposite, east, side of the Walbrook, the fort is one of the largest and most apparent structures representing the presence of the Roman administration in Londinium. But whereas the forum and basilica, and other public buildings and construction works such as the waterfronts, baths and the amphitheatre, have attracted much attention, resulting in a certain level of understanding about their roles, that of the fort and the nature of its relationship with the rest of Londinium and, indeed, the province as a whole, has never been properly resolved. As a result it seems at times to sit rather uneasily not only in the Roman landscape of Londinium but also in the copious amount of literature produced about Roman London over the last 60 years.

There has been of course much study and discussion about the level and nature of the military presence in 1st- and early 2nd-century AD Londinium, pre-dating the Cripplegate fort. This has largely focused upon potential conquest period remains in Southwark (equipment in particular) and the possible military origin of mid 1st-century features in the Aldgate area. To these can now be added the immediate post-Boudican remains of a fort on the Plantation Place site on the east side of the City near Fenchurch Street (FER97; Treveil 2003, 34–40; Dunwoodie et al in prep). Work too on the waterfront, *c* AD 64, has demonstrated military involvement with its construction (Brigham 1998, 25–7). To this can be added epigraphic remains (Chapter 11.2 contains a list of inscriptions from Roman London with military connections), the tombstone of the so-called 'Camomile Street' soldier, sadly lacking an inscription, but probably of Flavian or Trajanic date (Bishop 1983). And, of course, there is the reference to a soldier posted to London in a document from Vindolanda (Northumberland), *c* AD 100, detailing unit strengths (Bowman et al 1990). Military equipment abounds in Londinium, not just from the pre-Hadrianic period, and this too has attracted much study (Bishop et al in prep). However, many of these might be incidental occurrences of military involvement or, in the case of equipment, casual losses not related to garrisons. Firm evidence for the long-term military presence in Londinium during the second half of the 1st and early 2nd century AD has yet to be demonstrated.

The Cripplegate fort appears, as will be discussed below (10.5), during the Hadrianic period. Unfortunately, and it has to be admitted, the lack of any epigraphic evidence is a serious obstacle for researchers; the role and function – even a convincing indication – of its garrison is not forthcoming. When it is included in studies of 2nd-century Londinium it is conveniently used to give status to the city as being there to accommodate the soldiers serving on the governor's staff and bodyguard. Or is it the location of the procurator, or other senior military officials for the province as a whole? But, of course, there is a paradox here. If, as is also generally believed, the governor of the province was based in Londinium during the late 1st century AD, what precisely were the arrangements for housing his staff in the town? If, by the early 2nd century AD, an area of 11 acres (*c* 4.5ha) was required, is it not only logical to suppose that a similarly sized area was required for the late 1st-century garrison?

Attention has been refocused upon the Cripplegate fort recently by a succession of excavations by Pre-Construct Archaeology Ltd (PCA) and MOLA in the region. PCA examined a large area to the west of Noble Street, outside the city defences, in the re-entrant angle to the east of Aldersgate (Butler 2001). This was primarily concerned with the post-Roman sequence on the site, but it did reveal evidence of the Roman fort ditch – as well as a second, possibly parallel ditch, slightly further to the west suggesting that, at least on the west side, the fort had more than one ditch (Fig 122).

The work of MOLA, however, has been more substantial and has been focused upon the southern side of the fort, including large areas of the interior (Howe and Lakin 2004; Lyon 2004). The publications for these excavations are essential reading for researching the detail of activity in the Cripplegate area – much more so than the Grimes record presented here – but apart from producing a quality of data that enables a much more intensive interrogation than the Grimes material, the results regarding the fort sequence appear to corroborate much of Grimes's work. The accompanying discussions of the Roman sequence, however, are vital to the results presented here (Howe and Lakin 2004, 47–59; Lyon 2004, 165–6) and reference is made to them throughout the following account. These recent excavations have provided a clarity that, with hindsight, enables us to interpret better the data collected by Grimes (Fig 123).

Howe and Lakin (2004, 57–9) also include a revised assessment of the composition of the garrison of the fort based upon their better understanding of the layout and design of the buildings in the *praetentura* of the fort. This is a useful addition to the discussion about the complement of the fort, the first being produced over 30 years ago (Hassall 1973). A revision of this subject is included below (10.7).

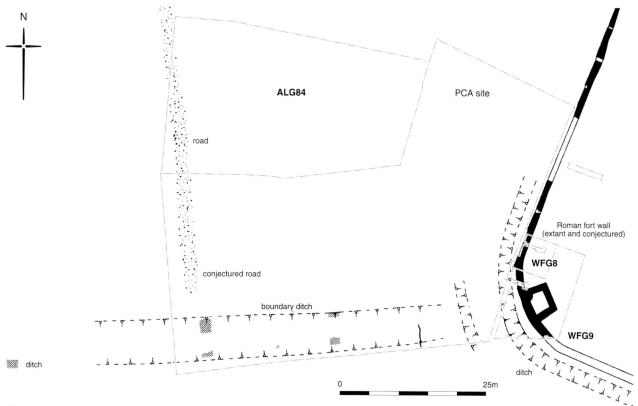

N

ALG84

PCA site

road

Roman fort wall
(extant and conjectured)

WFG8

conjectured road

boundary ditch

WFG9

ditch

ditch

0   25m

Fig 122 Plan showing Grimes, MOLA (ALG84) and PCA data for the west side of the fort (after Butler 2001) (scale 1:625)

Until the publication by Howe and Lakin (2004) the fort, which Grimes regarded as 'perhaps the outstanding event in the twentieth-century archaeological study of London' (1968, 38), had yet to be properly considered in all its varied aspects. It may be that others have been awaiting the detailed account of the archaeological sequence as recorded by Grimes, but it is significant that, until the work of Butler, Howe, Lakin and Lyon (above), there had been very little new, intensive archaeological work in the Cripplegate area during the second half of the 20th century.

Now that the results of new work are in the public domain, a repeat of the observations and conclusions made by the more recent commentators would be superfluous. However, there are some issues, which still need to be addressed, some of which concerned Grimes and led him to examine the fort in the way he did. There is also, of course, the date of the fort, which it can be argued can be provided more convincingly by the evidence from Grimes's work than by any site examined more recently.

To begin with, therefore, the discussion below examines the natural landscape and the earliest identifiable Roman occupation and the nature of the early Roman occupation not just under the 2nd-century fort but slightly beyond in the area of Aldersgate, including areas to the north and west. This area has been neglected in many of the recent studies of Roman London. In particular, the area west of the Walbrook and the available evidence does suggest that there was

occupation of varying levels of intensity throughout the area of Cripplegate and the region to the north and west.

There then follows a brief discussion about the relationship between the fort and the town, referring largely to the conclusions offered by Howe and Lakin (2004). This also looks back to the 1st century AD and suggests that the area to the west of the Walbrook, but further south of the later fort, may have been a zone in which the activities contained within the fort had previously been housed. This is followed by a discussion on the size and complement of the garrison by Mark Hassall with a review of later, 3rd-century, military occupation in Southwark.

The construction of the city wall and its effect upon the fort is discussed. A historical context for the instigation of this major building programme, which pertinently included the fort in its circuit, is briefly presented, but a more detailed discussion examining the full role and function of the landward city wall circuit is far beyond the scope of this volume. There is little doubt now that the fort ceased to be used during the 3rd century AD, perhaps as early as the beginning of the century. The evidence for occupation in the fort area, especially on Grimes's sites, during the 3rd and 4th centuries AD is assessed, but the question regarding where the military went during this period is, once again, beyond the scope of this volume. This discussion will not answer the many outstanding questions about the fort, but hopefully it will help to encourage the debate about its role.

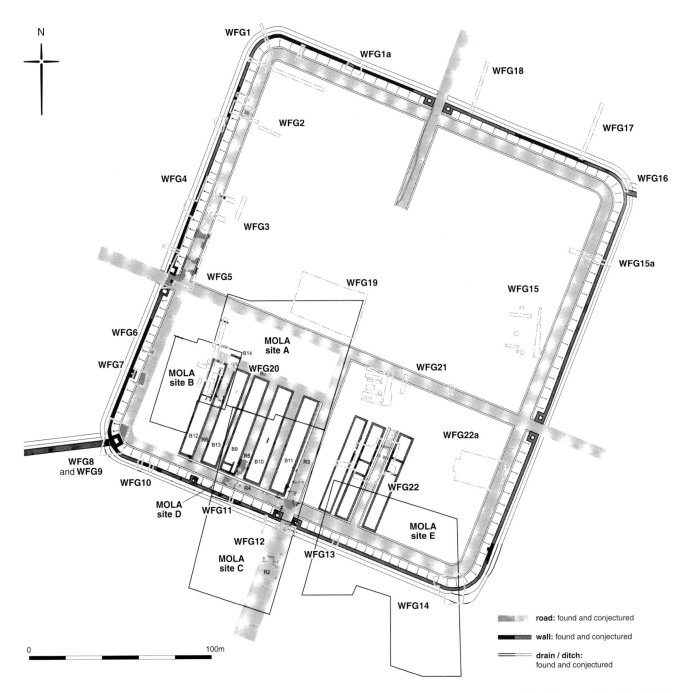

Fig 123 Plan showing Grimes and MOLA data (from sites A–E) merged on a single plan (after Howe and Lakin 2004) (scale 1:2000)

10.2 A survey of a marginal zone: the north-west area of the city in the 1st century AD

The natural soil throughout the Cripplegate area is brickearth overlying gravel. Grimes himself did not record the levels OD of the natural, but it has been possible to reconstruct these levels from a close examination of more recently examined sites in the LAARC. It would appear that the ground was reasonably flat north–south but it sloped down slightly to the east. The natural along Noble Street from the

tower in the south-west corner of the fort to the west gate is constant at *c* 12.70m OD. Natural in the area of the Rotunda of the Museum of London is *c* 13.50m and falls to *c* 12.00m in the Wood Street area, towards the centre of the fort. This area, therefore, can be seen as a relatively flat continuation of the westernmost hill, Ludgate Hill, of the city. It would appear that the area was well drained and that it was clear of any rivulets or marshy ground. This contrasts with much wetter areas which surround this locality, such as the area of the upper Walbrook valley to the east (Maloney 1990), the area around the hospital of St Bartholomew to the west (Bentley and Pritchard 1982) and the Blossom's Inn area to the south-east (Shepherd 1987, 18). Whatever the interpretation of the pre-masonry fort Roman features may be (below, 10.3), it is evident that the early 2nd-century fort was located on a well-drained, relatively flat area.

Evidence of prehistoric activity is present in the area, but this is very slight. Late Bronze Age sherds were found lying on natural brickearth under the west gate of the fort (WFG5, Chapter 5.6) and Bronze Age pottery was found at 24–30 West Smithfield (WES89; below, 10.3; Fig 124). The only possible pre-Roman feature recorded in this area is the round-bottomed ditch seen by Grimes just inside the city wall at Cripplegate Bastion (WFG1, Chapter 5.1). As discussed there, a sketch plan in the archive suggests that this was seen in two of the three trenches, which made up the WFG1 site, but it was only recorded in the main east–west section. The fills did not contain any dating material, not even Roman building material, and yet it was evidently a man-made feature.

The study carried out by Perring and Roskams (1991) of the area to the south and south-west of the Cripplegate fort, misleadingly called the 'West of Walbrook' even though only a part of that area was studied, revealed that the street-side developments were mainly residential, with some evidence for industry in the 1st century AD. The north of the city, in the area of the Walbrook valley, is also known to have been largely industrial at this time (Perring 1985, 94). The area under and to the west of the Cripplegate fort, however, was not included in that study – probably due to the disparate nature of the evidence (and of course Grimes's work was unpublished). However, a number of ideas have been put forward concerning its use in lieu of any detailed study. For example, see the following.

1 **Largely undeveloped**
It has been suggested by some that the area was entirely 'extramural' and formed no part of the settlement at all: 'It has often been suggested that the Walbrook would have formed a natural western boundary, but there was undoubtedly early occupation west of the Walbrook, especially in the neighbourhood of the main west road' (Merrifield 1983, 51).

2 **Ribbon development**
Another view has also been expressed in the above quotation, namely that any settlement in the north-west corner was solely concentrated in the area of the main west road that today is known as Cheapside.

3 **A timber fort**
Another opinion is that a timber fort possibly existed in the north-west corner as a predecessor to the early 2nd-century stone fort in that area (Grimes 1968; Perring 1985, 94). The discovery of a timber amphitheatre dating to the AD 70s has been used to support this view (Bateman 1998, 51; Bateman et al 2008, 19–38).

4 **Set aside**
Alternatively, the area could have acted as a 'set aside zone', that is to say an area that no one could occupy or enter because it was allocated for the military use and the building of the stone fort in *c* AD 120.

5 **Developed**
Finally, the area may have been used in a similar way to that in the south-west corner as found by Perring and Roskams (1991), consisting of planned streets and residential buildings with some industrial activity; in this case the later stone fort would have been superimposed upon the area.

However, due to the focus of attention upon the Roskams and Perring study, it has gone largely overlooked that there are an additional 43 excavated sites in the city to the north of their study area (Fig 124). These come from the GLA itself, those sites described in Chapters 5–9. Twelve of these can be shown to have evidence of definite 1st-century activity, however sparse it may appear in the records above. There are an additional seven sites from the Guildhall Museum Excavation Registers – sites and material collected mainly by Peter Marsden, field officer of the museum in the 50s and 60s. Finally there are three well-recorded and 15 other sites in the DUA archive, now part of the LAARC. The DUA's excavations have produced a large amount of 1st-century evidence, no doubt because of its ability to excavate in more detail, with better resources and a larger team, than the previous organisations. To these can now be added the information from the more recent PCA work on the west side of the fort (Butler 2001) and the MOLA work (five sites) in the interior and along the south wall of the fort (Howe and Lakin 2004; Lyon 2004).

In all, therefore, there have been 43 excavations and observations of 1st-century material in the north-west area in the last 60 years. The following is a brief summary of the main findings from these deposits.

10.3 Pre-Flavian evidence in the north-west corner of the City of London

Although there is some tentative pre-Flavian evidence on three of Grimes's sites in the Cripplegate fort area (WFG3, WFG5 and WFG14; Chapter 5.4, 5.6; Chapter 7.5), this evidence consists of very small assemblages of pottery sherds and their exact contexts are not known. They are not included in the summaries in Chapters 5–9. No finds or contexts specifically dating to the pre-Flavian period were recorded in any of the archive reports or Guildhall Museum publications on sites in the north-west part of the City.

However, the excavation carried out at the hospital of St Bartholomew by the late David Bentley in 1979 (BAR79; Fig 125) has produced some clear evidence

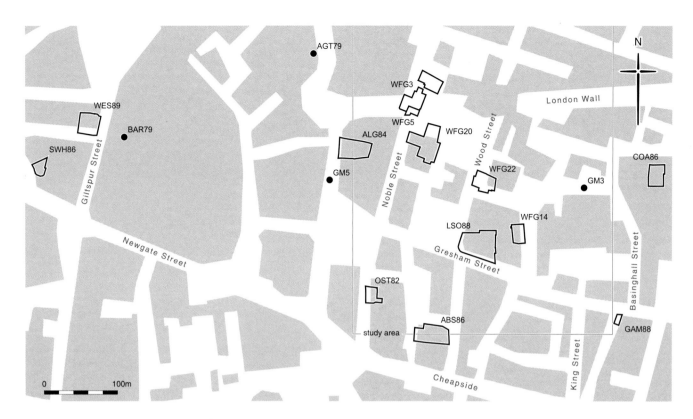

Fig 124 Location of sites discussed in the Cripplegate area in Chapter 10 (scale 1:5000)

for pre-Flavian occupation in the area to the west of Cripplegate. The first phase of activity (period 1, phase 1) was represented by flecks of charcoal and daub in the early stratigraphic sequence and in the later layers more occupation debris accompanied this: namely, oyster shells, fragments of animal bone, fine- and medium-sized pebbles and some pottery. Four out of the five sherds from this pottery group were Lyons ware (LYO CC), which is known to be of pre-Flavian date. Bentley believed that during period 1, phase 1, a natural gravel level had been removed from the area of excavation because the natural sand was very clean and there was a 'clear interface' with the surface above (Bentley and Pritchard 1982, 135–6).

Period 1, phase 2, consisted of four cut and depressed features, two of which are believed to be rubbish or cesspits from the nature of their fills and stratigraphic profiles. These included charcoal, red daub, pebbles, animal bone, iron fragments and some pottery sherds. They also included pre-Flavian Lyons ware and samian ware. Interestingly, one fill contained a sherd of Iron Age pottery. One of the other circular features was *c* 1m in diameter but had an unknown function. The other depression was described as having a 'strong greenish appearance' and a large amount of possible worm activity, which Bentley believed was likely to represent the edge of a waterlogged area, such as the edge of a pond or spring.

The activity represented in period 2, phase 1, would also support this interpretation (Bentley and Pritchard 1982, 136). This consisted of an effort to backfill and

'consolidate' the features found in period 1, phase 2. Bentley states that 'this rubble deposit represented a make-up and the first phase of building construction' (ibid). Therefore, it seems that the area was being prepared for a later building of some sort, with the introduction of a make-up layer comprising of a mixture of coarse sand and fine to medium pebbles.

It is possible to tell that this layer did not accumulate naturally because inclusions of shell, daub and pot fragments were found within it. These pot sherds included those of a pre-Flavian date. One context had a larger quantity of pot dating to the Neronian–early Flavian period, which suggests this levelling process took place over some time. Bentley states that the small size of the shell fragments indicates a large amount of 'tread' or human activity in this area, which seems likely.

A similar situation was encountered during the excavation at 7–10 Foster Lane, 5–6 Rose and Crown Court (OST82; Tobert 1983; Fig 125) where there was also pre-Flavian tread evidence and a 'mixed make-up levelling deposit' in preparation for a series of buildings and streets (period 1). Tobert states that pottery with the date *c* AD 60–75 was found at this site although the exact context was not made clear and this pottery was not recorded in the archive's spot-date records. However, stratigraphically the levelling deposits were earlier than the Flavian evidence in period 2, phase 2, at the site (ibid, chapter 4). Tobert believed that 'these deposits were seen to equate via sections exposed during the watching brief and constitute the deliberate

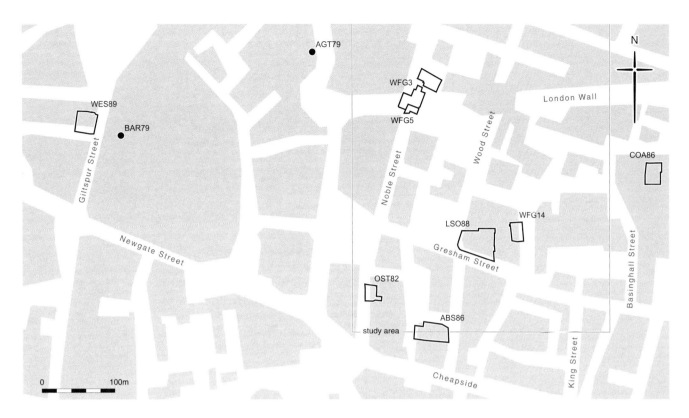

Fig 125 Sites in the Cripplegate area with evidence for pre-Flavian occupation (scale 1:5000)

consolidation and levelling of a quarry pit in preparation for the later street sequence' (ibid, 4).

The geology of the area suggests that brickearth was being quarried, perhaps for road or structural building elsewhere. If the quarry pit were deep enough, gravel could have been extracted as well, but the depth is not made clear in the archive report.

Period 1, phase 1, at OST82 is also likely to be pre-Flavian from its stratigraphic position and the nature of the deposits in period 2, phase 2. Evidence from phase 1 reveals the presence of a 'single north–south orientated cambered street, the western edge of which was defined in section by metalling' (Tobert 1983, 4). On the western side of this street a possible brickearth foundation slab was discovered which appears to be contemporary with the street surface. However, there was no evidence of any other structural elements associated with the slab and therefore it could be just another levelling deposit.

A quarry pit was also found to the west of the road that was backfilled at some stage. It is believed (Tobert 1983) that it was left open during the first stages of setting out the road, as preparation would have been needed only for those deposits underneath the proposed line of the road initially. An early 1st-century 'Colchester type' copper-alloy brooch (c AD 50–80), was also found during this excavation. However, as it comes from a much higher stratigraphic level it is likely to be residual (F Grew in Tobert 1983).

The 1986 excavation at St Albans House, Wood Street (ABS86; Chitwood and Hill 1987; Fig 125)

revealed pre-Flavian structural evidence in this area. However, the area was severely truncated and has proved difficult to interpret. The first phase of activity (period 1, phase 1) has been given a *terminus post quem* of c AD 40 and consisted of a poorly defined structure (A), which was found in the southern part of the excavation. This was represented by a possible brickearth slab, a scorched mortar surface above this, a cut aligned west-north-west–east-south-east and a stakehole. The fills of the latter contained mortar, charcoal and scorched daub which could indicate *in situ* fire debris.

The next phase (period 1, phase 2) has been given a *terminus post quem* of c AD 50. Another structure (B), represented by a north-east–south-west aligned scorched sill beam and stakeholes, replaced structure A. In the Flavian period an accumulation of silts built up to the east of B and several pits were dug. Chitwood and Hill (1987) suggest that two more timber and brickearth buildings (C and D), located to the north of the site of A/B, may have been contemporary with A and the later building B because of their stratigraphic position. These buildings were also destroyed by fire. Whether either structure A or structures B, C and D were destroyed in the Boudican fire is not clear, although one of the two could easily have been with the *termini post quem* of c AD 40 and c AD 50. However, alternatively they could have been destroyed just as easily in a domestic fire.

Excavations at 24–30 West Smithfield (WES89; Langton and Westman 1990; Fig 125) also revealed some pre-Flavian evidence. A prehistoric bucket urn in a very complete condition was retrieved from the site and was identified as a Deverel-Rimbury type dating to the Late Bronze Age (c 800–700 BC). Such a find is very unusual in London (but see the sherds from WFG5; Chapter 5.6) and no other prehistoric activity was found on the site. The earliest Roman activity at the site was represented by quarrying for sands and gravels, and several large quarry pits were found across the site. There is no dating evidence for this activity in the DUA archive. However, the author of the preliminary report feels it happened in conjunction with the initial settlement of London after AD 43, which is generally accepted as occurring c AD 50 (Milne 1995, 42).

Some possible pre-Flavian evidence also exists at 16 Coleman Street (COA86) and Leith House, Gresham Street (LSO88) in the form of pottery groups (Spence 1986) as well as possible cut linear features and a quarry pit (Hart 1988) (Fig 125).

In summary, therefore, the evidence presented above does show that the north-west corner of the City of London was in use during the pre-Flavian period, even if not to a great extent. The function of the area directly under the stone fort at this time still remains a mystery as a result of the truncation caused by this later stone development. However, the excavations carried out by Grimes (1968) have shown that the area does not seem to be a 'set aside zone', as groups of pottery were discovered and also some cuts, the function of which remains unclear.

Around the fort area the evidence is slightly clearer. From the DUA evidence, it seems that the area was largely used for quarrying gravels and brickearth in its early development, especially at the three most westerly sites. Additionally, COA86 and LSO88, if proved to have pre-Flavian evidence, would also have similar evidence to the above-mentioned sites.

Throughout the pre-Flavian period, site WES89 appears to maintain the same function, namely an area for quarrying. However, the sites at 174–176 Aldersgate Street (AGT79) and OST82 appear to change function during this period. It seems that at some point these areas were being prepared for permanent development. This preparation took the form of make-up dumps and, as can be seen from the evidence at OST82, permanent development started in the pre-Flavian period and took the form of a sequence of streets and a possible building foundation. Further development at AGT79 did not start until the Flavian period, so it seems that make-up dumps may have been placed here in the late pre-Flavian period.

Positive evidence for pre-Flavian domestic occupation also exists in the north-west corner. Although there is no direct structural evidence at AGT79, the presence of charcoal, daub and two rubbish/cesspits with fills of domestic refuse certainly suggests that occupation, either here or nearby, existed before the make-up dumps were deposited. The presence of animal bone could imply activities such as butchery were taking place, again here or nearby. Bentley's (1979) suggested pond or waterlogged area would also have produced a useful water supply for any nearby domestic establishment. The structures excavated at ABS86 show that this part of the north-west corner, at least, was constantly developed throughout the pre-Flavian period and the presence of three buildings in use at the same time agrees with the interpretation that this area was outside that of the Roman settlement but was still sparsely occupied as suggested by Merrifield (1983, 77).

From the location of this pre-Flavian activity it can also be seen that it was not solely concentrated along the main east–west road, now known as Cheapside, as suggested by Merrifield (1983, 51). Instead, it also lies to the north of this thoroughfare. The DUA sites, when plotted, do appear as a linear development, which could be interpreted as a westwards ribbon development and with some expansion northwards. The presence of the north–south road at OST82 and the foundational slab abutting on to this feature would confirm this theory.

Another interesting piece of evidence that has emerged from the pre-Flavian sites is the fact that some of the finds/features from the north-west corner do appear to be burnt. It is not possible to say with certainty whether the Boudican fire destroyed part of the north-west corner of the city as well as the Roman settlement to the south and east of this area. However, the dates given at ABS86 show that the area was occupied and a fire occurred at around the time of the revolt. The discovery of the coin hoard at WES89 could also suggest that the north-west area was under threat at this time. If this area was destroyed in the same way as the rest of the Roman settlement then this implies that the area was considered a part of Londinium and was worth attacking, thus proving that the north-west corner was integral with the rest of the city. It might also have been one of the routes north and north-west out of the area, and so would have suffered in much the same way at the hands of the rebels as the core of the town. However, as evidence for burning has not been mentioned at any of the other sites with pre-Flavian evidence it could be argued that domestic fires destroyed the buildings at ABS86. Note that Perring (1991, 10) states, in connection with the west of the Walbrook, that 'it is not yet clear if the traces of fire destruction found on these sites were due to the Boudiccan [sic] revolt or an unrecorded fire of the early Flavian period'.

10.4 Flavian evidence in the north-west corner of the City of London

The GLA has produced Flavian evidence from a large number of the sites in the Cripplegate fort area (Fig 126). This evidence consists of groups of pottery in the

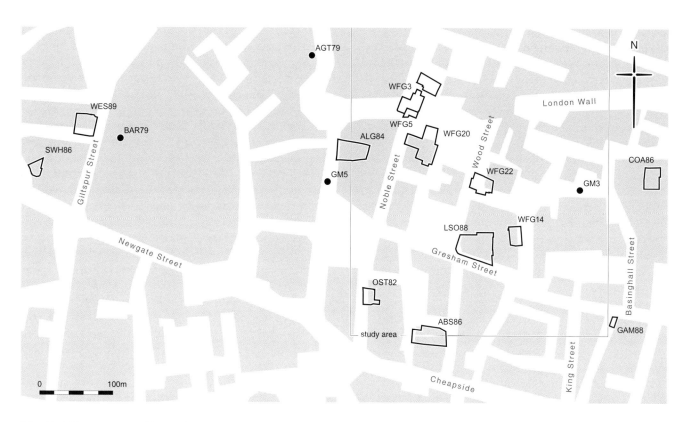

Fig 126 Sites excavated by MOLA in the Cripplegate area with Flavian occupation (scale 1:5000)

spot-date archive given the date range *c* AD 70–100 and is present at the sites shown on Table 2.

Table 2 Sites from the Grimes London Archive in the Cripplegate fort with pottery given the date range *c* AD 70–100

Site code	Size of sample
WFG2	small
WFG3	large
WFG4	small
WFG5	small
WFG9	small
WFG14	medium
WFG15	small
WFG18	small
WFG20	medium
WFG22	small
WFG22a	small

Most of the pottery from these sites was found from an unknown or unrecorded context – for this reason, not all of it is described in the catalogues published in Chapters 5–9. However, at Windsor Court (WFG3) it is known that some of the groups were found in cuts, although their function is not made clear. At Falcon Square (WFG5) and Aldermanbury (WFG14) two of the groups of pottery were very burnt. The cause of this burning is not clear, although looking at the date range it is likely to be as a result of a domestic fire unless there were any unrecorded early and late Flavian fires (eg Perring 1991, 72).

At 15–17 Silver Street (WFG20) most of the pottery groups had the general dates *c* AD 70–100 or *c* AD 70–120. However, one particular group had a more specific date of *c* AD 90–120, which is a very late Flavian–early Trajanic/Hadrianic date. It is possible that this group (and the later sherds in the *c* AD 70–120 groups) may represent the preparation of this area for the building of the fort in *c* AD 120. However, again the context of this group is not known so this makes any interpretation tentative.

It seems from sample size that the bulk of the Flavian activity existed in the areas of Windsor Court (WFG3), Aldermanbury (WFG14) and 15–17 Silver Street (WFG20) (Fig 126). However, the sample size could again depend upon factors such as methods of retrieval and truncation of the archaeology by later features. Therefore, the size of the sample may not necessarily represent the extent of the Flavian activity. Nevertheless, there is positive evidence for Flavian activity in this area before the fort was built.

Two of the Guildhall Museum sites have also produced Flavian evidence: namely, Three Nun Court, Aldermanbury (GM3; Marsden 1968, 5–6) and Aldersgate (GM5; Oswald 1939) (Fig 126).

At GM3 five gullies were discovered, cutting into the natural brickearth, all of which from their stratigraphic level appear to have been dug before the construction of the Cripplegate fort. One of the gullies produced sherds dating from c AD 70 to c AD 90, which suggests they were dug and in use during the Flavian period. Marsden (1968) also tentatively associates two of the gullies with two clusters of postholes which stratigraphically seem to date to the Roman period. Whether this forms any sort of structural evidence, however, is arguable. It is likely from the lack of any other evidence, that the gullies may have been used for drainage. However, the area was severely truncated by a modern cellar floor so there could have been more evidence originally. There was also a large concentration of pits in this area, the earliest of which can be dated to c AD 70–100. The nature of their fills suggests that they were rubbish pits.

At GM5 an excavation was carried out to find the city wall and the gate. It was found that below the stone construction there was positive evidence for the area being a hollow and marsh. This marshy area produced a substantial amount of Flavian pottery as well as some burning evidence and oyster shells. It is possible that this hollow acted as a convenient rubbish dump.

One other site has also produced positive Flavian evidence, namely St Albans House (GM66). Here a mid 1st-century pit was discovered by Marsden. This is the same site that has since been excavated by the DUA (ABS86; Fig 126).

The DUA sites have produced a great deal of Flavian (c AD 70–100) evidence in the north-west corner of the city. As already mentioned (above, 10.3), BAR79 has produced evidence for make-up deposits in the Neronian/early Flavian period. This levelling was in preparation for a timber and brickearth building, which was in use during the Flavian period (period 2, phase 2, at the site).

The evidence for this building, as cited by Bentley (1979, 4), was a north–south aligned brickearth sill as well as a 'conjectured' east–west wall at right angles to it. On either side of the sill there seem to have been a sequence of make-ups and brickearth floor preparations, as well as evidence for trample and a hearth. The floor preparations are different in content and the levels also differ which may suggest, according to Bentley (ibid), that they had different degrees of occupation or activity being carried out on them. The difference in floor level seems to be the above-mentioned east–west division in the building, which would mean there were originally four rooms. Although no archaeological evidence for this was found during the excavation, Bentley believed that upright planking might have separated the rooms. 'Total decay or the subsequent removal of the planking would account for the lack of wood traces' (ibid, 5). In one of the rooms, circular depressions were discovered in the floor, which may have acted as some kind of storage or holders for vessels. No other possible function is assigned to the other rooms, presumably because of the lack of archaeological evidence. However, it is also believed, through stratigraphic evidence (ibid, 6), that an

external area was attached to the building. This would have been useful as a work or storage area.

The pottery found from period 2, phase 2, dates mainly to the 1st century AD although there are some 2nd-century sherds as well. This evidence, as well as that from later periods, certainly suggests this area was in use for a long time and that long-term occupation/activity was being carried out throughout the Flavian period.

At OST82 (Tobert 1983) a continuation of development occurred around the north–south aligned street. It seems that the original pre-Flavian street had subsided into the quarry pit, which lay underneath. Therefore, in the Flavian period an effort was made to consolidate this by sealing the primary street level with make-up dumps of rubbish.

Above this 'make-up' deposit three successive road surfaces were built. All of them were metalled, cambered and kept the alignment of the original pre-Flavian street. Pottery from the levelling and the first of these road surfaces gave the date range c AD 70–100, which suggests this was in use during the Flavian period. The date of the two other road surfaces is not clear, although stratigraphically they appear earlier than the known 2nd-century deposits.

Alongside these street sequences it was found that 'two structural slabs' existed 'which were probably originally associated with a packed brickearth foundational sill' (Tobert 1983, 4). This brickearth sill has been given a 1st-century date and Tobert (ibid) suggests that the sill may have been laid down and a structure built before the laying of the street sequence. The street could then have been positioned against the structure's eastern face. Realistically, however, it does not seem very likely that one building would dictate the layout of a street. It seems more plausible that the previous street alignment would have dictated the Flavian thoroughfare especially as a series of later streets and related ditches continued to exist here, on the same alignment, in the 2nd century AD.

At 7–12 Aldersgate Street (ALG84) early Roman evidence was also produced in the lower stratigraphic levels, which Egan (1985) suggests may have resulted from brickearth quarrying being carried out in this area. Three individual cut features, believed to be gullies, were also discovered and it is possible that these were used for drainage. This hollow is consistent with the evidence produced by Oswald (1939) at Aldersgate itself (GM5).

Over these gullies a series of make-up deposits, made of redeposited brickearth, were found. As found on other sites, this may suggest that the area was undergoing a 'change of use' in the Flavian period. Structural evidence does exist in this area, so it was possible the area was being prepared for buildings. This evidence consists of three consecutive buildings, the first of which was timber (structure A) and all of which are known to date to before the end of the 2nd century AD (Egan 1985). It is unclear whether any date specifically to the 1st century AD, although looking at similar patterns in evidence at BAR79 and OST82 it seems likely that structure A belonged to the mid to late 1st century AD and was linked with the filling in of the gullies. Other features, often associated with structures, were found nearby, such as pegholes, a pit and a posthole, but these were 'too incomplete and isolated for detailed interpretation' (ibid, 3). Therefore, it is difficult to assign a date to them and confidently say that they were associated with structure A.

Also on the site several cuts were excavated which have been described as 'a series of large flat-bottomed ditches' (Schofield 1987, 28). Egan suggests (1985, 4) that these 'may have been to contain ground water, perhaps a considerable problem to judge by their size, which would have accumulated in this area, the earlier hollow still being reflected in the topography at this time'. It is interesting to note, however, that these ditches were found to run north–south and parallel to the alignment of the later city wall, which was built c AD 200. Could these have formed a type of city boundary and acted as a precedent for the later wall? A possible date for the digging of these ditches was not found. However, as in the case of the gullies they were filled in with a series of make-up deposits, one of which is known to give a date of c AD 70–200 (ibid). This certainly suggests they were dug in the 1st century AD and started going out of use during the Flavian period.

The 'make-up' of the area was in preparation for a sequence of roads on the same alignment as, but slightly to the east of, 'the wider and later road leading to the north from Roman Aldersgate' (Schofield 1987, 28). The date of this road sequence is not clear. However, as the make-up dumps rest on the natural it is likely to have an early date and Egan (1985, 4) suggests:

> The lower brickearth dumps seemed very close in nature to the natural soil on the site, and it seems reasonable to assume that these layers were redeposited natural, and therefore were laid down at an early point in the site's occupation (ie before the natural was covered with occupation deposits).

The nature of the stratigraphy certainly suggests a possible 1st-century date.

Egan (1985, 4) states that the road alignment, despite the evidence for traffic in the form of wheel ruts,

> was clearly not the main thoroughfare postulated as leading to the later gate. It may possibly provide evidence for an earlier smaller gate in the vicinity of the later city gate, but was clearly not designed for, or used by, large amounts of heavy traffic. It was certainly not as well built as most of the Roman roads discovered in the city, and may therefore have been intended as a temporary measure when originally built.

As mentioned above (10.3), the Flavian period at site ABS86 saw a continuation of use of the three structures built in the pre-Flavian period (Chitwood and Hill 1987). However, an external area or 'courtyard' was added with a *terminus post quem* of c AD 70 as well as a series of pits, probably for rubbish disposal.

Several rubbish pits were also excavated at 16 Coleman Street (COA86) in the eastern part of this study area (Spence 1986), the fills of which included pottery dating to the early and late 1st century AD. Unfortunately, pottery from other centuries was also included in these fills. It is possible these pits may have had some longevity of use especially as natural silting was present and no evidence for deliberate backfilling. However, Spence argues that these pits were in fact cut in the 2nd century AD and that the 1st-century finds are purely residual.

At 1–3 Snow Hill (SWH86), a number of pits were discovered cutting into the natural gravel (Maloney 1986). It is thought that these were used for gravel extraction/quarrying. All produced pottery of a Roman date. However, those sherds belonging to the 1st century AD mainly dated to the Flavian and Trajanic periods, proving that activity was taking place as far west as this site in the 1st century AD.

A similar situation was encountered at 52 Gresham Street/14 Ironmonger Lane (GAM88; Mackinder 1988; Fig 126) where a quarry pit was excavated with a *terminus post quem* of c AD 70. However, this period of gravel extraction was succeeded by the levelling of the area, which has been precisely dated to AD 70–85 by burnt pottery sherds belonging to this layer. It is not clear what the area was used for after this date in the 1st century AD as the next phase of levelling has been given a *terminus post quem* of c AD 230, which suggests the area was in a period of abandonment for c 150 years.

Leith House, Gresham Street (LSO88; Fig 126), has produced a great deal of evidence, which may help assign a function to the study area in the Flavian period. The earliest features at the site have been found to be cut into the natural, such as a quarry pit and several linear features. It is also believed (Hart 1988) that part of the site was used as an open area at this time. The exact date of these features is not clear, but the fill of the quarry pit, consisting of mainly destruction debris, gives a date to the Flavian period. This suggests the features may have been created in the pre-Flavian period and a programme of 'levelling' was adopted c AD 70. As a result of destruction debris existing in the fill, Hart (1988) suggests that buildings probably existed nearby. The discovery of a brickearth sill in a similar stratigraphic horizon to the quarry pit certainly suggests that this was the case, although its date remains uncertain and it is possible the quarry pit's fill could have been brought in from elsewhere.

Features at the site, which can definitely be assigned to the Flavian period, succeed this levelling deposit and include a possible working surface associated with a pit. The large amount of mortar found in the fill of the pit and trampled into the adjoining surface leads Hart (1988) to believe that the feature acted as a mortar-mixing pit for this period. He suggests, 'the mortar was used in the initial construction of buildings in the immediate vicinity' (Hart 1988, 6). Its fill also included iron slag and charcoal which suggests some industry may have been carried out here.

Several postholes and stakeholes appear to provide structural evidence, as well as floor surfaces, a robber trench and a rubbish pit with a *terminus post quem* of *c* AD 70 (Hart 1988). A trackway, possibly leading between two buildings, was also laid on top of the redeposited brickearth. An open area appeared to be contemporary with the construction of this trackway. Two parallel ditches were also discovered. Their function is not clear, but it is possible that they were used for drainage (ibid). It is thought that the building and trackway may have been the two reasons for the levelling carried out at the beginning of the Flavian period: 'as undoubtedly such a laborious task as levelling would not have been undertaken without a major use/re-use of the levelled site clearly in mind' (ibid, 6).

From excavation it appears that WES89 continued to be a non-residential area in the Flavian period (Langton and Westman 1990). It seems, after quarrying took place in the pre-Flavian period, that

> possibly contemporary with or immediately post-dating the sand and gravel quarrying, [activity] also included light industry, perhaps animal slaughter. The site was also used for the disposal of refuse at this time. No associated early Roman structures were found on the site, so it might be suggested that this marginal area could have been set aside deliberately for activities such as that mentioned above, rather than for settlement. (ibid, 5)

From the above-mentioned evidence it can be seen that development occurred on a larger scale in the north-west corner during the Flavian period. In the fort area there is a dramatic increase in the number of pottery groups being found which again suggests that this area was not a 'set aside zone' during the 1st century AD. As in the case of the pre-Flavian period it is still not clear what types of activity were being carried out in this area although again there are cuts of unknown function present.

It seems on the whole that there is an increase in the amount of domestic occupation and activity during the Flavian period. The make-up deposits already laid down in the pre-Flavian period had now been built on, for example at AGT79, and new sites were also undergoing development, for example at LSO88. At OST82 and ALG84 more houses join on to the north–south aligned streets, suggesting that some form

of northern ribbon development may have existed before this period of denser population. The large amount of rubbish pits, for example at GM3, also suggests an increase of domestic activity.

It seems that during the Flavian period industrial activity also began. This is supported by the find of iron slag, possibly representing the practice of metalworking, and the mortar mixing pit, for construction work, at LSO88. The discoveries of external yards at AGT79, ABS86 and LSO88 also show that working surfaces were in use during this period. The presence of large animal bones at WES89 could also suggest butchery was being carried out in this area.

One interesting factor is the mention of the large, flat-bottomed ditches at ALG84 by Egan (Schofield 1987, 28). It is possible that these were used for drainage, like the gullies found at GM3, but it is equally possible that they had a more important role, such as a boundary marker. Whether they formed a marker for the city boundary is arguable. This does seem unlikely, despite their matching alignment with the later city wall, as there is much 1st-century activity to the west of this area which seems to be included in the settlement. It seems more likely, therefore, that they may have formed some type of property boundary.

Evidence for property boundaries does appear to exist elsewhere as structures can be seen to be built on the same plots time and again. This is apparent at ALG84 when buildings were replaced, and also at OST82 and ALG84 when the road surfaces were replaced. These kept the same alignment well into the 2nd century AD, which suggests an element of town planning was involved with their construction.

As can be seen from the above evidence, a wide variety of archaeological discoveries have been made in the north-west corner of the City of London. These findings can be divided roughly into two groups. Firstly, there is evidence for the preparation of the area and making the north-west corner serviceable. This includes evidence for the digging of quarry pits to provide brickearth and gravel, deforestation for land clearance and the provision of timber, make-up dumps for levelling the area and also the building of streets and roadways to provide easy access in and out of this area. Secondly, there is evidence of domestic occupation. This comes in the form of pottery groups, hearths, rubbish pits, structural evidence, features such as a pond (Bentley 1979) and possible industrial activity. This second group of activities appears to occur as a direct result of the first.

The concentrations of these activities vary during the 1st century AD. The evidence found dating to the pre-Flavian period stretches in a 'line' westwards and northwards alongside the two recorded roads, whereas the Flavian evidence has a more even spread over the whole north-western corner.

In terms of the early development of the area it seems that it was quite sparsely inhabited during the pre-Flavian period. There is positive evidence for domestic structures at ABS86 and possible evidence that buildings once existed at AGT79, as daub and domestic refuse were found in the rubbish pits there. Other than that it appears that the area was used for quarrying and, if the pottery groups found at Grimes's excavations are not connected with domestic occupation in this area, possibly for rubbish disposal.

At the end of the pre-Flavian period, however, there does seem to be a conscious effort to prepare for the further development of this area. This comes in the form of make-up dumps and levelling deposits. The consistency of this process of development, in both the pre-Flavian and Flavian periods, suggests a certain amount of planning, perhaps by a central authority, was involved with this area. During the Flavian period it can be seen that an increase of occupation occurs in this area. The sites already occupied produce an increase of structural evidence and in some cases more permanent structures. More sites are given over to quarrying and then domestic occupation follows. An increase of pottery in the Cripplegate fort area also supports this increased density of activity in this area.

The evidence found also shows the area was affected by fire on more than one occasion. Pre-Flavian burnt pottery and the fire at ABS86 during this period could be attributed to the Boudican fire, although this is arguable due to the small amount of evidence. Perring (1991, 10) has already suggested there may have been an unrecorded Flavian fire, which also caused large-scale destruction. Alternatively, it is possible that domestic fires or those started by industrial production caused the destruction.

With regard to the function of the area, it can be seen clearly from the archaeological evidence that the north-west corner was not a 'set aside zone'. There is obviously activity going on inside the area of the later Cripplegate fort, even if it is not clear what kind of activity exactly, during the pre-Flavian and Flavian periods. Outside this area it can be seen that occupational evidence exists close to the fort area and as far away as West Smithfield, which indicates a substantial area was in use.

From the excavations studied it can be seen that there is no direct evidence for a timber predecessor to the Cripplegate fort. This is further confirmed by the more recent work by Howe and Lakin (2004) in the internal area of the fort. The bulk of the 1st-century evidence was destroyed by the later stone fort and the only real evidence left appears to be pottery and some cuts of unknown function. Whether any of these cuts could have been substantial postholes for a timber fort remains unclear. There is also no direct evidence for there being any sort of military settlement, as suggested by Rowsome (1998), during the 1st century AD in this area.

The argument that any development in the western part of Londinium belonged solely to a western ribbon development can be disproved by the fact that occupational evidence existed to the north of the Roman east–west road as early as the pre-Flavian period. The presence of the north–south road at OST82 and its adjoining structure, and the slightly later predecessor to Aldersgate (AGT79), suggest that a northern ribbon development may have also existed and formed an early part of the settlement.

Largely it seems that the evidence reflects that found in the south-west corner of the city by Perring and Roskams (1991). Similarities exist between the two areas, such as the quarrying of brickearth and gravel, and the preparation for buildings and streets by the deposition of make-up dumps. Also, the style of buildings constructed and the materials used appear to be very similar. The fact that many buildings join on to roads in the south-west corner is mirrored in the north-west corner, for example at OST82 and ALG84, although on a smaller scale. Both areas have evidence for industry in the form of hearths and slag, although this is on a smaller scale in the north-west area. Additionally, both areas have a similar style of planning, with marker ditches being laid out first for roads and large flat-bottomed ditches being used as possible property boundaries. It is interesting to note that these boundaries are adhered to throughout the 1st century AD, in both areas, even when buildings are replaced.

One main difference between the two areas is that the south-west corner has more evidence for the existence of town houses. These are high-status timber buildings, with *opus signinum* or mosaic floors. They may also have stone wall foundations (Perring and Roskams 1991, 28). No evidence for mosaic flooring was discovered. More masonry structures start to appear in the early 2nd century AD. Also, in the north-west corner there is no direct evidence for industry being carried out on as large a scale as in the south-west and the structural evidence also appears less dense.

One possible explanation for this is that the south-west may have started to be developed first and, therefore, the north-west has a 'staggered' development compared to it. It does seem likely that the changes in this area occurred slightly later than in the south-west. It is possible, as suggested by Perring and Roskams (1991, 62), that as other areas became more populated with the increased economic stability of London, development started to 'spill over' into the less inhabited north-west corner as there was more room. As in the case of the south-west area, the more comfortable people became with the area, the more permanent their homes became. This 'spilling over' into the north-west seems to have started in the Flavian period, as there is an increase of archaeological evidence and, therefore, activity at this stage. It appears to come to a head with the construction of the fort in the early 2nd century AD and is reflected in the archaeological record by the presence of masonry structures at this time.

One other point worthy of mention is the occupation based in the West Smithfield area in the 1st century AD. In the pre-Flavian period this area was a considerable distance from the other domestic occupation found at OST82 and ABS86. The evidence at WES89 and the cemetery evidence suggest this area was peripheral and it seems likely that AGT79 may have been an independent structure in this peripheral area. One suggestion is that it could have been an independent farmstead. The presence of redeposited brickearth, such as that noted there, has been interpreted at other sites as evidence for ploughing. One certainty is that during the Flavian period this arguably 'separate' area of domestic occupation was then linked with the rest of the town. This may have occurred in the same way as expanding towns absorb surrounding villages as their suburbs today.

Finally, it does seem from the evidence available in the north-west corner that the Cripplegate fort was an entirely intrusive feature when it was built in the early 2nd century AD. Its alignment when it was constructed would also suggest that this was the case, as it does not really align with the rest of the settlement. One possible reason for its strange alignment is the fact that it lies on a region of high ground and this was the only convenient area on which it could have been built.

As has already been mentioned, it is known from archaeological excavations at GM5 that a hollow was found just to the west of the site of the later fort. It can be seen on modern maps today that a contour skirts the western edge of the fort and this is likely to correspond with the above-mentioned hollow. Therefore, it is probable that natural topography influenced the fort's position. If the fort can be proved to be intrusive, which does seem likely, then this shows that some change of town planning must have taken place in the late 1st century AD, as a fort is a dramatic feature to impose on an area already in use.

It is interesting to note, however, that the majority of the sites outside the fort area in the north-west continue their occupation in the 2nd century AD, even to the west of the fort. This, therefore, still suggests that they form a part of the Roman settlement at this time. It is also known that the south-west corner continued its development in the same way during a large part of the 2nd century AD (Perring and Roskams 1991, 64).

10.5 The building of the fort

As mentioned above (10.4), it is clear from the large amount of information available for 1st-century occupation in the vicinity of Cripplegate that the construction of the fort would have required some considerable displacement of activities already going on in the area. It is unlikely that their disruption would have been either a concern to the authorities or would have had much of an effect upon the economics of the town. However, there is the possibility – and here it will

simply be left as that – that the fort was constructed following the well-recorded Hadrianic fire, a period when disruption was universal for a greater part of the population of the town.

The evidence from Grimes's sites, especially Barber-Surgeons' Hall (WFG2), Windsor Court (WFG3), Falcon Square (WFG5) and St Alban's church, Wood Street (WFG22), emphasises the early 2nd-century construction date of the fort. Samian ware dated to the Trajanic and Hadrianic period occurs deep in the sequence, especially the lowest levels of the fort bank, giving a useful *terminus post quem*, and the assemblages that were contemporary with the fort suggest that it was in use during the Hadrianic and Antonine periods at least.

As for the reason why a fort was constructed in the first place, Grimes's interpretation was that, from the early 2nd century AD at least, the city was made up of two parts, to be made into one at the time of the construction of the city wall. In a report to the RMLEC Executive Committee in 1950, Grimes wrote that:

> For some time, therefore, military fort and civil settlement were physically distinct. But the latter undoubtedly grew with the years and when in the second century the wall was thrown round the city the fort was incorporated in the enclosed area. The main city wall was carried to its northeast and southwest corners and the north and west walls of the fort then became part of the external defences. Whether or not the fort continued to enjoy a separate existence remains to be seen.

Grimes maintained this view in his 1968 volume (38–9):

> London in the early second century AD must now be visualised as made up of two parts. Centred on the eastern hill but spreading gradually from it was the redeveloping city, perhaps replanned after the Boudiccan [*sic*] destruction. Away from the civil settlement, though the houses were creeping towards it, and apparently occupying an area, which had previously carried some civilian occupation, the fort took up the slightly higher ground to the northwest. Fort and city reflect the separateness of military and civil which is a feature of Roman organisation in the frontier provinces, but the fort was so placed that it was within easy reach both of any part of the city and the port, and of the most important roads that fanned out from the crossing of the Thames towards the interior of Britain.

This concept of 'separateness' is a phenomenon that appears to have been disregarded or discounted without debate in subsequent studies of Londinium.

While Wacher was ready to suggest the presence in London of a short-lived fort dating to the earliest period of the city's history, and to express some affinity with Merrifield's suggestion (1965, 39) that Londinium grew up from the *vicus* of this hypothetical early fort, he saw the construction of the fort at Cripplegate simply as 'the next stage in the establishment of London as a provincial capital'. Its role was to house the guard and staff of the governor but 'we cannot say ... where they were accommodated before the fort was built' (Wacher 1974, 94).

Merrifield repeats the statement that the adoption of Londinium as the capital required quarters for a considerable military establishment, but does not suggest where they had been housed before *c* AD 120 or the conditions which prevailed which necessitated the construction of the fort (Merrifield 1983, 77). It is 'yet another manifestation of its transformation into the provincial capital' (ibid).

It is evident, therefore, that Wacher and Merrifield, amongst others, saw the construction of the Cripplegate fort as a phenomenon related to the important status of Londinium. However, this interpretation makes the status of Londinium throughout the Empire a very special one. Rome had its own garrison, so did Carthage, but no other provincial capital was equipped with such a lavish facility for the governor's guard, and so forth. This would have been very lavish provision, because in Britannia the governor would not have been in residence throughout the year in the capital, but would probably have spent much of his time in the frontier zones.

Perhaps the explanation is much simpler and is not related to the status of Londinium, but its location. There was no pre-Roman settlement in the city area from which Londinium grew up. It was a new foundation, *c* AD 50, which took advantage of the excellent communications, of road and river, at a point where there was raised, accessible and dry ground on the river's edge. We are aware that, at the time of Boudica's rebellion, Londinium was a place 'not distinguished indeed by the title of *colonia*' and that it was a centre of trade and commerce (Tacitus, *Annals*, XIV, 33). Following the destruction by Boudica, London appears to have taken on a new importance. It may well be that the original arrangement, with a capital placed at Camulodunum – an important centre in the pre-Roman period – was no longer necessary. Any political or strategic advantages this had probably no longer existed after the rebellion. Boudica and her supporters had destroyed the pro-Roman lobby in the three main centres at this time, and it is probable that the location of the earliest town at Camulodunum had the interests of these in mind. The destruction of Boudica's army, once teeming with the anti-Roman element, then enabled the incoming Roman administration to relocate their main administrative centre. London had already showed itself, in the ten years or so since its foundation, to be a prime site for

communication with the Continent and the rest of the province. Its development as the capital city, therefore, might have been part of a fresh start.

Other than the short-lived post-Boudican fort at Plantation Place (Dunwoodie et al in prep), however, there is no evidence during the Flavian period for anything resembling the Cripplegate fort for the housing of the staff and garrison, which a governor and procurator would have required. However, it is certain that such individuals would have existed. Even if the senior representatives of Rome were not always present in Londinium, the city would still have had to carry out the functions of a capital, in particular the calculation, storage and export of tax revenues. It may be significant, therefore, that Londinium does contain a number of houses which reflect a very strong Italian influence and which were presumably occupied by wealthy and highly Romanised members of the community. The best example of this is at Watling Court (WAT78). The period IV buildings there contain numerous mosaic floors and wall paintings of the Flavian period. Indeed, building D has been described as 'one of the best Romano-British town houses of the first century to have been discovered' (Perring and Roskams 1991, 105). It is possible that such a building could have been the residence of someone engaged on the emperor's business. It may be of further significance, therefore, to note that the destruction debris of this building, destroyed in the Hadrianic fire, contained a fragment of a bronze military diploma.

If this hypothesis is correct, that the buildings at Watling Court, and perhaps similar buildings to the immediate west at Watling House, 12–16 Watling Street, 31–37 Cannon Street (GM213), and Gateway House, 1 Watling Street (including the site of St John Evangelist church) (GM160; Shepherd 1986), housed some of the staff engaged in administrative duties, then the location to the immediate south of the large bath complex at Dominant House, 85 Queen Victoria Street/205 Upper Thames Street (DMT88), may be connected. Rather than there being a walled zone for the use of the governor's and procurator's staff, they may have been housed in the area on the west side of the Walbrook, with their own bathing establishment and, to the north, a timber amphitheatre. One reason for a change to this arrangement, as suggested above, may well be the Hadrianic fire which devastated the buildings described above. Whether, however, the construction of the fort was in direct response to the loss of these buildings or the fort had already just been introduced immediately before the fire, the building of the fort does represent a definite restructuring of whatever arrangements had existed beforehand. From the early 2nd century AD, it appears that the expectation was for all formal activities requiring military personnel to be centred upon the fort.

This then returns us to the observations made by Grimes, that the fort and town were essentially separate entities throughout the 2nd century AD. The fort was located away from the civil zone, with its own amphitheatre, a small bathhouse at Cheapside and, perhaps, a larger complex at DMT88. It may be of significance to note that the street pattern to the south and east of the fort do not show the regular planning that can be seen on the east side of the city. Is it possible, therefore, that the area immediately adjacent to the fort, that is between the fort and the road at Cheapside and the Walbrook to the east, came under the control of the senior officer of the fort? This would suggest that this area could be called a *vicus*, although the precise title must remain in doubt.

There are a number of elements in the area around the fort, which suggest that this zone was not part of the formal civil area. Firstly, the presence of industry in the upper Walbrook valley might not be surprising, but the scale of this industry would appear to be far greater than the needs of the town. Evidence there of tanning, leather working, glass working, bone working and some pottery production could have been taking advantage of military contacts and contracts as well as satisfying local demand. The large glass-working assemblages at Guildhall Yard and Basinghall Street are good examples of this. At Guildhall Yard (GYE92) a cullet dump (glass to be recycled) of *c* 50kg of broken vessel glass, window glass and glass-working debris suggests a large-scale operation (Perez-Sala and Shepherd 2008). It is not surprising to find the evidence that glass was being collected for recycling in any town, but this dump contains the fragments of over 2000 vessels. It is probable that it was collected over a very short period of time. If this is so, it is most unlikely that such a large number of vessels could have come from Londinium. It is possible, however, that this broken glass was entering the city along the same routes that the finished products were leaving. In other words, glass may have been coming in from many parts of the province, especially the military zones, and finished vessels were being exported to the same areas. Also, at Basinghall Street (BAZ06), a large deposit of glass-working waste suggests a scale of production that was probably much greater than the demands of the citizens of Londinium alone would require. In excess of 70kg of waste was recovered (McKenzie et al in prep).

It may also be significant that the boundaries of this part of the city do not appear to have remained constant. A 1st-century boundary is suggested as extending southwards from the later position of the south-west corner of the fort to the Thames. The presence of this can be surmised by the location of graves in the St Martin's le Grand and St Paul's area (Shepherd 1988, 11). In addition, a slight kink has been suggested in the alignment of the main east–west road as it passes through the position of this supposed boundary. However, this boundary, if it existed, moved westwards. Cremations of 2nd-century date in the Warwick Square cemetery (Tylor 1884), which are incidentally of the highest quality, suggest another

limit, although their location may be due to topographical considerations. Whatever the case, it is evident that, with the construction of the city wall in *c* AD 200, this and earlier boundaries had been discounted. On the east side of the city, however, the boundary appears to have remained constant. This different treatment may be a further indication of the separation of the two areas, one on either side of the Walbrook.

10.6 The building of the city wall and the late Roman period

Merrifield sought a historical context in which to place the construction of the city wall. He suggested that, as Londinium was the seat of the governor, this city was given priority during the Albinian rebellion so that, while other towns received earthworks, London received a stone wall (Merrifield 1983, 166–7). It is difficult to be certain of this but it would appear unlikely that a usurper who wished to claim Rome would take such a defensive posture. Indeed, the historical account shows that Albinus took the earliest opportunity to leave his province and cross the channel to prepare for the engagement with Severus. It is certainly beyond the scope of this publication but it is perhaps important to consider that the new, Severan administration is well recorded as having a major impact on the economies and administration of other areas of the Western Empire following his defeat of Albinus.

Considering the role that Londinium must have taken during the civil war, no doubt a main supporter of Albinus, it is likely to have been treated with a firm hand by the incoming Severan administration. Also, considering the range of problems between Britain and the rest of the Empire from *c* AD 180 it is not surprising that a new emperor might try to 'regularise' the situation. It has been argued elsewhere (Bédoyère 2001, 117) that the town walls of cities were primarily tariff boundaries, intended to control tax gathering and the movement of people and goods. Such a role might have been intended for the Londinium city wall – that is that it was a boundary linking together the gates and not a primary defensive circuit. The absence of any measure on the riverside might support this.

The evidence for a continuation of the arrangements in place during the 2nd century AD simply does not exist in the 3rd century AD. The barrack blocks were no longer in use and the defensive ditch on the south side of the fort was filling up with silt and rubbish during the same period. This is probably of greater significance since it would suggest that the defences of the fort in that area were no longer being maintained, which in turn would suggest that the fort was not being maintained also. In fact, it would appear that the fort no longer existed to function in the same way. It is most probable, as suggested above, that the construction of the city wall was carried out as a means to remove the need for a fort in this area.

The problem of defining the state of the south and east defences of the fort in the 3rd century AD and beyond is, therefore, difficult to resolve. Work by MOLA on the south side of the fort (Lyon 2004) revealed that the wall was extensively robbed, but exactly when this occurred is difficult to ascertain. Some evidence exists that it was carried out in the medieval period – but this need not necessarily mean that the wall survived to its full height until then. Rather, it could simply mean that the large foundations or stubs of the wall were removed at that later date.

This being so, there are important implications regarding the presence of the fort in this area and the nature of the post-Roman topography in this particular region of the city. Grimes admitted that the later history of the fort was unresolved by his own work. As has been seen above, he favoured the idea that the fort held a separate existence to the rest of the city at least until the construction of the city wall (c AD 200). Whether it remained in use during the 3rd century AD or the south and east walls were dismantled, he was not prepared to surmise. But the evidence now suggests that this was the case. However, Grimes (1968, 39) felt that the second of these alternatives, that the south and east walls were dismantled, was unlikely

> … on general grounds and such evidence as there is seems to be against it. This relates entirely to the survival in modified form of the street plan of the fort which might be expected to have suffered more drastic alteration if it had gone out of use before the end of the Roman period, to reappear when after the lost years of the early dark ages the city was reoccupied.

However, there no longer appears to be the need to see a continuity of the fort plan until the early medieval period (Milne 2001). The most important features in this respect are the city wall itself (the old west and north sides of the fort) and the position of the late Roman gate at Cripplegate (on the site of the north gate of the fort). The early medieval road system grew up on the Thames side and then expanded in planned phases northwards to the city wall. Each planning stage filled up a new zone. This reached the Cripplegate area during the 12th century and respected the city wall and gate at Cripplegate. The street plan, therefore, is only related to the fort plan in as much as the main topographic features of the area derive from the west and north sides of the fort. The street which passed through Cripplegate into the city was perpendicular to the city wall, which would have been the case for the 2nd-century fort road. The east–west alignments of Silver Street, especially, and Addle Street owe more to their positioning as interconnecting roads, although Silver Street may have been a lane which passed through a postern on the site of the old west gate of the

fort. The distribution of medieval pits at Windsor Court (WFG3) and Falcon Square (WFG5) seems to respect the route through the gateway (Fig 127).

The fort and the area in which it was placed have been considered in some detail here. It can be shown that the 1st-century occupation in the area, by no means as extensive as along the course of the main roads, was certainly considerable. It is likely that the imposition in the Hadrianic period of a major public building programme here would have caused some disruption. But whether this occurred before or after the Hadrianic fire is debatable. A case can be made for both occasions. The fort did not survive for long, however, and within a hundred years or so it may have gone out of use, or been replaced by a new garrison arrangement in the city. It is more than likely that this coincides with the building of the city wall, the purpose of which is beyond the scope of this publication. However, little comment has been made about the life of the fort itself, which naturally centres our attention upon the garrison. To conclude, therefore, it is appropriate to review the evidence for the military in Londinium and to examine once again the potential complement of Cripplegate fort.

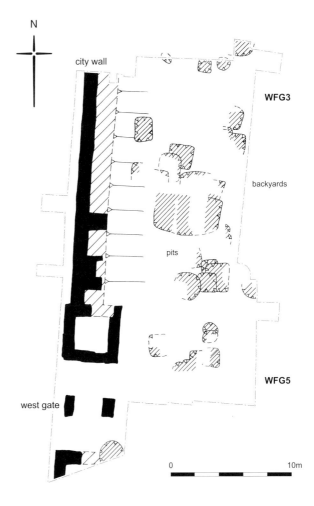

Fig 127 WFG3 and WFG5, general plan of the early medieval features on the site (scale 1:300)

10.7 The 2nd-century AD garrison of Londinium

Mark Hassall

There is no direct evidence as to the identity of the unit in garrison at the Cripplegate fort. Even such an apparently simple statement begs a number of questions. Firstly, it is a truism that the garrison of fort sites often changed in response to the needs and requirements of the Roman military, and the same could, in theory at least apply here. Secondly, though less well known, a significant number of Roman forts did not house single, discrete units, but either parts of units, more than one different unit, or parts of more than one different unit (Hassall 1998). For both of these reasons, therefore, a single unit may not be in question. Thirdly, recent work in analysing the small finds in one of the early barrack blocks at Vindolanda has shown the presence of women and children in two of the *contubernia* (Driel-Murray 1995; Hassall 1998), and if women and children, then why not other civilians? It would be better then to rephrase the opening statement as, there is no direct evidence as to the identity of the soldiers and (possibly) others accommodated in the Cripplegate fort.

In attempting to answer this question, there are two lines of approach that can be followed, the one a priori and the other deductive. The a priori approach considers London as the provincial capital and argues from the analogy of other, better-documented provinces as to the likely presence there of certain categories of soldiers and others who could have been accommodated in the fort. The deductive takes as its starting point the actual presence in London of soldiers attested to by tombstones or other forms of evidence, who *could* have been accommodated in the fort. Here the emphasis will be on the soldiers, for, despite the caveat about civilians given above, they will surely have been the major element in the fort. Finally, and based on both these lines of approach, the attempt is made to answer the question who occupied the Cripplegate fort and why they were stationed there.

London as a provincial capital

That London was the capital of the province in succession to Colchester there can be no doubt (Hassall 1996) (Fig 128). The only respect in which this was not true was that the centre of the imperial cult remained at Colchester, where the great temple of the

Fig 128 Reconstruction of Londinium, provincial capital, in the early 2nd century AD, looking north-west (by Peter Froste)

deified Claudius was rebuilt after its destruction by Boudica's rebels. Since the provincial council was intimately connected with the cult of the emperor, this too will have continued to meet at, or more probably just outside, Britain's 'premier' colony. The permanent offices of the governor's staff (*officium*) will have relocated to London soon after the revolt was crushed in AD 60–1, while the financial staff of the procurator had probably moved there even earlier. There was a sharp division between the two branches of the administration: the position of both governor (*legatus Augusti pro praetore*) and procurator were in the emperor's gift, and both men were directly responsible to the emperor. There, however, the resemblance ended. The former was a Roman senator, an ex-consul, and a man who had now been personally selected to serve the emperor in his public capacity as the highest officer of the Roman state – just as other legates assisted the proconsuls, men who were theoretically the emperor's peers, of Asia and Africa. The procurator on the other hand was an 'equestrian' who came from the second order of Roman society, the Roman knights, and though entrusted with public monies, served the emperor more in the manner of a personal steward.

The members of the staff of the procurator were of a status appropriate to this role, and will have largely consisted of imperial freedmen and slaves, collectively known as *Caesariani*, a term that has cropped up on one of the Vindolanda tablets (Bowman and Thomas 1996, appendix 326–8, sheet 1, lines 8–9). In contrast, the staff (*officium*) of the governor, who was both the highest administrative official and the commander-in-chief in the province, were freeborn soldiers on secondment from the military units, especially the legions, under his command and as such were known by the 4th century AD and probably earlier as *cohortalini* (Hassall 1996, 25). In considering the possible garrison of an overtly military establishment like the Cripplegate fort, it is the subordinates of the legate only which should be in question, a group which will also have included the somewhat enigmatic *beneficiarii* and *stratores consularis*. Further, and most significantly, as commander-in-chief of the legions and auxiliaries in the province, the governor was accorded a guard of infantry and cavalry drawn from the auxiliary cohorts and *alae* stationed in the province, and these may be presumed to have comprised the major element, if not the only, present in the fort (Hassall 1973; Davies 1976; Speidel 1978).

The governor's *officium, beneficiarii, stratores* and guards

The *officium* of the governor of an 'imperial province', such as Britain, that is one which fell within the remit of the emperor who acted through a deputy, the legate, will have consisted of clerks, accountants, short-hand writers and so on largely seconded from the legions. In absolute terms it will have been very small considering the administrative responsibilities of the governor, and has been reckoned in total as numbering some 200 men (Jones 1949). At its head will have been a seconded legionary centurion, known as the *princeps praetorii*. There will also have been a registry (*tabularium*) under a chief secretary (*scriba*), of whom one is actually attested for the British province, a certain Gaius Julius Justus, who died in post (*ILS*, no. 1883), and various functionaries such as five *lictores* who attended the legate on official business, or the *speculatores*, literally scouts, who were seconded, ten from each legion under his command to act as military policemen and executioners (Hassall 1973).

In addition to the above, London may have been the home base for two further groups of soldiers, the *beneficiarii consularis* and *stratores consularis* (Hassall 1996, 21–2). The *beneficiarii consularis*, literally 'beneficiaries of the consular (governor)', may have been concerned with military supply. They ranked below the post of centurion, and like centurions there were probably 60 *beneficiarii consularis* per legion. Inscriptions from Britain show that they were normally outposted, both to the northern frontier zone and to the civilian south. The *stratores consularis*, or 'grooms of the consular (governor)' were seconded auxiliary troopers. They were also outposted and there is some evidence to show that they were concerned with the supply of remounts to the army. The number of *stratores* is unknown, though they may have been sufficiently numerous to have been transformed en bloc into regular fighting units known as *stablesiani* during the crisis of the 3rd century AD (Speidel 1974). A unit of *equites stablesiani* was based at Burgh Castle (Norfolk) on the Saxon shore, but if its numbers are unknown, it is reckoned that there will have been either 180 or 240 *beneficiarii consularis* attached to the governor before the division of Britain in the early 3rd century AD, depending on whether there were three or four legions stationed in the province.

The final group to consider are the governor's horse and foot guards, the *equites* and *pedites singulares* (Hassall 1973; 1996, 22; Speidel 1978). These men were selected – hence the name *singularis* – from the auxiliary units serving in the province, but remained on the books of their parent unit. Both infantry and cavalry detachments were normally under the command of seconded legionary centurions, with the title *praepositus* or *curam agens* (Speidel 1978, 26–8). There is no hard evidence as regards numbers, though Speidel has argued (ibid, 13) that they equated to regular *alae* and cohorts in size – that is 480 or 800 for the infantry and 480 (or possibly 720) for the cavalry – and thus it was that the detachment of the British foot guards, or to give them their official title, the *numerus singularium Britannicianorum* could, without difficulty be incorporated into one of the local provincial armies, after having been transferred to the Danube front in the late 1st century AD (Birley 1953). This unit never returned to Britain but a newly enrolled corps will have replaced it there. If a suggestion that the 1500 picked spearmen who were sent to Rome towards the end of the reign of Commodus to enforce the demands of the army in Britain (Dio, *Epitome* LXXXIII, 88) were identical with the governor's *pedites* and *equites singulares* is correct (Hassall 1973; rejected by Davies 1976; accepted by Speidel 1978), then the detachment of *pedites* will have been milliary (nominally 1000, in practice 800) and the detachment of *equites* quingenary (nominally 500 in practice 480). The question of numbers is an important one which will be raised again below.

To summarise, it is likely that the Cripplegate fort housed the governor's bodyguard, perhaps 800 infantry and 450 cavalry troopers with their mounts. In addition it could have held the governor's *officium* of *c* 200 men, the *tabularium* of unknown size but presumably considerably smaller, and possibly 180 *beneficiarii* (or 240 if the 1st-century timber fort existed), and an unknown but presumably comparable number of *stratores*. It is time to look at the evidence from Britain in general and more particularly from London itself.

The evidence for soldiers in Roman London

The evidence for soldiers in Roman London ranges from the archaeological such as items of military equipment, of which there is a surprisingly large amount (Bishop et al in prep), to the epigraphic (Chapter 11.2). Some items defy easy categorisation: one such is the famous tombstone found incorporated into the Camomile Street bastion (Bishop 1983), which shows a soldier in 'undress' uniform, equipped with a sword and carrying what appears to be a bundle of writing tablets; it has lost the inscription which would have placed it firmly in the epigraphic category. Another is a spearhead which would naturally be classed as an archaeological find were it not for the presence of an inscription (*RIB* 1991, 2427.3). In dealing with the archaeological evidence a problem arises in difficulties of attributing specific types of armour or weaponry to specific classes of troops – for example legionary or auxiliary. Thus, for example, it has been shown (Maxfield 1986, 66–7) that *loricae segmentatae* (cf the significant element from a set of armour of this type from the site of the Bank of England, Threadneedle Street, excavated in 1926–36: Robinson 1975, 174–5; Wilmott 1991, 51–4), were not used exclusively by legionaries despite repeated assertions to the contrary.

The epigraphic material is normally much more explicit, although even here there can be doubt: in the case of the inscribed spearhead cited above, the inscription, C VER VICT, can be interpreted as *C(enturiae) Ver(i)*, *Vict(oris)*, '(property) of Victor, in the century of Verus', but it is uncertain whether Verus was legionary or, as is more probable, an auxiliary centurion. In this particular instance there would be no problem if one could attribute the use of the spear exclusively to auxiliary infantry and *pila* to legionaries, but this is an assumption that is not justified. Neglecting such ambiguous cases, the epigraphic (and other written) evidence can be used to show the presence of both legionaries and auxiliaries in Roman London.

Legionaries

Soldiers from Legions II Augusta, VI Victrix and XX Valeria Victrix are all attested. Of these the following are of particular significance.

1   Tombstone of Vivius (=Vibius) Marcianus centurion (probably) of Legion II Augusta (<MI6>, Chapter 11.2).
2   Tombstone of Celsus, a *speculator* (military policeman) in Legion II Augusta set up by three colleagues from the same legion (<MI3>, Chapter 11.2).
3   At least 24 serving soldiers from at least three cohorts of an unknown legion listed on an inscription, cut on fine sheets of marble found at the site of Winchester Palace (<MI12>, Chapter 11.2). The inscription is not directly dated but since many of those mentioned have the nomen Aurelius it will date to the 3rd century AD, after the decree of Caracalla awarding citizenship to all freeborn provincials, when this, the emperor's nomen, became extremely common.

The presence of <MI6> need not be significant, although it would not be difficult to find a role for a legionary centurion at the provincial capital, either as commander of the *pedites singulares*, or as *princeps praetorii* (head of the governor's *officium*), or in some other senior administrative role. The presence of the group of *speculatores*, <MI3>, however, is of unquestionable significance. If these men were present at the provincial capital on secondment from their legion, then *speculatores* from all the legions in the province will have been there also – theoretically a total of 40 (or 30 after the legionary establishment in the province was reduced from four to three). These are just the sort of men that one would expect to see accommodated within the Cripplegate fort. Significant too will have been the men listed on the Winchester Palace inscription, <MI12>. Because of the fragmentary nature of the inscription, we do not know the reason for their presence in London, but it is highly probable that it was linked with its role as the provincial capital. The suggestion has been made that they may have been *beneficiarii consularis* seconded from each of the centuries of one of the legions in the province, for whom London was their home base (Hassall 1996, 23). An alternative might be even to see them as the *cohortalini* of the governor's *officium*, but whoever they were, it is unlikely that they were quartered in the

Cripplegate fort, rather than at some as yet unlocated spot in Southwark in the immediate vicinity of Winchester Palace.

Auxiliaries

The presence of auxiliaries in London is less well attested, but of particular interest are the following.

1 A writing tablet from Vindolanda records that 46 men and one centurion were detached from the First Cohort of Tungrians for service with the governor's bodyguard (destination not stated) and one centurion detached (? with them) for service in London (Bowman and Thomas 1994, no. 154; Hassall 1996, 22).
2 The military diploma (certificate of Roman citizenship and 'marriage licence' normally awarded to veterans on discharge after 25 years' service) of an unnamed veteran of an unknown unit, dated to an unknown year between AD 96 and AD 108, was found in 1978 during excavations at Watling Court, 41–53 Cannon Street (WAT78; <MI10>, <MI11>; Chapter 11.2).

The first point to note is that even if the centurion did not serve with the 46 infantrymen, the latter were almost certainly present with him at the provincial capital – London. Can anything more be extracted from this brief but tantalising notice? Despite the fact that Cohors I Tungrorum had only six centurions and presumably six centuries, so that it had the structure of a quingenary cohort, it was probably a *cohors peditata milliaria*, that is to say was composed entirely of infantry and had a nominal strength of 800 men. Forty-six men would represent about 5.75% of the total strength of the unit. Does this figure help in estimating the size of the unit of *pedites singulares* attached to the governor? Probably not since there are so many imponderables, but assuming that this was on average the sort of number deducted from all auxiliary units in the province – and it is a big assumption – it should be possible to estimate the approximate number of *pedites singulares* in the governor's bodyguard if one knew the total number of auxiliary infantrymen who served in the province. In AD 122, for which year our evidence is best, there were at least 50 auxiliary units in the province (CIL 1936, 69). Of these, 37 were either infantry cohorts or cohorts to which a cavalry element had been added (*cohortes equitatae* a term conventionally translated as 'part-mounted cohorts'). Cohorts of both sorts were either 'quingenary' with a nominal strength of 480 infantry, or 'milliary' with a nominal strength of 800 infantry, probably irrespective of whether they had a cavalry element attached or not. Of the 37 cohorts, then, as far as the evidence presently available goes, 33 were 'quingenary' with a combined nominal strength of 15,840 infantry, and four were milliary with a combined nominal strength of 3200 for

a grand total of *c* 19,000 (Holder 1982, appendix 104–24). And, for what it is worth, 5.75% of this figure comes to 1092.

If the (lower grade) cavalry troopers in the part-mounted units were not drawn upon to serve as *equites singulares*, and these were only selected from the troopers in the *alae* (the *alares*), a similar calculation would be based on a pool of 12 'quingenary' *alae* (of 480 men each) totalling 5760 and one 'milliary' *ala* of (probably) 720 men, that is 6480. If 5.75% of this figure was deducted to form the *equites singulares*, the figure would come to 372. If the total number of *equites* were available, including the cavalry elements from the part-mounted cohorts, the figure would, of course, rise. There were three milliary part-mounted cohorts with a cavalry element of 240 each, so adding another 720 troopers and 18 quingenary units with a cavalry element of 120 each, for a total of 2160, giving a total of troopers in the part-mounted cohorts of 2880, which when added to the number in the *alae* gives a grand total of 9360. If 5.75% of these men served as governor's guards, the total would come to 538. These figures, of course, cannot be taken literally, but they are not inconsistent with a force of *c* 800 *pedites singulares* or *c* 480 *equites singulares*. Or put another way, if the unit of *pedites* was milliary, and that of *equites* quingenary, the Tungrians at Vindolanda would seem to have been fairly typical in supplying 5–6% of their strength for service in them.

Turning to the find of the auxiliary diploma <MI10> and <MI11>, it presumably indicates that in the early years of the 2nd century AD one veteran from an auxiliary unit chose to settle in London. There could be all sorts of reasons why this was so, but the most natural one is that he had previously served there, and on present evidence this can only have been as a member of the governor's guards – the *singulares*.

Others

1 At the outset of the Boudican revolt in AD 60 or AD 61, Decianus Catus, the provincial procurator, sent 200 half-armed men to Colchester (Tacitus, *Annals*, XIV, 32). Since he was clearly not at Colchester himself, and since the later seat of the procurator appears to have been in London (Hassall 1996, 20), this group could well have come from London.
2 One of the documents found at Vindolanda (Bowman and Thomas 1994, no. 310) is a letter from a certain Chrauttius to Veldedeius, the governor's groom (*equisio consularis*) at London.
3 There may have been a detachment of the British fleet (*Classis Britannica*) based in London as suggested by Milne (1996, 53).

It is unlikely that the force of '200 half-armed men' under the command of a 1st-century procurator, or their successors in the early 2nd century AD, were housed along with personnel connected with the governor given the independent nature of their spheres and the animosity that existed between the two imperial functionaries. An example of the latter is the hostile report sent back to Nero by the procurator Julius Classicianus on the conduct of the governor Suetonius Paulinus. Similarly, antipathy between the procurator and the legate is implied by Tacitus's statement that the model governor Agricola when in Aquitaine always got on well with *his* procurator (Tacitus, *Agricola*, 9). The fact that the men were 'half armed' perhaps suggests a scratch force raised from the *Caesariani*, the clerks among others on the procurator's staff.

Again, members of the governor's immediate staff, like Veldedeius, were presumably closely attached to the governor person. The existence of the supposed palace of the governor at Cannon Street Station has recently been disproved by Milne (1996), but no doubt it existed somewhere, and it is there, in a stable block attached to the *praetorium* that Veldedeius (and his castrating shears!) may well have been found. Finally, while it is more than likely that a detachment of the fleet was based in London, their presence would be expected closer to the naval dockyards, wherever they were located.

To conclude, a consideration of the situation to be expected in London as the capital of the province, suggests that a force of 800 foot guards and 480 horse guards with their mounts were quartered in the vicinity of the city, which in effect means the Cripplegate fort. In addition, the *c* 200 men of the governor's *officium* also may have been accommodated in the fort. The situation as regards *beneficiarii* (180 or 240 men) and *stratores* (an unknown number) is uncertain. It is unlikely that the *Caesariani* of the procurator were housed within the fort. Turning to the archaeological and, in particular, the epigraphic and documentary evidence from Britain, the Vindolanda documents give some slight support to the figures suggested for the number of guardsmen present. The tombstones, particularly that of the *speculator* Celsus, reinforce the presumption that the members of the governor's *officium* and other seconded legionary personnel *were* present at the provincial capital, but since they come from the cemeteries they are of no value in locating their whereabouts there. The Winchester Palace inscription (<MI12>, Chapter 11.2), however, is a different matter. It may, as suggested above, show that the permanent base of the *beneficiarii consularis*, or conceivably the site of the governor's *officium*, lay somewhere in Southwark, rather than in the Cripplegate fort. If the inscription does not refer to either, it would seem to show the presence of a significant number of legionaries, perhaps 60 or more – six or seven men from all ?ten cohorts of one of the British legions – were based south of the river. It is unlikely that the personal attendants of the governor or men of the fleet were stationed in the fort. The

conclusion that emerges is that the two major elements in the fort's garrison were the governor's foot and horse guards – perhaps 800 infantrymen and 480 troopers and their mounts – some 1280 men and 480 horses in a fort of some 11 acres (4.5ha). For comparison, the 720 troopers of the *Ala Petriana* and their mounts were housed at Stanwix on Hadrian's Wall in a fort 3.8ha in size. Comparisons should not be pushed too far, since densities of occupation can vary considerably, but this sounds about right.

It is unfortunate that not more is known of the plan of the fort. It may have resembled that of the fort of Echzell in Upper Germany, though there the barrack blocks were set out parallel to the four sides of the fort. The comparison is a particularly happy one given the mixed garrison of an auxiliary infantry cohort (though quingenary rather than milliary as suggested for London) and a cavalry *ala* (Hassall 1996). One other fort in southern Germany which might also be cited is the little fort at Ellingen occupied by the *pedites singulares* of the governor of Raetia in the later 2nd century AD. Here the barracks of more or less conventional design consisted of 12 *contubernia* instead of the expected ten required for an infantry century of ten sections, and there is no headquarters building (*principia*). The latter feature can be explained by the fact already observed in the case of the *singulares* despatched from Cohors I Tungrorum at Vindolanda, that men selected for service in the governor's guard remained 'on the books' of their original unit, so that administrative requirements of units of guards will have been minimal (Hassall 1996, 23). The second could be explained if two of the *contubernia* had been set aside as married quarters, as also happened at Vindolanda (cf Driel-Murray 1995). So this survey concludes with two questions: was there or was there not a *principia* at the Cripplegate fort and were women accommodated – on a regular basis that is – within the barracks?

10.8 Conclusion

The work of Grimes in the Cripplegate area described in this volume and the subsequent work by MOLA archaeologists in the 1990s (Howe and Lakin 2004) emphasise that the construction of the fort was a new project in the first few decades of the 2nd century AD. Earlier activity cannot be assigned to a military function, unless it was associated with the construction gangs for the fort itself, but there is compelling evidence to suggest that some of this pre-fort occupation (eg at WFG22) occurred during the later quarter of the 1st century AD, long before a fort appears to have been planned for this area of Londinium.

The life of the fort during the 2nd century AD is not well documented by Grimes's work. Indeed, it is still very difficult to determine the original complement housed in the fort itself. There is nothing among the finds assemblages here – or from the 1990s campaign –

to assist in their identification. It is evident, however, that the fort must have played an important role, but it is most likely that this role was of provincial significance rather than just local or regional. The fort needs to be read as part of the national network of fortifications and works carried out during this period, including of course the construction of Hadrian's Wall. It would be misleading to see it as part of a parochial attempt at defence, although of course its position did protect important lines of supply and communication.

The fort does not appear to have existed during the 3rd century AD, and it can be argued that the construction of the city wall *c* AD 200 was the catalyst for the removal or dispersal to other areas of the city of the garrison – Southwark perhaps. The area of the fort remains largely *dishabitatio* and it is unlikely that the correlation of the road network in the fort and later, medieval street systems indicate continuity. Rather, the latter represents a use of the gates of the fort and the resulting through routes coinciding with the earlier Roman roads.

The work conducted by Grimes in the 1950s and 60s in the Cripplegate area was remarkable in that so much was revealed with so few resources. His careful selection of sites in order to retrieve the plan of the fort, while also excavating at the temple of Mithras, St Bride and elsewhere, demonstrates the careful research and thought that went into this campaign of work. Without a doubt, his archive has suffered over the years and had he published closer to the time of discovery then morc detail might have been forthcoming. This publication, however, puts on record the main results of his work and will allow, with the results of the more recent work by MOLA, a more detailed assessment of the role of the Cripplegate fort to be undertaken in the future.

11 Appendices

11.1 Excavations at Noble Street, 1973

Patrick Allen

This section was dug in December 1973 by staff of the DUA during landscaping of visible remains of the Roman fort surviving along the west side of Noble Street. The section extended eastwards from the line of the fort wall and crossed the associated bank, internal wall thickening and intramural street. These features had already been identified by the RMLEC (WFG6 and WFG7, Chapter 6.1). The section and its accompanying archive note are included here as a comparison with Grimes's work. The section (Fig 129) was drawn by Peter Ellis and Gustav Milne. The survey work was carried out at various intervals by Patrick Allen, Trevor Brigham, Derek Gadd and John Maloney.

NOB73, 29 Noble Street

DUA 1973 (Fig 73; Fig 74); NGR: TQ 3222 8149

Phase 1

The surface of the natural brickearth [21] was recorded at the bottom of the section. It was nearly level, undulating very gently between 12.53m and 12.65m OD.

Above the natural ground surface was a substantial layer, 0.15–0.25m thick, of grey clay containing lenses of sand and gravel in the east and traces of mortar in the west ([12], [20], Fig 129). This layer extended the full length of the section, but was so undulating that it is unlikely to have formed a ground surface. It was sealed by an equally thick and extensive layer of clean red brickearth containing horizontal lenses of mortar at its western end ([11], [19]). This was evenly laid and formed a nearly level surface at 12.90–12.95m OD. This levelling represents a major ground preparation for subsequent development.

In the west the levelling was sealed by a massive deposit of orange clay (?brickearth) containing lenses of grey clay, loam and gravel [18], which formed a bank 2.40m wide and 0.95m high, with its top at 13.85m OD. To the east the bank sloped down at a ratio of between 1:1 and 1:2, but to the west it was recorded as lying up against a ragstone wall ([22], below, phase 2), sealing its offset foundation.

If true, this relationship causes considerable problems of interpretation, as the sequence represented would be completely different to sequences recorded to the immediate north and south. The bank is similar in every respect, especially in its position and the clean material of which it was composed, to the bank built up against the original wall of the fort (Grimes 1968, 17). However, wall [22], with which the bank is apparently associated, is clearly related, both by position and alignment, to the secondary reinforcement of the fort wall (ibid). The line of the fort wall itself lies just beyond the western limit of the section, where it has been cut away by modern cellaring. On balance, the correlation of the bank and wall lines with those recorded to both north and south suggests that the bank can only have been the primary bank associated with the original fort wall, with wall [22] in fact a later construction. The most likely explanation of the evidence on the section is that it was misrecorded, and that the foundation trench for wall [22] (ibid, 21 and figs 3, 10) was missed. Significantly, the bank was affected by modern disturbance in the immediate vicinity of the wall.

If this interpretation is accepted, there is no doubt that the levelling and the construction of the bank were both directly related to the initial construction of the fort. As to the north (Grimes 1968, 17), the top of the levelling contained spreads of mortar adjacent to the fort wall, and presumably related to its construction.

Cut into the tail of the bank was a shallow feature, 0.45m wide and 0.15m deep, with a curved profile and a bottom at 12.79m OD [23]. Further east, a thin layer of loose pale gravel [10] was laid above the

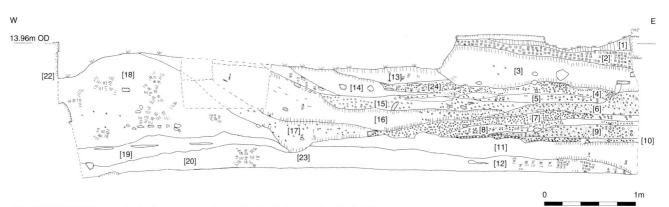

Fig 129 NOB73, south-facing section through the defences (scale 1:40)

levelling sequence and formed a nearly level surface at 12.95–12.98m OD (Fig 129). Its western edge was 1.55m from the cut feature, but its eastern edge lay beyond the limit of the section. These two features must represent the first surface of the intramural street (Street 1), and a shallow drainage gully at the tail of the fort bank.

While the bank and gully survived in their original form the street was resurfaced on three occasions.

A thick layer of coarse sandy gravel [9], which formed the surface of Street 2 at 13.09m OD, sealed Street 1. Street 2 was thickly and evenly laid for the most part, but sloped down at its western edge to the surface of the underlying Street 1.

Above Street 2 a mixture of clay and gravel [8] was more thinly laid to form the surface of Street 3 at 13.15m OD. Street 3 was more thickly laid towards its western edge, which extended beyond the edge of Street 2, so that the street was restored to its original width.

Above Street 3 hard-packed gravel [7] was laid to form the surface of Street 4 at 13.19–13.25m OD. Like its predecessor, Street 4 was quite thinly laid at its centre, but more thickly laid at its western edge, which extended some 0.80m beyond that of the earlier streets. The edge of the street was consolidated with a square-cut stone. Street surfaces continued to be laid above Street 4, but only Streets 1–4 were related to the bank and gully in their original form. Overall, the features of phase 1 represent the initial construction of the fort defences and intramural street, and their continued maintenance without any change to the initial layout.

Phase 2

The bank and gully of phase 1 were sealed by a layer, 0.15m thick, of loam mixed with gravel [17], which marginally overlapped the western edge of Street 4 (Fig 129). This layer followed the profile of the bank, merely building it up a little, but to the east it levelled off at 13.10m OD and extended beyond the tail of the bank to form a common surface with Street 4. Patches of clay in the base of the layer filled the gully, suggesting that it had become clogged up before being sealed over. Street 4 remained unsealed and must have continued in use.

In the east, the street was partially resurfaced with loose reddish sandy gravel [6], which formed Street 5 at 13.25–13.30m OD. This street was quite thickly laid, but sloped down abruptly at its western edge, which was well short of the edge of the underlying Street 4. The exposed portion of Street 4 must have remained in use as part of Street 5, and the street at this time would have been distinctly cambered, with its centre built up c 0.30m higher than at its edges.

To the west, loam containing charcoal flecks [16] represents a further, more substantial addition to the bank, which extended for 2.5m beyond its original eastern edge. Towards its eastern end the loam was very gravelly and not only sealed the exposed portion of Street 4, but also overlapped the edge of Street 5, representing considerable encroachment of the street.

Above this, light sandy gravel (with a patch of cinders and brick at its surface) [15] extended from the surviving western edge of Street 5 for a distance of 1.75m, and formed a surface continuous with it at exactly the same level. This surfacing was actually cut into the underlying loam, and must represent a deliberate widening of Street 5 by cutting into the tail of the bank.

The widened Street 5 was partially resurfaced with compact gravel mixed with clay [5], probably no more than a local repair. Above this, fine red sandy gravel [4] was laid more extensively to form Street 6, whose surface was truncated at c 13.50m OD.

The very western edge of Street 6 was overlapped by loam mixed with clay, containing charcoal flecks and tips of brick and stone [14], which represents yet another addition to the bank. The tail of the bank again encroached upon the street, though to a lesser extent than before.

Above Street 6, sandy gravel containing patches of clay [24] formed a surface at 13.66m OD. This surfacing was cut into the tail of the bank in similar fashion to the widening of Street 5, and represents a further attempt to restore the street to its full width. The surface was cut away to the east by modern disturbance, so that it is impossible to say whether it represents a completely new street metalling or merely a repair at the edge of Street 6.

The latest street surface was sealed by loam mixed with clay and gravel [13]. This layer followed the profile of the bank and is likely to have been a further addition to it.

Overall, material accumulated or was dumped over the bank to a height of at least 0.60m, and successive deposits encroached upon the intramural street. The street itself was repaired and resurfaced, and on two occasions a deliberate attempt was made to re-establish the original street edge by cutting into the tail of the bank. This is in complete contrast to phase 1, when it was possible to maintain the street and gully without encroachment from the bank.

The ragstone wall [22] at the extreme east end of the section is certainly related to the secondary reinforcement of the fort wall, and it is assumed that its relationship with the original bank has been misrecorded (above, phase 1). On this basis, wall [22] presumably cut the original bank and was part of the changes taking place in phase 2. Unfortunately though, the relationship between the wall and the various additions to the bank, and by extension the later streets to the east, was truncated by later intrusions.

The latest, modern, surfaces of phase 2 were sealed by loam mixed with stone and brick rubble [3]. This deposit was apparently cut into the underlying stratigraphy. Above it was a thick layer of clay [2] and a thin layer of soil [1] which formed a make-up for the concrete slab of the Victorian cellar floor at just over 14m OD.

11.2 Epigraphic evidence for the military in Roman London

A corpus of epigraphic and sculptural evidence for military equipment from London is currently being compiled (Bishop et al in prep). The selection below includes only those items which have or are likely to have had inscriptions of a military nature.

Propraetorian legate

<MI1> Limestone altar; 3rd century AD (possibly AD 251–9)
Found reused in the 3rd-century riverside wall, Upper Thames Street, 1976
Museum of London (acc no. 77.57)
IN H(onorem) D(omus) D(ivinae) /
M(arcus) MARTIAN /
NIVS PULCH /
ER V(ices) F(unctus) LEG(ati) /
AVGG(ustorum) PRO /
PRAET(ore) TEMPL(u)M /
ISIDIS C[...] /
TIS VETVSTATE /
COLLABSVM /
RESTITVI PRAE /
CEPIT
'In honour of the divine imperial house, Marcus Martiannius Pulcher, deputy (?) imperial propraetorian legate of the two emperors ordered the temple of Isis...... which had fallen down through old age, to be restored'.
Reference: A full discussion can be found in Hassall 1980, 195–8, pl 57.

Centurion

<MI2> Purbeck marble tombstone, late 1st–2nd century AD
From Bishopsgate
Museum of London (acc no. A25458)
[D(is) M(anibus) /
[....SEMPRO]NIO SEMPRO[NIANO /
CEN]TVRIONI LEG(ionis) /
[...VI]XIT ANNOS LI /
[ET FRATRIB]VS SEMPRONIIS /
[.......] ET SECVNDO /
[LIBER]TI EIVS /
[PATRONIS BENE ME]REN /
[TIBVS POS]V[ERV]NT
'To the spirits of the departed and to Sempronius Sempronianus, centurion of the ... Legion who lived 51 years and to his brothers Sempronius ... and Sempronius Secundus; his freedmen had this set up for

their well-deserving patrons'.
References: RCHM(E) 1928, 172–3; *RIB* 1965, 15.

Speculator

<MI3> Limestone tombstone, 3rd century AD
From Playhouse Yard, Blackfriars, 1843
British Museum (acc no. PRB 1855, 0804, 21)
[DIS MANI]BVS /
[...]R L(uci) F(ilius) C[L(audia tribu)] CELSV[S] /
[...S]PEC(ulator) LEG (ionis) [II A]VG(ustae) AN /
[TONINIA]NE DARDAN[I]VS CV[R /
SOR R]VBRIVS PVDENS /
[...]S PROBVS SP[E]C(ulatores) L(egionis)
'To the spirits of the departed; [...]r Celsus, son of Lucius, of the Claudian voting tribe, [from ...], speculator of the Second Legion Augusta Antoniniana; Dardanius Cursor, Rubius Pudens and [...]s, spectolatores of the legion (set this up)'.
References: RCHM(E) 1928, 173; *RIB* 1965, 19; Hassall 1973.

Beneficiarius

<MI4> Limestone tombstone, late 1st or early 2nd century AD
Barter Street/Bloomsbury Court/High Holborn, 1963
British Museum (acc no. PRB 1961, 0704, 1)
DIS MANIBVS /
G(aii) POMPONI /
G(aii) F(ilii) VALENTIS /
VICTRICENS[IS] /
[B(ene)F(icarii)] TRIB(uni) [.] LE[G(ionis)...
'To the spirits of the departed and to Gaius Pomponius Valens, son of Gaius, from Colchester, beneficarius of the legionary tribune....'
References: Painter 1963.

<MI5> Limestone tombstone, late 1st/early 2nd century AD
Camomile Street bastion with other sculptural and architectural fragments, 1876
Museum of London (acc no. 3366)
No inscription but the figure is that of a legionary soldier, sometimes identified as a *beneficiarius*. The figure is wearing a tunic and cloak, with a short sword and studded strap terminating in a crescent-shaped ornament hanging from his belt. His left hand holds a case of wooden writing tablets, perhaps indicating that his duties were partly clerical. The soldier was probably a non-commissioned officer seconded from his legion to serve on the headquarter's staff of the governor.
References: Price 1880; RCHM(E) 1928, 45; Bishop 1983.

Legionary soldiers

<MI6> Limestone tombstone, 3rd century AD
Found during the rebuilding of St Martin's church,

Ludgate Hill, 1669
Museum of London (acc no. L162, on permanent loan from the Ashmolean Museum)
D(is) M(anibus) /
VIVIO MARCI /
ANO LEG(ionis) II /
AVG(ustae) IANVARIA /
MARTINA CONIUNX /
PIENTISSIMA POSV /
IT MEMORIAM
'To the spirits of the departed and to Vivius Marcianus of the Second Legion Augusta, Januaria Martina his most devoted wife set up this memorial'.
The soldier wears a tunic with a military belt and a long cloak draped over his left shoulder. He holds a staff in his right hand and perhaps a scroll in his left. The staff may indicate that he was a centurion.
References: RCHM(E) 1928, 173; *RIB* 1965, 17; Hassall 1996, 21.

<MI7> Slate tombstone, 3rd century AD
From Goodman's Fields, Minories
Museum of London (acc no. 29.90; on loan from the Society of Antiquaries)
D(is) M(anibus) /
FL(avius) AGRICOLA MIL(es) /
LEG(ionis) VI VICT(ricis) V(ixit) AN(nos) /
XLII D(ies) X ALBIA /
FAVSTINA CONIVGI /
INCONPARABILI /
F(aciendum) C(uravit)
'To the spirits of the departed; Flavius Agricola, soldier of the Sixth Legion Victrix, lived 42 years, 10 days; Albia Faustina had this made for her incomparable husband'.
References: RCHM(E) 1928, 171; *RIB* 1965, 11.

<MI8> Stone tombstone
From Church Lane, Whitechapel, 1776
Now lost
D(is) M(anibus)
IVL(ius) VALENS /
MIL(es) LEG(ionis) XX V(aleriae) V(ictricis) /
AN(norum) XL H(ic) S(itus) E(st) /
C(uram) A(gente) FLAVIO /
ATTIO HER(ede)
'To the spirits of the departed; Julius Valens, Soldier of the Twentieth Legion Valeria Victrix, aged 40, lies here. His heir Flavius Attius saw to it being done'.
References: RCHM(E) 1928, 172; *RIB* 1965, 13.

Auxiliary soldier

<MI9> Fragment of limestone tombstone
From unknown London site
Museum of London (acc no. 23083)
No inscription, but may have had one originally.
The figure is carved in low relief and wears a helmet, cloak and tunic. He is armed with a spear and the oval shield of an auxiliary infantryman. An alternative interpretation of the figure is that it is of Mars.

<MI10> Copper-alloy diploma of an auxiliary veteran, AD 96–108

<MI11> Second tablet as <MI10>
From Watling Court, 41–53 Cannon Street, 1978
Museum of London (acc no. WAT78 [225], <380>)
Fragments of two tablets of an auxiliary soldier's official release or retirement diploma. It was issued to soldiers after 25 years of service. The tablets have been fused together by fire.
References: Roxan 1978, no. 83; 1983, 67–72; Hassall and Tomlin 1983, 344–5 no. 34; *RIB* 1990, 2401.5.

Military guilds

<MI12> Fragmentary marble building inscription, 3rd century AD
Found during excavations of Winchester Palace, 1983–4
Museum of London (acc no. WP83)
Seven fragments of inscription consisting of names. The inscription lists personnel drawn from ten cohorts of a legion. It is uncertain whether they were in London for a special occasion, on garrison duty or were men seconded from one of the legions to serve on the governor's staff. Because of the 3rd-century date, the men may have come from the Twentieth Legion or the Twentieth Legion Augusta, both of which were known to be in Britannia Superior at that time.
References: Hassall and Tomlin 1985; Hassall 1996, 22–3, pls 26 and 27; Yule 2005, 69–73, 75; *RIB* 2009, 3016, note also 3017, a list of centurions, and 3018, probably a fragment from a further list of names of centurions or legionaries, both from the same context.

The century – legionary equipment with inscriptions

<MI13> Copper-alloy helmet, mid 1st century AD
From the Walbrook or Thames
British Museum (acc no. PRB 1950, 0706, 1)
There are four instances of punched graffiti on the neckguard:
>(centuria) M(arci) VAL(erii) VRS(i) L(uci) DVLCI
'(Property) of Lucius Dulcis in the century of Marcus Valerius Ursus'
>(centuria) MART(ialis?) L(ucius) POSTVMUS
'In the century of Martialis, Lucius Postumus
>(centuria) SCR(iboni) RVFI
'(Property) of Rufus in the century of Scribonius'
>(centuria) MA(rtialis?) AVL(i) SAVFEI
'(Property) of Aulus Saufeius in the century of Martialis'.
References: British Museum 1951, pl XXV.5; Wright 1951, 142–3, no. 11; Robinson 1975, 32; *RIB* 1991, 2425.2.

<MI14> Iron spearhead, late 1st century AD
From Bucklersbury House, Walbrook, 1954
Museum of London (acc no. 19233)
>(centuria) . VER(i) . VICT(oris)
'The century of Verus Victor' or '(belonging to) Victor in the century of Verius'.
References: RIB 1991, 2427.2; Wilmott 1991, 147.

<MI15> Lead tag
From Courages, Park Street, Southwark, 1984
Museum of London (acc no. COSE84 [4087], <696>)
C.Q.CORNIILI VIIRIICVNDI
'The century of Quintus Cornelius Verecundus'.
References: Hassall and Tomlin 1994, 304; Cowan 2003, 172–3, <S152>.

The armourer

<MI16> Copper-alloy shield boss
From Fenchurch Street/ Gracechurch Street
British Museum (acc no. PRB 1940, 0405, 1)
Stamped near the rim:
COCILLVS F(ecit)
'Cocillus made (this)'.
References: Jackson 1984; *RIB* 1991, 2426.3

11.3 Visible remains of the Roman fort and city wall in the Cripplegate area

1) St Alphage Gardens

Section of northern wall and Roman fort, subsequently incorporated into the Roman city wall. The wall fell into disrepair during the Saxon period. In the 11th century, a church dedicated to St Alphage was built against the city wall, the inner face of the wall serving as the north wall of the graveyard.

The overall surviving length of the wall is *c* 46.5m with its full post-medieval height of 7m. At the eastern end, the face of the wall is set back to a mainly brick post-medieval face. At the point of the offset, the Roman fort wall (with medieval facing) and later Roman internal thickening is visible. The vertical butt joint between the two is clearly visible.
References: RCHM(E) 1928, 90; Bell et al 1937, 3, 9, 10; Merrifield 1965, W40; Grimes 1968, 27, 78–82; Chapman et al 1985, site 12.

2) Wallside, St Giles Cripplegate

Roman fort wall at the base of a stretch of early medieval rebuild of the city wall. Most of the surviving stonework dates to the early medieval period with battlements rebuilt in brick in the late 15th century. The foundations of Bastion 11A survive, projecting northwards from the face of the wall. Bastion 12 lies to the west of Wallside, standing *c* 9m high and forms the

edge of a lake in the Barbican development.

A stretch of wall, *c* 32m in length and *c* 4m high, reaches as far as Bastion 11A. The thickness of the original fort wall is *c* 1.25m. The later Roman internal thickening has been removed.
References: RCHM(E) 1928, 104; Bell et al 1937, 10, 102; Merrifield 1965, W41, W42, B12; Grimes 1968, 17–20, 64–79; Chapman et al 1985, site 14.

3) Barber-Surgeons' Hall

Most of the Roman wall was completely rebuilt in the medieval period. The Roman fort wall survives below ground level. The internal city wall thickening has been removed.

The stretch of wall runs southwards from the Barbican lake for *c* 37.5m and stands to a height varying from 2m to 7m. The wall is much obscured. Earth is banked up against the outer face of the wall, part of the graveyard of St Giles Cripplegate. The lower levels of a 13th-century tower (Bastion 13) survive adjacent to Barber-Surgeons' Hall. In 1607, the Barber-Surgeons' Company built a courtroom (designed by Inigo Jones) which incorporated the tower as an apse at its western end.
References: RCHM(E) 1928, 104; Bell et al 1937, 104–5; Merrifield 1965, B13; Grimes 1968, 17–20, 64–9; Chapman et al 1985, site 16.

4) Museum Gardens

The line of the original outer face of the Roman fort wall is represented by later brickwork. The Roman fort wall and the city wall thickening is visible across the diameter of Bastion 14.

The city wall, 25m long and 2m high, has a 13th-century tower (Bastion 14), 6m high with the remains of several arrow slits. Against the tower, on the external face, up to four courses of medieval rubble core are visible behind a 19th-century brick arch.
References: RCHM(E) 1928, 104; Bell et al 1937, 35–6; Merrifield 1965, W41, W42, B14; Grimes 1968, 17–20, 64–79; Chapman et al 1985, site 17.

5) Underground car park, Bastion House, London Wall

The foundations of the west gate of the Roman fort survive. Only the northern tower can be seen, providing a guardroom and access to the sentry walk. To the south lies a gravel road, divided into two by stone piers. Running northwards from the gate tower is *c* 5.35m of fort wall, 1.2m thick and 1.5m high. The internal thickening (1.65m wide) lies behind. Most of the facing has been robbed.

Set in an underground car park, opening times are limited to two half-days each month. For opening times check with the Museum of London Press Office.
References: Wright 1957, 219–20; Merrifield 1965, W43, G4; Grimes 1968, 29–32, 78; Chapman et al 1985, site 18.

6) Noble Street

The line of the Roman city wall survives, with the foundations of a corner and intermediate tower of the fort visible. The surviving length of the wall is *c* 66m. The north section of Noble Street shows the base of the Roman wall, supporting a 19th-century brick wall. The Roman wall consists of the fort (1.2m wide) and internal thickening (1.25m wide). Part of the core of this thickening still survives to the height of 2.4m with ragstone laid in herringbone courses. The outer face of the wall, however, shows differing medieval building techniques and stands to *c* 7.6m. The foundations of an inner intermediate tower lies *c* 12m from the south-west corner.

In the southern section of Noble Street (south of Plaisterers' Hall), the surviving walls form the south-west corner of the fort with the foundations of a rectangular corner tower. A Roman brick-lined culvert cuts through the base of the city wall just west of its fort wall junction. The foundations for an intermediate tower lie to the north.

References: RCHM(E) 1928, 104; Wright 1950, 107–9; Bruce-Mitford 1956, 126–7; Wright 1958, 144; 1959, 126; 1960, 229; Merrifield 1965, 161, 198, W44–8, B15; Grimes 1968, 20–1, 33–4, 48–50, 67, 76; Chapman et al 1985, site 19 and 20; Westman 1988.

Bibliography

Manuscript sources

London Metropolitan Archives (LMA)

Cross and Tibbs Collection, cat nos m0018650d and m0020324cl

London County Council (LCC), war damage maps sheet 62

Photograph Collection, cat no. m0026674d

Museum of London, London Archaeological Archive and Research Centre (LAARC), London

GLA Grimes London Archive

The National Archives (TNA): Public Record Office (PRO)

MINISTRY OF WORKS

WORK 14/2200 1954/1960, minutes of meetings of the Ancient Monuments Board for England held on 5 October 1956 and 7 December 1956

Printed and other secondary works

Aitken, G, and Aitken, N, 1982 Excavations on the Library site, Collington Park, Dorchester 1961–3, *Proc Dorset Natur Hist Archaeol Soc* 104, 93–126

Allason-Jones, L, 1996 *Roman jet in the Yorkshire Museum*, York

Anon, 1847 Proceedings of the Association, *J Brit Archaeol Ass* 2, 265–368

Atkinson, D, 1914 A hoard of samian from Pompeii, *J Roman Stud* 4, 27–64

Arthur, P, and Marsh, G (eds), 1978 *Early fine wares in Roman Britain*, BAR Brit Ser 57, Oxford

Baddeley, J J, 1921 *Cripplegate ward: one of the twenty-six wards of the City of London*, London

Bailey, D M, 1988 *A catalogue of lamps in the British Museum: Vol 3, Roman provincial lamps*, London

Barber, B, and Bowsher, D, 2000 *The eastern cemetery of Roman London: excavations 1983–90*, MoLAS Monogr Ser 4, London

Bateman, N, 1998 Public buildings in Roman London: some contrasts, in *Roman London: recent archaeological work* (ed B Watson), J Roman Archaeol Suppl Ser 24, 47–57, Portsmouth, RI

Bateman, N, Cowan, C, and Wroe-Brown, R, 2008 *London's Roman amphitheatre: Guildhall Yard, City of London*, MoLAS Monogr 35, London

Bédoyère, G de la, 2001 *The buildings of Roman Britain*, Stroud

Bell, W, Cottrill, F, and Spon, G, 1937 *London Wall through 18 centuries*, London

Bémont, C, 1977 Marques sur céramiques sigillées au Musée du Louvre. Mélanges de l'École Française de Rome, *Antiquité* 89, 169–218

Bentley, D, 1979 Excavations at St Bartholomew's hospital, unpub MOL rep

Bentley, D, and Pritchard, F, 1982 The Roman cemetery at St Bartholomew's hospital, London, *Trans London Middlesex Archaeol Soc* 33, 134–72

Biddle, M, and Hudson, D, with Heighway, C, 1973 *The future of London's past: a survey of the archaeological implications of planning and redevelopment in the nation's capital*, Rescue Publ 4, Worcester

Bird, J, 1988 Decorated samian ware [from 199 Borough High Street], in *Excavations in Southwark 1973–6, Lambeth 1973–9* (ed P Hinton), Joint Publ London Middlesex Archaeol Soc/Surrey Archaeol Soc 3, 249–75, London

Bird, J, Hassall, M W C, and Sheldon, H (eds), 1996 *Interpreting Roman London: papers in memory of Hugh Chapman*, Oxbow Monogr 58, Oxford

Birley, E, 1953 *Roman Britain and the Roman army: collected papers*, Kendal

Bishop, M, 1983 The Camomile Street soldier reconsidered, *Trans London Middlesex Archaeol Soc* 34, 31–48

Bishop, M C, Hall, J, and Wardle, A, in prep *A corpus of military objects from Roman London*, MOLA Monogr Ser

Blockley, K, Blockley, M, Blockley, P, Frere, S S, and Stow, S (eds), 1995 *Excavations in the Marlow car park and surrounding areas: Vol 1*, Archaeol Canterbury 5, Canterbury

BMC, 1975 (1923–62) Mattingly, H, and Carson, R A G, *Coins of the Roman Empire in the British Museum*, vols 1–6, rev edn, London

Bowman, A K, and Thomas, J D (eds), 1994 *The Vindolanda writing tablets: Tabulae Vindolandenses II*, London

Bowman, A K, and Thomas, J D, 1996 New writing tablets from Vindolanda, *Britannia* 27, 299–328

Bowman, A K, Thomas, J, and Adams, J, 1990 Two letters from Vindolanda, *Britannia* 21, 33–52

Brigham, T, 1998 The port of Roman London, in Watson (ed) 1998, 23–34

British Museum, 1951 *Guide to the antiquities of Roman Britain*, London

Bruce-Mitford, R L S (ed), 1956 *Recent archaeological excavations in Britain*, London

Butler, J, 2001 The city defences at Aldersgate, *Trans London Middlesex Archaeol Soc* 52, 41–112

Cal Husting Wills Calendar of wills proved and enrolled in the Court of Husting, London, AD 1258–AD 1688 preserved among the archives of the Corporation of the City of London, at the Guildhall: Part I, AD 1258–AD 1358 (ed R R Sharpe), 1889–90, London

Cal Pat R Calendar of patent rolls (65 vols, 1232–1509, 1547–82), 1891–1986, London

Chapman, H, Hall, J, and Marsh, G, 1985 *The London Wall walk*, London

Chenet, G, 1941 *La Céramique gallo-romaine d'Argonne du IVe siècle et la terre sigillée décorée à la molette*, Mâcon

Chitwood, P, and Hill, J, 1987 Excavations at St Albans House, 124 Wood Street, unpub MOL rep

CIL, 1936 *Diplomata militaria ex constituionibus imperatorum de civitate et conubio militum veteranorumque expressa* (ed H Nesselhauf), Corpus Inscriptionum Latinarum 16, Berlin

Cowan, C, 2003 *Urban development in north-west Roman Southwark: excavations 1974–90*, MoLAS Monogr Ser 16, London

Crowley, N, and Betts, I M, 1992 Three *classis Britannica* stamps from London, *Britannia* 23, 218–22

Crummy, N, 1983 *The Roman small finds from excavations in Colchester 1971–9*, Colchester Archaeol Rep 2, Colchester

Crummy, P, 1997 *City of victory*, Colchester

Davies, R W, 1976 *Singulares* and Roman Britain, *Britannia* 7, 134–44

Davies Pryce, T, 1932 The decorated samian, in Bushe-Fox, J P, *Third report on the excavations of the Roman fort at Richborough, Kent*, Rep Res Comm Soc Antiq London 10, 94–123, London

Davies Pryce, T, 1945 Report on the burnt samian from Regis House, in Dunning, G C, Two fires of Roman London, *Antiq J* 25, 48–77

Dio, Cassius, *Epitome Dio's Roman history: Vol 9* (trans E Cary), Loeb Classical Library, 1927, London

Driel-Murray, C van, 1995 Gender in question, in *Theoretical Roman archaeology: second conference proceedings* (ed P Rush), 3–21, no place

Dunwoodie, L, Harward, C, and Pitt, K, in prep *Roman fortifications and urban development on the eastern hill: excavations at Plantation Place, City of London*, MOLA Monogr Ser

Egan, G, 1985 Excavations at 7–12 Aldersgate Street, EC2, unpub MOL rep

English Heritage, 1991 *Management of archaeological projects*, London

Evening Standard, 1944 [article discussing need for controlled archaeological examination of bomb-damaged sites in London prior to redevelopment], 8 May

Fowler, E, 1960 The origins and development of the penannular brooch in Europe, *Proc Prehist Soc* 26, 149–77

Gillam, J P, 1970 *Types of Roman coarse pottery vessels in northern Britain*, 3 edn, Newcastle upon Tyne

Gilson, A, 1981 A group of Roman surgical and medical instruments from Corbridge, *Saalburg Jahrbuch* 37, 5–9

Greep, S J, 1995 Objects of bone, antler and ivory from CAT sites, in Blockley et al (eds) 1995, 1112–52

Grimes, W F, 1930 Holt, Denbighshire: the works-depôt of the 20th legion at Castle Lyons, *Y Cymmrodor* 41, 1–235

Grimes, W F, 1956 Recent discoveries in the City of London, in Bruce-Mitford (ed) 1956, 111–45

Grimes, W F, 1968 *The excavation of Roman and mediaeval London*, London

Hansard Hansard parliamentary debates, Commons, vol 558, 1955–6; vols 580, 583, 588, 590, 1957–8; vol 6098, 1958–9, London

Harben, H A, 1918 *A dictionary of London; being notes topographical and historical relating to the streets and principal buildings in the City of London*, London

Hart, D, 1988 Excavations at Leith House, 47–57 Gresham Street, London EC2, unpub MOL rep

Hassall, M, 1973 Roman soldiers in Roman London, in *Archaeological theory and practice: essays presented to Professor W F Grimes* (ed D E Strong), 231–7, London

Hassall, M, 1980 The inscribed altars, in Hill, C, Millett, M, and Blagg, T, *The Roman riverside wall and monumental arch in London: excavations at Baynard's Castle, Upper Thames Street, London 1974–6* (ed T Dyson), London

Middlesex Archaeol Soc Spec Pap 3, 195–8, London

Hassall, M, 1996 London as a provincial capital, in Bird et al (eds) 1996, 19–26

Hassall, M, 1998 Units doubled and divided, in J Bird (ed), *Form and fabric: studies in Rome's material past in honour of B R Hartley*, Oxbow Monogr 80, 1998, 31–9, Oxford

Hassall, M, and Tomlin, R S O, 1983 Roman Britain in 1982: Part 2, Inscriptions, *Britannia* 14, 336–56

Hassall, M, and Tomlin, R S O, 1985 Roman Britain in 1984: Part 2, Inscriptions, *Britannia* 16, 317–32

Hassall, M, and Tomlin, R S O, 1994 Inscriptions, *Britannia* 25, 293–314

Hattatt, R, 1985 *Iron Age and Romano-British brooches*, Oxford

Hattatt, R, 1987 *Brooches of antiquity*, Oxford

Hattatt, R, 1989 *Ancient brooches and other artefacts*, Oxford

Henig, M, 1978 (1974) *A corpus of Roman engraved gemstones from British sites*, BAR Brit Ser 8, 2 edn, Oxford

Hermet, F, 1934 *La Graufesenque (Condatomago)*, Paris

Holder, P A, 1982 *The Roman army in Britain*, London

Howe, E, and Lakin, D, 2004 Roman and medieval Cripplegate, City of London: archaeological excavations 1992–8, MoLAS Monogr Ser 21, London

Illustrated London News, 1865 [revealing Bastion 14], 19 August

Illustrated London News, 1957 [bomb damage, view west from Moorgate], October

ILS, 1962–74 *Inscriptiones Latinae selecta* (ed H Dessau), Dublin

Jackson, R, 1984 A Roman stamped shield-boss from London, *Britannia* 15, 246–50

Johnson, D, 1980 *The City ablaze*, London

Jones, A H M, 1949 The Roman civil service (clerical and sub-clerical grades), *J Roman Stud* 39, 38–55

Knorr, R, 1919 *Töpfer und Fabriken verzierter Terra-Sigillata des ersten Jahrhunderts*, Stuttgart

Knorr, R, 1952 *Terra-Sigillata-Gefässe des ersten Jahrhunderts mit Töpfernamen*, Stuttgart

Langton, B, and Westman, A, 1990 Archaeological investigations at 1–4 Giltspur Street and 18–20 Cock Lane, London, EC1, unpub DUA archive rep

Loeschcke, S, 1919 *Die Lampen aus Vindonissa*, Zurich

LRBCII, 1960 *Late Roman bronze coinage: Part II, Bronze Roman imperial coinage of the later Empire AD 324–498* (eds R A G Carson and J P C Kent), London

Lyon, J, 2004 New work on the Cripplegate fort: excavations at 25 Gresham Street, *Trans London Middlesex Archaeol Soc* 55, 153–82

McKenzie, M, Shepherd, J, and Wardle, A, in prep *Excavations at 35 Basinghall Street, City of London*, MOLA Archaeol Stud Ser, London

Mackinder, A T, 1988 Excavations at 52 Gresham Street/ 14 Ironmonger Lane, unpub DUA archive rep

Maloney, C, 1986 Excavations at 13 Snow Hill, London, EC1, unpub MOL rep

Maloney, C, with de Moulins, D, 1990 *The archaeology of Roman London: Vol 1, The upper Walbrook in the Roman period*, CBA Res Rep 69, London

Marsden, P, 1968 Guildhall extension site, *Trans London Middlesex Archaeol Soc* 22, 4–10

Marsden, P, 1980 *Roman London*, London

Mary, G T, 1967 *Novaesium I: die südgallische Terra-Sigillata aus Neuss, Berlin*, Limesforschungen 6, Berlin

Maxfield, V A, 1986 Pre-Flavian forts and their garrisons, *Britannia* 17, 59–72

Merrifield, R, 1965 *The Roman city of London*, London

Merrifield, R, 1983 *London: city of the Romans*, London

Milne, G, 1995 *English Heritage book of Roman London: urban archaeology in the nation's capital*, London

Milne, G, 1996 A palace disproved: reassessing the provincial governor's presence in 1st-century London, in Bird et al (eds) 1996, 49–55

Milne, G, 1997 *St Bride's church, London: archaeological research 1952–60 and 1992–5*, Engl Heritage Archaeol Rep 11, London

Milne, G, with Cohen, N, 2001 *Excavations at medieval Cripplegate, London: archaeology after the Blitz, 1946–68*, Engl Heritage Archaeol Rep, Swindon

Ministry of Information, 1942 *Front line 1940–1: the official story of the civil defence of Britain*, London

Oldenstein, J, 1976 Zur Ausrüstung römischer Auxiliareinheitung, *Bericht der Römisch-Germanischen Kommission* 57, 49–284

Oswald, A, 1939 GM5 archive report, unpub MOL rep

Oswald, F, 1936–7 Index of figure types on terra sigillata ('samian ware'), *Annals Archaeol Anthropol* 23, 1–4; 24, 1–4, Liverpool

Oswald, F A C, and Pryce, T D, 1920 *An introduction to the study of terra sigillata, treated from a chronological standpoint*, London

Painter, K S, 1963 A Roman tombstone from Holborn, *Antiq J* 43, 123–8

Perez-Sala, M, and Shepherd, J, 2008 The cullet dump and evidence of glass working, in Bateman et al 2008, 142–6

Perring, D, 1985 London in the 1st and early 2nd centuries, in *Roman urban topography in Britain and the western Empire: proceedings of the third conference on urban archaeology: organised jointly by the CBA and the Department of Urban Archaeology of the Museum of London* (eds F Grew and B Hobley), CBA Res Rep 59, 94–8, London

Perring, D, 1991 *Roman London*, London

Perring, D, and Roskams, S P, with Allen, P, 1991 *The archaeology of Roman London: Vol 2, Early development of Roman London west of the Walbrook*, CBA Res Rep 70, London

Price, J, 1995 Glass counters and gaming pieces, in Manning, W H, Price, J, and Webster, J, *Reports on the excavations at Usk 1965–76: the Roman small finds*, 129–34, Cardiff

Price, J E, 1880 *On a bastion of London wall, or, excavations in Camomile Street, Bishopsgate*, London

Ramsey, W G (ed), 1988 *The Blitz then and now: Vol 2*, London

RCHM(E), 1928 Roy Comm Hist Monuments (Engl), *An inventory of the historical monuments in London: Vol 3, Roman London*, London

Rees, H, Crummy, N, Ottaway, P J, and Dunn, G, 2008 Tools, in *Artefacts and society in Roman and medieval Winchester: small finds from the suburbs and defences, 1971–86*, 146–53, Winchester

RIB, 1965 Collingwood, R G, and Wright, R P, *The Roman inscriptions of Britain: Vol 1, Inscriptions on stone*, Oxford

RIB, 1990 *The Roman inscriptions of Britain: Vol 2 fasc 1, Instrumentum domesticum: the military diplomata, metal ingots, tesserae, dies, labels and lead sealings (RIB 2401–11)* (eds S S Frere, M Roxan and R S O Tomlin), Gloucester

RIB, 1991 *The Roman inscriptions of Britain: Vol 2 fasc 3, Instrumentum domesticum (personal belongings and the like): brooches, rings, gems, bracelets, helmets, shields, weapons, iron tools, baldric fittings, votives in gold, silver and bronze, lead pipes, roundels, sheets and other lead objects, stone roundels, pottery and bone roundels, other objects of bone (RIB 2421–41)* (eds R S O Tomlin and S S Frere), Gloucester

RIB, 2009 *The Roman inscriptions of Britain: Vol 3, Inscriptions on stone; found or notified between 1 January 1955 and 31 December 2006* (eds R S O Tomlin, R P Wright and M W C Hassall), Oxford

RIC, 1923–94 *Roman imperial coinage* (eds H Mattingly and E A Sydenham), 10 vols, London

Ricken, H, and Fischer, C (eds), 1963 *Die Bilderschüsseln der römischen Töpfer von Rheinzabern: Textband mit Typenbildern zu Katalog VI der Ausgrabungen von Wilhelm Ludowici in Rheinzabern 1901–14*, Materialen zur römisch-germanischen Keramik 7, Bonn

Robinson, R, 1975 *The armour of imperial Rome*, London

Rogers, G B, 1974 *Poteries sigillées de la Gaule centrale: Tome 1, Les Motifs non figurés, Gallia* Suppl 28, Paris

Rowsome, P, 1998 The development of the town plan of early Roman London in Watson (ed) 1998, 35–8

Roxan, M, 1978 *Roman military diplomas 1954–77*, Inst Archaeol Occas Publ 2, London

Roxan, M, 1983 A Roman military diploma from London, *Trans London Middlesex Archaeol Soc* 34, 67–72

Schofield, J (ed), 1987 Museum of London: Department of Urban Archaeology: archive catalogue, unpub MOL rep

Schofield, J, with Maloney, C (eds), 1998 *Archaeology in the City of London, 1907–91: a guide to records of excavations by the Museum of London and its predecessors*, MoL Archaeol Gazetteer Ser 1, London

Shepherd, J, 1986 The Roman features at Gateway House and Watling House, City of London 1954, *Trans London Middlesex Archaeol Soc* 37, 125–44

Shepherd, J D, with Rowsome, P, 1987 The pre-urban and Roman topography in the King Street and Cheapside areas of the City of London, *Trans London Middlesex Archaeol Soc* 38, 11–58

Shepherd, J D, 1988 The Roman occupation in the area of Paternoster Square, City of London, *Trans London Middlesex Archaeol Soc* 39, 1–30

Shepherd, J D, 1998a *The temple of Mithras, London: excavations by W F Grimes and A Williams at the Walbrook*, Engl Heritage Archaeol Rep 12, no place

Shepherd, J D, 1998b *Post-war archaeology in the City of London, 1946–72: a guide to records of excavations by Professor W F Grimes held by the Museum of London*, MoL Archaeol Gazetteer Ser 3, London

Simpson, G, 1976 Decorated terra sigillata at Montans (Tarn) from the manuscript of Elie Rossignol at Albi, *Britannia* 7, 244–73

Speidel, M, 1974 *Stablesiani*: the raising of new cavalry units during the crisis of the Roman Empire, *Chiron* 4, 541–6

Speidel, M, 1978 *Guards of the Roman armies*, Antiquitas ser 1, vol 28, Bonn

Spence, C, 1986 Excavations at 16 Coleman Street, unpub DUA archive rep

The Sphere, 1947 [post-war excavations at Bastion 12, London], November, London Illustrated Newspapers, London

Stanfield, J, 1929 Unusual forms of terra sigillata, *Archaeol J* 86, 113–51

Stanfield, J A, and Simpson, G, 1958 *Central Gaulish potters*, London

Stow, J, 1956 (1598) *The survay of London* (ed H B Wheatley), London

Tacitus, *Agricola The Agricola and the Germania* (trans H Mattingly; rev S A Handford), 1970, Harmondsworth

Tacitus, *Annals* (trans J Jackson), 1962, Cambridge, Mass

Terrisse, J-R, 1968 *Les Céramiques sigillees gallo-romaines des Martres-de-Veyres (Puy de Dôme)*, Paris

Terry, J, 1906 On the Cripplegate Bastion of London Wall, *Trans London Middlesex Archaeol Soc* 1, 356–9

Thompson, A, Westman, A, and Dyson, T (eds), 1998 *Archaeology in Greater London 1965–90: a guide to records of excavations by the Museum of London*, MoL Archaeol Gazetteer Ser 2, London

Tobert, N, 1983 7–10 Foster Lane: finds appraisal report, unpub MOL rep

Treveil, P, with Dunwoodie, L, Harward, C, and Pitt, K, 2003 Plantation Place, London, EC3: an archaeological post-excavation assessment and updated project design (FER97), unpub MOL rep

Tylor, A, 1884 New points in the history of Roman Britain, as illustrated by discoveries at Warwick Square, in the City of London, *Archaeologia* 48, 220–45

Wacher, J, 1974 *The towns of Roman Britain*, London

Watson, B (ed), 1998 *Roman London: recent archaeological work*, J Roman Archaeol Suppl 24, Portsmouth, RI

Westman, A, 1988 Archaeological examination of the city wall at Noble Street, EC2 (CWN87), unpub MOL rep

Wilmott, T, 1991 *Excavations in the middle Walbrook valley, 1927–60*, London Middlesex Archaeol Soc Spec Pap 13, London

Wright, R P, 1950 Roman Britain in 1949: Part I, Sites explored, *J Roman Stud* 40, 92–114

Wright, R P, 1951 Roman Britain in 1950: Part II, Inscriptions, *J Roman Stud* 41, 140–5

Wright, R P, 1957 Roman Britain in 1956: Part I, Sites explored, *J Roman Stud* 47, 198–226

Wright, R P, 1958 Roman Britain in 1957: Part I, Sites explored, *J Roman Stud* 48, 130–49

Wright, R P, 1959 Roman Britain in 1958: Part I, Sites explored, *J Roman Stud* 49, 102–35

Wright, R P, 1960 Roman Britain in 1959: Part I, Sites explored, *J Roman Stud* 50, 210–36

Yule, B, 2005 *A prestigious Roman building complex on the Southwark waterfront: excavations at Winchester Palace, London, 1983–90*, MoLAS Monogr Ser 23, London

Index

Compiled by Margaret Binns